Lecture Notes in Computer S

Commenced Publication in 1973
Founding and Former Series Editors:
Gerhard Goos, Juris Hartmanis, and Jan van Leeuwen

T0238814

Eitan Frachtenberg   Uwe Schwiegelshohn (Eds.)

Job Scheduling Strategies for Parallel Processing

13th International Workshop, JSSPP 2007
Seattle, WA, USA, June 17, 2007
Revised Papers

 Springer

Volume Editors

Eitan Frachtenberg
Powerset, Inc.
475 Brannan St., San Francisco, CA 94107, USA
E-mail: eitan@powerset.com

Uwe Schwiegelshohn
Technische Universität Dortmund, Institut für Roboterforschung
Otto-Hahn-Str. 8, 44227 Dortmund, Germany
E-mail: uwe.schwiegelshohn@udo.edu

Library of Congress Control Number: 2008924626

CR Subject Classification (1998): D.4, D.1.3, F.2.2, C.1.4, B.2.1, B.6, F.1.2

LNCS Sublibrary: SL 1 – Theoretical Computer Science and General Issues

ISSN   0302-9743
ISBN-10   3-540-78698-8 Springer Berlin Heidelberg New York
ISBN-13   978-3-540-78698-6 Springer Berlin Heidelberg New York

Springer is a part of Springer Science+Business Media

springer.com

© Springer-Verlag Berlin Heidelberg 2008
Printed in Germany

Typesetting: Camera-ready by author, data conversion by Scientific Publishing Services, Chennai, India
Printed on acid-free paper   SPIN: 12243488   06/3180   5 4 3 2 1 0

Preface

This volume contains the papers presented at the 13th workshop on Job Scheduling Strategies for Parallel Processing. The workshop was held in Seattle, WA, USA, on June 17, 2007, in conjunction with ICS 2007.

All submitted papers went through a complete review process, with the full version being read and evaluated by an average of five reviewers. We would like to thank the Program Committee members and additional referees for their willingness to participate in this effort and their excellent, detailed reviews: Nazareno Andrade, Su-Hui Chiang, Walfredo Cirne, Alvaro Coelho, Lauro Costa, Dror Feitelson, Allan Gottlieb, Andrew Grimshaw, Moe Jette, Richard Lagerstrom, Virginia Lo, Reagan Moore, Bill Nitzberg, Mark Squillante, John Towns, Jon Weissman, and Ramin Yahyapour.

The accepted workshop papers in recent years show a departure from the supercomputer-centric viewpoint of parallel job scheduling. On the one hand, the field of supercomputer scheduling is showing some signs of maturity, exhibited in many widely accepted practices for job scheduling. On the other hand, many nontraditional high-performance computing and parallel environments are emerging as viable solutions to many users and uses that cannot or need not access a traditional supercomputer, such as Grids, Web services, and commodity parallel computers. With the growing ubiquity of these technologies, the requirement to schedule parallel jobs well on these various architectures also grows.

Some of the papers in this and recent JSSPP proceedings address these contemporary architectures, such as Balle and Palermo's paper on resource management with awareness of multi-core and multi-threaded parallel processors, and whole sessions devoted to Grid scheduling. We plan to follow through with these shifts in parallel architectures and related scheduling in JSSPP. Opening this collection, we present a detailed exposition of recent technological trends in parallel computing, and how they affect, and are affected by, parallel job scheduling. To remain a relevant field of study in the face of constant progress in the underlying technology, we are currently expanding the scope of JSSPP to include these trends, as described in the introductory paper.

We call for the researchers in the JSSPP community and related fields to contribute from their experience with traditional parallel job scheduling, and to participate in the description, generalization, and resolving of the contemporary scheduling challenges. We hope to continue the long tradition of this workshop, which has now reached its 13th consecutive year. We would also love to hear from authors with any questions or suggestions regarding the future direction of JSSPP.

December 2007

Eitan Frachtenberg
Uwe Schwiegelshohn

Organization

Workshop Organizers

Eitan Frachtenberg   Powerset, Inc.
Uwe Schwiegelshohn   Dortmund University

Program Committee

Su-Hui Chiang   Portland State University
Walfredo Cirne   Google
Dror Feitelson   The Hebrew University
Allan Gottlieb   New York University
Andrew Grimshaw   University of Virginia
Moe Jette   Lawrence Livermore National Lab
Richard Lagerstrom   Cray Inc.
Virginia Lo   University of Oregon
Reagan Moore   San Diego Supercomputer Center
Bill Nitzberg   Altair Grid Technologies
Mark Squillante   IBM T. J. Watson Research Center
John Towns   NCSA
Jon Weissman   University of Minnesota
Ramin Yahyapour   Dortmund University

Table of Contents

New Challenges of Parallel Job Scheduling

Eitan Frachtenberg[1] and Uwe Schwiegelshohn[2]

[1] Powerset, Inc.
eitan@powerset.com
[2] Robotics Research Institute,
University Dortmund, Otto-Hahn-Strasse 8,
44221 Dortmund, Germany
uwe.schwiegelshohn@udo.edu

Abstract. The workshop on job scheduling strategies for parallel processing (JSSPP) studies the myriad aspects of managing resources on parallel and distributed computers. These studies typically focus on large-scale computing environments, where allocation and management of computing resources present numerous challenges. Traditionally, such systems consisted of massively parallel supercomputers, or more recently, large clusters of commodity processor nodes. These systems are characterized by architectures that are largely homogeneous and workloads that are dominated by both computation and communication-intensive applications. Indeed, the large majority of the articles in the first ten JSSPP workshops dealt with such systems and addressed issues such as queuing systems and supercomputer workloads.

In this paper, we discuss some of the recent developments in parallel computing technologies that depart from this traditional domain of problems. In particular, we identify several recent and influential technologies that could have a significant impact on the future of research on parallel scheduling. We discuss some of the more specific research challenges that these technologies introduce to the JSSPP community, and propose to enhance the scope of future JSSPP workshops to include these topics.

1   Introduction

The last few years have brought about many radical changes in the technologies and platforms that exhibit the same salient challenges that JSSPP focuses on—all in the family of flexible allocation and management of multiple computer resources. These technologies, however, depart from the traditional supercomputer model of relatively homogeneous architectures and applications, and add new dimensions to those that are already being studied within JSSPP's scope. This paper therefore has two main goals: (1) To present some of the major technological changes and to discuss the additional dimensions they add to the set of JSSPP challenges; and, (2) to promote and suggest research topics inspired by these dimensions in the JSSPP community.

Such dimensions include, for example, reliability and resource allocation across multiple sites (Grids), workloads that are a mixture of parallel, sequential, and

E. Frachtenberg and U. Schwiegelshohn (Eds.): JSSPP 2007, LNCS 4942, pp. 1–23, 2008.

interactive applications on multi-core desktops, and data-intensive applications on Web servers that exhibit little or no communication. Although the traditional topics of interest of JSSPP are still relevant and will likely continue to attract high quality papers to the workshop, we feel the need to introduce these new topics to JSSPP's scope at this time, for two main reasons:

1. The field of parallel job scheduling, while still evolving, is showing signs of maturity.
2. New technologies are exhibiting many characteristics of the problems that the JSSPP community tackles. We believe that the JSSPP community's expertise can produce meaningful contributions for these technologies.

By introducing these new but related topics to the scope of JSSPP, we hope to expand its impact and attractiveness to researchers with little or no past exposure to traditional parallel job scheduling. After discussing these topics with our peers, we present here a nonexhaustive list of research topics and questions to which we believe the JSSPP community can add significant contributions.

Paper organization. We have loosely grouped these topics into four technological trends:

- Commodity parallel computers (Section 2): Parallel environments mainly consisting of desktops and laptops with multi-core chips
- Grids (Section 3): Large-scale, heterogeneous, distributed, partially shared computing environments
- Web servers (Section 4): Large-scale, latency-sensitive online services, and the offline data infrastructure behind it
- Virtualization (Section: 5): Resource management inside and among multiple virtual machines

These categories are not sorted, and in fact, under the umbrella of parallel scheduling, have much more in common with each other than what sets them apart. Section 6 discusses the similarities and overarching scheduling considerations that affect most or all of these contemporary technologies. Finally, Section 7 concludes the paper.

2   Commodity Parallel Computers

The largest shift towards parallel computing is actually occurring right now. A large majority of the desktop and notebook computers sold today for everyday use employs dual-core and quad-core chips. Several server, console, and special-purpose processors even contain between 8 and 96 cores, and the trend to increase on-chip parallelism is expected to continue in the foreseeable future [20].

As MIT's Leiserson writes: [41]

> The Age of Serial Computing is over. With the advent of multi-core processors, parallel-computing technology that was once relegated to universities and research labs is now emerging as mainstream.

Commodity hardware is growing increasingly more complex, with advances such as chip heterogeneity and specialization, deeper memory hierarchies, fine-grain power management, and most importantly, chip parallelism. Similarly, commodity software and workloads are becoming more concurrent and diverse, encompassing spreadsheets, content creation and presentation, 3D games, and computationally intensive business and scientific programs, among others. With this new complexity in hardware and software, process scheduling in the operating system (OS) becomes more challenging. Nevertheless, many commodity OS schedulers are based on design principles that are 30 years old [20]. This disparity may soon lead to significant performance degradation. Particularly, modern parallel architectures such as multi-core chips require more than scalable OSs: parallel programs need parallel-aware scheduling [21]. Although the effort to produce more scalable scheduling is already producing some results (both in task scheduling [41] and process scheduling [24]), there is still much research and implementation work needed before commodity parallel computing fulfills its performance promises.

Scheduling for a mixed workload. The arrival of ubiquitous parallel hardware leads to complex workloads with complex scheduling requirements, especially as software becomes increasingly more parallel. Although the transition to parallel software on the desktop is not immediate, it is already taking place. Popular programming languages such as C++ and Java offer increasingly sophisticated support for parallel programming [41], while the emerging parallel hardware creates a stronger incentive for concurrency. Some contemporary applications already benefit from parallel computing power, for example, parallel searches in terabytes of data, 3D games, photo and video editing filters, and technical computing in science and industry. Consequently, the typical desktop workload, already highly variable and difficult to characterize, becomes even more complex as parallel desktop applications grow in number. The scheduler designer must now contend with an unpredictable mix of conflicting scheduling requirements, such as:

- Media applications that require few resources, but at precise intervals and with strict process inter-dependencies.
- Parallel applications that need synchronization and/or co-scheduling.
- Low-priority background tasks such as virus scanning.
- Interactive applications that require high responsiveness, like web browsers or word processors.

Taking a more general view, we observe that parallelization poses two principal challenges to the commodity scheduler: (1) processes competing over resources suffer from degraded performance when coscheduled, and (2) collaborating processes suffer from degraded performance when *not* coscheduled. To design effective schedulers for such mixed workload, we must first understand the workloads. The job scheduling community has a rich history in characterizing and modeling supercomputer workloads, and can employ some of the experiences and techniques from that effort to similarly describe parallel desktop workloads.

Priorities. Within a mixed workload we must often deal with priorities, fairness, and user experience. Unlike a large computing center handling multiple users with conflicting priorities and with economic constraints desktops typically have a single user with his attention primarily focused on a single application at a time. This additional constraint on the scheduler requires that it does its best effort in guessing temporal user priorities and prioritizing processes accordingly without sacrificing other scheduling goals. The dynamic nature of personal computer usage makes this goal more difficult, because it requires the scheduler to respond quickly to changes in user attention. This challenge again is not a new one [12], but the introduction of parallel resources and synchronized parallel programs complicates it beyond the scope of most existing solutions.

Power management. Power consumption in chips is one of the largest challenges faced by chip manufacturers today and has itself instigated the arrival of the multi-core processors. Since the temperature and power of a chip is directly related to the chip's power consumption, the chip clock's speed is limited by its operational thermal envelope. To further minimize and control the power output, modern chips can selectively turn off and/or throttle down the speed of unused logic. Increasingly, this fine-grain power control functionality is exposed to the OS. This is where scheduling can play a vital role in managing the trade-offs between performance and power consumption. Although some initial work has already shown that scheduling can have a significant impact on power consumption, there are as of yet no mainstream desktop schedulers that explicitly try to optimize this factor. As the number of cores increases in the future, and as the granularity control that the hardware exports to the OS grows finer, this research area will likely grow more complex and challenging. On the other hand, the rising importance of power management will also make the fruits of this research more rewarding.

Asymmetric cores heterogeneity. Merely duplicating cores in a chip is not always a sufficient solution to the ever-increasing demand for performance. Limiting factors such as power budget, cooling capacity, and memory performance will still require innovative design solutions such as heterogeneous cores with selective shutdown, use of specialized coprocessors, and moving computation closer to memory. The highly popular Cell processor, for example, comprises nine cores of two different designs and purposes [27]. Other emerging architectures include a relatively large number of special-purpose computing cores, such as the Clear-Speed 96-core chip for mathematical processing, and the Azul 24-core chip for Java applications [31,46]. Memory hierarchies are also growing more complex due to the use of multi-core and hyper-threaded chips. Such computers are essentially nonuniform memory access (NUMA) machines, and as such, may impose special scheduling requirements [6]. On another end of the computing spectrum, ubiquitous computers, such as mobile phones, portable music and video players, and media-convergence appliances that have strict minimum service requirements on a low-power, low-performance platform could further stress the resource management requirements.

These architectures will require OS support to allocate their resources intelligently. There is already an ongoing effort to hand tune applications and schedulers to specific architectures [54], but this effort may not be enough. Heterogeneous chip environments are challenging to schedule on, but also present many opportunities for a scheduler that can map tasks to different chip components appropriately.

Generalizing the Challenges

We noted that the introduction of parallel applications to the desktop workload challenges the commodity parallel scheduler with potentially conflicting requirements. Moreover, architectural changes also produce additional constraints for scheduling, such as heterogeneity/asymmetry, power management, and NUMA. But unlike classical parallel computers, the presence of various classes of applications in a single workload mix—including interactive and single-threaded applications—poses a significant additional challenge on top of the specific application requirements. Ignoring these scheduling constraints can lead to poor application performance because of lack of synchronization, as well as poor system-wide performance because of contention for resources [1,14,30,49]. Future research on parallel commodity computing must take these factors into account.

Most contemporary commodity schedulers are challenged at all levels of parallel execution, from the thread [6,49], through the SMP [1,16], the cluster [14,23], all the way to supercomputers [30]. In particular, parallel programs may suffer tremendously from lack of coscheduling[1] [14,30] as processes in parallel programs—as opposed to sequential and distributed programs—rely on frequent synchronization for their progress. Supercomputers, with a more uniform workload of parallel applications, typically operate in batch mode [15]. For commodity computers and workstations that host a multiuser, time-sharing system, this is not an acceptable solution [36]. We believe however that effective scheduling for a mixed workload is not only necessary, but also within reach, and could incorporate lessons learned from scheduling parallel jobs on large homogeneous systems.

Better scheduling is achieved when the OS has intimate understanding of the hardware's capabilities and the software's requirements. With regard to hardware, the OS should arbitrate between multiple and possibly heterogeneous resources, while considering cache and memory-pressure factors. With regard to applications, the OS needs to be cognizant of all levels of parallel execution: thread, process, and parallel program, in addition to sequential and interactive programs. Schedulers can manage these workloads by applying principles from such fields as parallel and multimedia scheduling. Particularly, cooperation, adaptivity, and classification can play a decisive role in achieving optimal user experience and utilization on next-generation computers.

---

[1] Coscheduling refers to scheduling all of a job's processes at the same time, to facilitate synchronization [37].

3   Grids

Most supercomputer workloads contain a large number of sequential applications or applications with little parallelism [38]. With few exceptions due to exhibitive memory consumption, most of these applications can run as well on common desktop or server systems not requiring a parallel machine with its expensive internal network. Therefore, executing these jobs on supercomputers is not efficient in general although a limited number of them is welcome as they do not affect the completion time of parallel jobs but increase utilization of the machine. The actual number depends on the characteristics of the workload. Many parallel applications can exploit different degrees of parallelism, that is, they are malleable or moldable [15]. In many of these cases, it is acceptable to forgo the maximum degree of parallelism if a system with fewer nodes is readily available. Therefore, it is often more efficient to acquire a Grid of machines with different numbers of processors instead of investing a significant larger amount of money into a big supercomputer with the same total number of processors. This is one reason for the increasing popularity of Grids [18]. Moreover, it is often difficult for user groups of a small enterprise to fully utilize a large parallel machine with their own applications. However, if many of those user groups share several parallel machines an improved average utilization can be achieved. As there are many different resource owners in a Grid, every such Grid represents a market in which different application owners compete for processors or other resources of different providers. On the one hand this is likely to lead to some form of bidding system [11]. On the other hand it increases the dynamics of machine availability as many resource owners may additionally have high priority local users.

Unfortunately, job scheduling on Grids is significantly more difficult than job scheduling on single parallel machines. The most obvious reason is the separation of the scheduling problem into two interdependent problems:

- machine allocation
- scheduling on the selected parallel processor

This problem separation is known from many parallel job scheduling problems [39] but it becomes more complicated in the presence of rigid parallel jobs without multisite scheduling [51]. In addition, some properties of Grids also influence job scheduling. We discuss these properties and their consequences to job scheduling in the following paragraphs.

Heterogeneity. Manufacturers offer a large number of configurations for their supercomputers. This may include different types of nodes, like single processors or SMP nodes, differences in the network connection, or different amounts of memory. But in practice, most supercomputer installations have only a few nodes that are specially equipped, (for example, to execute server tasks), while almost all worker nodes are identical [28]. As the supercomputer has a single owner, the node equipment is governed by a single policy resulting in similar hardware and mostly identical software on each node. Despite the rapid development in processor technology, few institutions abstain from mixing new and old processors within the same machine. Instead they rather invest in a new machine if the performance of the old one is no longer sufficient.

From the perspective of scheduling, supercomputers therefore exhibit little node heterogeneity. Hence, most job scheduling research on supercomputers assumes homogeneous nodes. But of course, heterogeneity exists among the various resources available at a single node, like processing power, memory, or network bandwidth [50].

In Grids, the situation changes completely: Since a Grid comprises different installations with different owners, there is a large amount of heterogeneity in Grids. The individual computers are typically not installed at the same time, resulting in the use of different processor technology. Moreover, the various machine owners in a Grid have different objectives when buying their computers, leading to different hardware and software equipment in the nodes of different machines in the Grid. Finally, the network performance within a machine is usually much better than the network performance between different machines. This characteristic of Grids particularly affects so called multisite jobs [9] that are executed on several machines in parallel. But in practice, the performance of these multisite jobs is bad in comparison to single site execution [3] and they only occur rarely.

The heterogeneity within a Grid is one of the main advantages of Grid technology, since installations with many users (such as large compute centers in universities) can never satisfy all users when selecting the next machine to buy. Grid technology allows users to look within the Grid for the machines that are best suited to execute their jobs. This selection increases overall efficiency, since applications that perform poorly on local machines can be forwarded to other better-suited machines, possibly in exchange for other applications. On the one hand, there are system properties that are mandatory for the execution of an application, like the availability of a certain software. Clearly, the scheduler can easily consider these constraints. On the other hand, an application may run best on certain processors which are in high demand while other readily available processors will result in a reduced performance. In such situations, it is difficult for the scheduler to make an allocation decision, since critical job information like the execution time on the available machines may only be partially available.

Further, the above mentioned heterogeneity in supercomputers also exists in Grids: A Grid often comprises resources of different types like storage resources, computing installations and networks connecting the other resources. Therefore, Grids are, for instance, well suited for applications analyzing large amounts of data, like evaluations of experiments in particle physics. For reasons of cost and efficiency, experiment data are stored in large data centers that are specially equipped with hardware. An application requires the transfer of these data to an appropriate computing facility. Therefore, the execution of such an application consists of a workflow with several stages [19]. While most scheduling problems on parallel processors deal with independent jobs, Grid scheduling uses precedence constraints and scheduling routes through different resources effectively transforming job scheduling problems into a kind of job shop scheduling problems [39]. This property of Grid scheduling problems directly influences the scheduling techniques on parallel processors: For instance, to consider the processing time of the data transfer, computer resources must be reserved in advance. Hence, simple batch job scheduling is not sufficient anymore, and most Grid schedulers support *advance reservation* [48].

Because of the existence of different resource owners in a Grid, the Grid scheduler is not run by these resource owners as in the supercomputer case, but rather by an independent broker. This Grid scheduler may then interact with the local schedulers that are run on each machine and also support local users that do not submit their jobs via the Grid [45].

Service Level Agreements. A supercomputer typically has a single owner and is governed by a single policy that determines the rules and constraints of scheduling. The users must accept these rules unless they are able to manually submit their applications to other supercomputers. However, this alternative does not affect the scheduling process. In Grids, there are often several independent owners which have established different rules and restrictions for their resources. Note that this assertion may not be true for so-called Enterprise Grids [26], that belong to a single enterprise with many different locations and resource installations. But if the Grid comprises similar resources from different owners, users expect that the machine allocation decision considers the rules and policies of the various owners. Especially when being charged for the resource usage, users want the allocation and schedule properties of their applications to be guaranteed in form of so-called *service level agreements* (SLA) [34].

In addition to static components, like the level of security, those service level agreements typically contain various dynamic and job-specific properties, like the amount of available resources within a time frame, the start time of a time frame, and the cost of the resource per occupied time unit. The actual values of these SLA components are closely related to the actual schedule. They may depend on the amount and the type of job requests as well as on the amount and type of available resources. Dynamic parameters of an agreement are typically determined with the help of a negotiation process [58]. Therefore, Grid scheduling may also include a negotiation component [32]. Moreover, global scheduling objectives, like makespan, average utilization, average throughput, or average (weighted) response time have a different meaning and relevance in a scenario that involves independent resources providers and independent job owners. For instance, if the utilization of a specific machine in the Grid is low then the owner of this machine may decide to drop the resource price in order to attract more applications.

A Grid scheduling system that supports SLAs must include processes that automatically generate SLAs based on possibly complex directives of owners and users [52]. It must also be able to support complex objective functions in order to decide between different offers for a job request. Therefore, even if we ignore the machine allocation problem, the local machine scheduling becomes significantly more complex than the scheduling of a single parallel processor. Assuming that in the future, many parallel processors will also be part of a Grid, the Grid poses new challenges even for job scheduling on parallel processors. Also if an independent broker runs the Grid scheduler he may define additional SLAs with resource providers and job owners.

Finally, there is always the possibility that an SLA cannot be satisfied. If such a problem is foreseeable and there is still enough time to react then some form of rescheduling [4] may provide some help. These considerations will again influence the Grid scheduler. However, if the violation of the SLA is only determined after the execution of the job, such as too few resources were provided within the promised time frame, then either the SLA contains some clause to handle this problem, or a mediator in the Grid is needed. In this case however, the Grid scheduler is not affected unless we speak of an SLA that covers the actual scheduling process.

Accounting and Billing. Since traditional supercomputers typically have a single owner, their accounting and billing is rather simple. It is sufficient to log the job requests and the actual resource utilization of the jobs. As the rate is typically invariable, the cost can easily be determined. Because of the monopoly of the machine provider, a best-effort strategy usually suffices. Therefore, the user has few options if the resources are suddenly not available or other problems occur.

However, in a Grid environment, resource providers may be willing to provide guarantees that are marked down in an SLA. To verify whether the conditions of the SLA have been satisfied, the entire process from job request submission to the delivery of the results must be recorded [40]. Therefore, accounting becomes more complicated than for isolated parallel processors. Similarly, billing is not equivalent with multiplying a fixed rate with the actual resource consumption but requires the considerations of the SLAs including possible penalties for violating parts of the agreement. The Grid scheduling system is part of the above-mentioned process. Therefore, a scheduling system must be transparent to enable validating the correct execution of an agreement.

As already mentioned, a broker [53] in a Grid system may be bound by agreements with resource providers and job owners. This is especially true if several brokers compete with each other in a single Grid. Then the details of the scheduling process must be recorded to determine whether the guarantees of the SLA covering the scheduler have been satisfied.

Security. There are significant security concerns in a Grid as an application of a user may run on a distant resource. Most resource policies require some form of user screening before a user is admitted to a resource. In case of a local compute center with a few carefully selected remote users, this policy can be enforced with relatively little effort. In Grids, this policy is not feasible and must be replaced by some form of trust delegation. This task is often handled by so-called virtual organizations (*VO*) [17]. Although security has a significant impact on the Grid infrastructure it does not affect the scheduling system to a large extent. But security concerns may prevent schedulers from providing information about future schedules freely, and thus reduce the efficiency of Grid schedulers. This problem is particularly relevant for rearrangement tasks that try to save an SLA in case of unexpected problems.

Reliability and Fault Tolerance. In large systems, occasional failures are unavoidable. If the system is subject to a best-effort policy such a failure is a nuisance to the users but has no other consequences. For important applications, users can try to secure a second resource if they accept the additional cost. In Grids, users may try to push the responsibility toward the resource providers by negotiating appropriate SLAs. In case of a failure, the resource provider typically attempts to use rescheduling in order to avoid or at least reduce the penalty costs. Therefore, reliability directly influences Grid scheduling as well [29].

Virtualization. As already discussed user may benefit from the heterogeneity of Grid systems. However, this heterogeneity also comes with a disadvantage: Only few systems in a Grid may actually be able to execute a given application due to all the constraints involving application software, system software and hardware. This may lead to bottlenecks even in large Grids. Users can partially avoid this problem by *virtualization*, that is, by providing an execution environment together with their application, see Section 5. This concept receives increasing interest on the operating system level and is recently considered in Grids as well. As with security, virtualization has little direct influence on Grid scheduling. It opens new scheduling opportunities (as discussed in Section 5), but predictions of execution parameters become less reliable. However, virtualization directly affects scheduling on the operating system level.

Workloads. From supercomputers, we know that only few theoretical results provide benefits for job schedulers in real systems [44]. Instead, the development of new schedulers for parallel processors and the improvement of given schedulers is often based on discrete event simulations with recorded workloads as presented in numerous publications of previous JSSPP workshops, for instance [25,5]. Therefore, a lot of work in the domain of JSSPP has been devoted to workloads in recent years. As there is only a limited number of recorded traces, this work focuses on the characterization of these workloads and on scaling them so that an appropriate workload can be provided for a new installation [10].

Since there are few Grids running in production mode, only few real Grid workloads are available yet [35]. Nevertheless, there is some effort to record Grid workloads (see `http://gwa.ewi.tudelft.nl`), which may lead to a comprehensive archive in the future. However, it is likely that these workloads will depend to a large extend on the community running the Grid. Generally it is very difficult to optimize a Community Grid by using a workload from another Community Grid. Similarly, it is unclear how to scale traces as there may be strong dependencies between the machine composition in a Grid and the workload.

In general, simulation with workloads are only meaningful if the properties of the individual jobs remain invariant. To a large extend, this is true for job execution in a rigid and exclusive fashion on a parallel processor. If the job is malleable or moldable a simulation requires the prediction of the processing time for a certain degree of parallelism from the recorded processing time using the original degree of parallelism. Theoretical studies often assume a divisible load characteristic which holds in practice only for bag-of-tasks of embarrassingly-parallel jobs, while jobs with extensive communication between processors show a different behavior [42]. In Grids, similar problems occur in connection with heterogeneity. It is difficult to predict the processing time of a job on certain processors if only the recorded processing time on other processors is available. The different speed model (Q_m) of scheduling theory generally does not apply to processors, see the results of the SPEC benchmarks (`http://www.spec.org/benchmarks.html`). Therefore, it is very difficult to optimize a Grid scheduler even on the same system that was already used to record the applied workload.

Metrics and Evaluation. Since parallel computers are expensive, they are usually not available for extensive experiments to optimize system components. Instead, simulations are frequently applied on models that have a sufficiently close relationship to the real system. Then only some final tuning must be performed on the real system. As already discussed, this approach has been successfully executed on parallel computers. It requires a given metric that can be evaluated with the help of simulations. For parallel systems, the most common metrics are utilization, average throughput, and average weighted response time [15]. All these metrics depend on the completion time of the jobs which is provided by the simulations.

In Grids, we must consider the various (dynamic) objectives of resource providers and application owners. Therefore, scheduling becomes a multi-objective problem since it is very difficult to combine these objectives into a single scalar metric [57]. Moreover, as the objectives are not static, it is not possible to simply evaluate another schedule unless the objective functions and the negotiation process are invariant and predictable. However, this assumption will not hold in many real situations. Hence, it is not realistic to assume that a real Grid scheduling system can be optimized with the help of simulations even if appropriate workloads and sufficient computing power is available. In Grid scheduling, we face a problem that is similar to the optimization of the performance of a stock broker. But while the Grid is some form of a market it is likely less volatile than the stock market. We may therefore try to optimize single parts of this complex scheduling system and assume that the rest remains unchanged. Once enough workloads and sufficient data on the dependencies between the various components are available, we may start to model and simulate a whole system.

Generalizing the Challenges

Grid scheduling is a very complex problem that uses common job schedulers for parallel processors as subcomponents. Even if job scheduling for parallel processors has reached some degree of maturity, many subproblems in Grid scheduling are not yet solved.

Grids typically consist of machines with different numbers of processors. As small machines with few processors cannot efficiently execute highly parallel jobs unless multisite scheduling with performance loss is supported, large machines with many processors should be reserved for those highly parallel jobs. On the other hand, load balancing may require to use those large machines also for sequential jobs or jobs with little parallelism. The machine allocation algorithm must find a suitable tradeoff between both objectives.

Heterogeneity transforms job scheduling problems into job shop problems. In addition, the comparison between different schedules may become rather difficult as the prediction of execution properties on other machines is subject to a significant amount of uncertainty.

Service level agreements introduce new dynamic objectives into the scheduling problems resulting in multi-objective problems. Moreover, the objective functions of the various job and resource owners may not be available for the evaluation of a scheduling system. In order to satisfy SLAs even in the case of machine failure, the scheduling system should support rescheduling which can be considered as a deterministic problem that must be solved within a rather short time frame.

Other properties of Grid systems, like security or virtualization, pose significant challenges to Grid infrastructures but have limited influence on the scheduling system.

Finally, there are not yet enough public workloads traces on Grid systems. It is also not clear how to use such workloads in new systems with different sizes or on systems which belong to a different community. With respect to the evaluation, the common metrics of parallel processors may not be applicable to Grids. But it is not clear how to determine an objective that can be used for evaluation and sufficiently represents the multi-objective character of the real Grid scheduling problem.

4   Web Services

Large-scale web services are one of the fastest-growing sectors of the computer industry since the mid 1990s. This growth is expressed not only in revenue and market share, but also in the scale of the problems solved and the infrastructure required to provide the solutions. Generally speaking, large-scale web services have three usage models with strong relevance to our field:

1. Online service–this is the part that is most visible to users, where they interact with the system through queries or requests. This aspect is latency-sensitive, and typically relies on parallelism to provide the shortest response time and the highest reliability. Much of the parallel logic behind these large-scale transactional systems is devoted to resilient resource management and load balancing, and less to computation. Using a search engine as an example, the online service represents the user query page, where a query is received, parsed, and distributed to query servers, and the results are aggregated, ranked, and presented to the user in HTML form.

2. Offline processing–this is the part that gathers and processes the data that is used in the online service. It is typically less sensitive to latency and more sensitive to throughput, not unlike the Grids mentioned in Section 3. Load balancing and fault tolerance play a larger role in the economics of the service than in the online service. Additionally, the offline processing can potentially be significantly more reliant on computing and I/O resources than the online service. These differences translate to different scheduling and resource-management requirements between the online and offline parts. In the search engine example, this part represents the crawling, indexing, reversing the search engine index as well merging, and distributing it.

3. Research and Development (R&D)–large web service companies are always looking for ways to improve and expand their services. Developing newer services and features often requires similar resources to those that are already used by the production services, whether online or offline, and for large companies, the scale of the resources required for R&D approximates the scale of the production systems. Unlike the production systems though, resource management can be more lax on the one hand (neither latency or throughput is as critical as on production systems), and more strained on the other (more users are competing for the same resources in a less-predictable environment). Going back to the search engine environment, this part represents the ongoing work on improving crawling algorithms, ranking, database/index representations, and performance tuning to mention just a few aspects.

The following paragraphs give a breakdown of some of the main resource management challenges in large-scale web services.

Economy. Because of the large scale of some web serving farms and the business nature of the companies that run them, economical issues become a primary consideration in web server resource management. For example, choices such as how requests are distributed and balanced across a cluster, the degree of redundancy in request execution, and which nodes to route the request to in a heterogeneous cluster, have an effect not only on the cost per request, but also on the server's reliability and responsiveness, themselves being part of the company's business model. Thus, the algorithms used for balancing and managing these resources can have a significant impact on the company's bottom line. Resource managers have to respond to temporal cycles in load, as well as peak and average load, while aiming to minimize overall costs of hardware, power, and human maintenance [7]. Complicating the economical models further are the potential large differences between different services and the resources they need to manage, making a generalized solution hard to develop.

Power management. The rising concern about power consumption in microprocessors (Sec. 2) has permeated virtually all systems where microprocessors are used. Multiply the power consumption of a single microprocessor by the thousands of microprocessors that typically comprise a large web serving farm, and you get an expensive power bill and significant excessive heat that further taxes the reliability and economic balance of the farm. The larger the scale of the server, the worse the problem becomes, as is demonstrated by Google's move to a more efficient power supply component of their own design (see `http://services.google.com/blog_resources/PSU_white_paper.pdf`). Scheduling, however, can play a significant role in increasing the power efficiency of a large-scale farm [7]. For example, outside of peak hours, jobs can be all scheduled on a subset of nodes, while suspending the remaining load until peak increases. Or jobs can be distributed across multi-core nodes so that some cores remain in low-power idle mode until requested.

Resource sharing. Despite the occasional peaks in request loads to web services, most load exhibits cycles and peaks, based on diurnal cycles, weekly cycles, external events, etc. [59]. Web server loads can be hard to predict, and there is still plenty of room for research in characterizing and modeling their workloads. Still, even with a complete understanding of the workloads, it is reasonable to assume that most servers will operate below capacity some of the time. It is desirable to manage the shared resources of the online system with the R&D activities, so that lightly-loaded production machines can run R&D tasks, while still being highly available if load suddenly increases.[2] Oversubscribing online resources to handle R&D tasks touches many interesting and familiar topics in parallel job scheduling such as load balancing, managing priorities, service guarantees, predictability and modeling of load, and dynamic management of responsiveness.

Resilience and fault tolerance. If there is one working assumption that holds true for large data stores and web servers it is "Everything Fails. Everything!"[3]. Many thousands of commodity components typically comprise a large web service, and as their number increase, so does the probability of a component failure at any given time. Resource management algorithms therefore cannot have the luxury of dedicated supercomputer middleware that often assumes a reasonably reliable hardware. Redundancy, fault-tolerance, and graceful degradation under load and failures must be built into the resource manager. One example is the offline work distribution algorithm MapReduce [8], that can transparently and scalably replicate tasks and re-execute them if required. Online resource management requires different scheduling for resilience, since service latencies are more important than throughput. As servers grow even larger and the services grow more complex, the importance of fault tolerance will similarly grow and require novel resource management solutions.

Heterogeneity. One of the distinguishing characteristics of large-scale web servers, as opposed to most supercomputer and to a lesser extent, Grid environments,

---

[2] We assume that offline production systems have a more predictable load and operate at near capacity most of the time.

[3] Quoted Sivasubramanian and Vogels' talk "Challenges in Building an Infinitely Scalable Datastore" in the 2007 Google Scalability Conference `http://www.google.com/events/scalability_seattle/`

is that server farms are rarely acquired at once to serve a predetermined capacity. Instead, servers are expected to constantly grow as the required capacity increases over time. Web servers grow by adding nodes that correspond to the optimal balance between price and required performance at the time, and because of the dynamic nature of the industry, these nodes are likely to differ from the previous acquisition or the next one. Consequently, a large-scale web server consists of at least a few different types of nodes–possibly with varying degrees of performance, memory, storage space, I/O capabilities, or all at once. Dynamically allocating tasks to these servers has to take into account this heterogeneity in order to meet the expected performance requirements. The evolving nature of the cluster, as well as the constant changes in configuration resulting from node failures, suggest that a very dynamic approach to resource management is needed, as opposed to most supercomputers and Grids. Although here too some initial studies have addressed these issues [7], there is still much room for research in the area.

Workload characterization. The workloads of the online and offline environments are typically quite different from each other, as well as from traditional supercomputer workloads. Perhaps the most significant difference from supercomputer workloads is that Web-server workloads tend to be embarrassingly parallel: loosely-coupled, with little or no synchronization between parallel tasks. This removes an important constraint that facilitates the development of efficient scheduling. On the other hand, other workload characteristics make scheduling more challenging than with supercomputer workloads. For example, both the offline and online systems are often data-bound and require access to information that is distributed across the compute nodes. Scheduling tasks to compute close to the data they operate on reaps a significant performance benefit in these cases. Other idiosyncratic workload characteristics include the dynamic nature of offered load on the online system, which is largely determined by uncontrolled agents outside of the system (the users). Devising better scheduling for the environments requires that we understand and characterize workloads for the online and offline parts of the web servers, as we do for more traditional parallel environments.[4]

Generalizing the Challenges

Probably the single most challenging and representative factor in large-scale web service scheduling is the unprecedented huge scale of most aspects involved with it: the size of the clusters; the number of users; the rate of transactions; the amount of data, files, and I/O required to service these requests; and the network resources used internally and externally. Scheduling and resource management are further complicated by the dynamic nature of the underlying infrastructure, with heterogeneous resources being added and removed constantly. Because of

---

[4] The workload of the R&D environment usually consists of a mix of online and offline applications, and is probably even harder to generalize.

these factors, as well as the different workloads, scheduling for web services might require some different approaches, compared to Grids or supercomputers. For example, the already mentioned MapReduce algorithm introduced by Google [8] does a good job in managing dynamic resources for the offline aspect of Google's search engine, but would perform poorly with the typical fine-grain, tightly coupled supercomputer workload. Nevertheless, many scheduling principles, as well as work on metrics, workloads, and methodological issues, have much in common with other parallel environments.

5   Virtualization

Virtualization in this context refers to running multiple operating system environments in one or more nodes concurrently. Typically, a node would have a host OS that can run a "guest OS" as an application, often by emulating a complete hardware environment for each guest OS. Although the commoditized virtualization technology is relatively new, it is quickly becoming widespread, and new software and hardware is quickly being developed to support more features and provide better virtualization performance.[5]

One of the lingering challenges in managing virtualized environments efficiently is scheduling: since the host and guest OSs often operate with no coordination and knowledge of each other's scheduling, mis-scheduling issues continue to crop up. For example, an interactive application in a guest OS might be scheduled correctly by the guest OS, but since the host OS is unaware of the application's requirements, the guest OS (and by extension, the application) could be mistakenly scheduled as a noninteractive program.

The area of scheduling research for virtualization is still in its infancy, and it may be too early to explore well-developed scheduling issues with virtualization. Nevertheless, we identify the following topics where job scheduling research can benefit virtualized environments:

 - Scheduling inside the guest OS: Currently, a guest OS schedules its processes oblivious of any host OS constraints, as demonstrated in the previous example with interactive applications. Scheduling research can address this class of problems by (1) characterizing the scheduling needs of different processes; (2) characterizing the scheduling constraints and services that the host OS can guarantee; and (3) communicating and matching these requirements and constraints to create an acceptable schedule in the guest OS within the host environment.
 - Similarly, the guest OS is oblivious of any other guest OSs or processes running on the same host, creating more scheduling mismatches. The problem can thus be generalized to creating a schedule within the host OS that takes into account the requirements of all host processes and guest OS processes.

---

[5] Refer for example to Intel's new hardware support for virtualization in its latest architecture (code-named Penryn).

– Looking at a larger scale still, virtualization is often used in Grids and multi-host environments to provide dynamic allocation of customized computing images in the form of virtual images[6]. This extension creates additional meta-scheduling issues for the virtualized environment, not unlike those discussed in Section 3, but with additional consideration for the moldable and malleable nature of virtualized resources.

Generalizing the Challenges

Research into the implications of virtualization has only yet begun. We believe that scheduling will play an increasingly important role in virtualized environments where performance and utilization matter. One of the keys to the successful scheduling of such heterogeneous workloads and execution environments is the ability to characterize clearly the scheduling requirements of different processes, and scheduling them accordingly. The literature already contains examples of process characterizations for several scheduling domains, such as multimedia and parallel processing [2,12,24,55]. We think the time is ripe to create and generalize additional characterizations that would fit the virtualized environments as well. Such characterizations need to take into account the entire process stack, from the multi-threaded guest process at the one end to the host OS or meta-scheduler at the other. Eventually, these characterizations may even help define a standard of communication of scheduling information between host and guest OSs.

6   Overarching Considerations

There are several considerations from those listed above that span most or all of the new scheduling challenges. In this section, we will briefly generalize these considerations.

Workload. Virtually all scheduling and performance evaluations start with a workload, and all use cases described above require good workloads for research progress. While a good workload often depends on the use case in general, useful workloads for research contain long enough traces (or model-derived data) for metrics to stabilize, and are detailed enough to allow multiple factor analyses. For classical supercomputers, a handful of such workloads has been collected and maintained by Feitelson [38]. An effort to collect Grid workloads is also underway, but it is in its early phases (see http://gwa.ewi.tudelft.nl). For other use cases, however, we are not aware of any centralized effort to collect such workloads. The workload challenge does not end with collection, but merely starts: To be useful for researchers and to enable performance evaluation, workloads need to be analyzed, characterized, and possibly classified and modeled. By understanding and generalizing data from multiple workloads, we can develop

---

[6] For example, Amazon's *Elastic Compute Cloud*
(http://www.amazon.com/gp/browse.html?node=201590011)

better scheduling schemes, as well as a better understanding of the similarities between scheduling scenarios in Grids, web servers, supercomputers, and the like.

Heterogeneity. Unlike traditional supercomputers, most contemporary parallel architectures offer some degree of heterogeneity: from the single chip level with parallel execution modules and simultaneous multithreading, through the single node and its heterogeneous components such as accelerators, through the cluster and the Grid with their heterogeneous nodes. Scheduling for all levels now needs to take into account unequal resources to manage which complicates both the optimization problem and the metrics themselves being optimized.

Scheduling for power. Power constraints now appear in resource management schemes at virtually all levels, from keeping the temperatures on the surface of a multi-core chip controlled and equally distributed, to lowering the power and cooling bills of large web servers and Grid farms. In some instances, power consumption is the single most influential resource management constraint of a parallel installation, and every percent saved translates to significant cost and emission savings. Scheduling can play an important role in power saving by incorporating power considerations into the bigger resource management question. Although work on this incorporation started several years ago [47,33], scheduling for power saving is still a relatively unexplored research topic.

Security. Security is a fast-growing concern in today's computing environments. Most of the scenarios described above involve multiple users, or at least multiple applications. Protecting the data and resources of one user or application is vital for the successful deployment of parallel and shared computing resources [56]. To some extent, security considerations affect scheduling. For example, some applications may request to run without sharing any memory or network resources with other applications. Security considerations can also conflict with scheduling considerations, such as the "black-box" approach of virtualized images, that discourages shared resource-management and scheduling decisions. A large research gap exists in the area of scheduling with/for security considerations in these new domains.

Economy. Just like security considerations, economy considerations affect, and sometimes even govern, the shared use of compute resources. Large data bases may not be available for free if they are useful for commercial activities, like weather forecast and traffic data for logistics. Moreover, an increasing number of users and user groups need information systems which will become more complex and more expensive in the future, for instance, due to power consumption. This may lead to a shortage of resources and result in user priorities based on the price a user is willing to pay for the provided information service. It may not be the task of scheduling systems to determine market prices of information resources but scheduling systems certainly need to convert a given policy into the distribution of resources.

Metrics. Properly using meaningful metrics is an inseparable part of performance evaluation. Although scheduler performance evaluations typically use well-publicized metrics such as average response time and throughput, these metrics are not always used correctly or do not describe the performance picture adequately [13,22]. Moreover, metrics will have to be somewhat adjusted to account for some of the newer use cases described above. For example, Grid users may care more about fairness than response time [43]. Scheduling on heterogeneous architectures requires different treatment of run time and resource utilization for performance than for billing, since not all resources are equal. There is therefore a need to extend and unify current scheduling evaluation metrics in order to be useful and meaningful for the actual use cases.

7   Conclusion

Scheduling for traditional multiprocessors is still a hard problem that is actively researched. The recent introduction of several architectures with different types of parallelism and a wide spectrum of uses, workloads, requirements, and hardware, poses an even harder challenge to the scheduling community. If parallel job scheduling can be viewed as a multi-dimensional optimization problem, these new architectures now add several more dimensions to the problem.

Nevertheless, this challenge is also a great opportunity. The scheduling community can evolve and incorporate lessons learned over many years of research (much of which has been published in JSSPP), and advance the state of the art in the new emerging fields. Despite the various architectures, there are many shared issues between the different scheduling domains: workloads, requirement characterization, resource management, meaningful metrics, power consumption, and others. All these topics are inter-related and are studied by contributors to JSSPP. The time is ripe now for this community to generalize these scheduling characterizations to the emerging domains in parallel job scheduling.

References

1. Antonopoulos, C.D., Nikolopoulos, D.S., Papatheodorou, T.S.: Scheduling algorithms with bus bandwidth considerations for SMPs. In: 32nd International Conference on Parallel Processing (ICPP), October 2003, Kaohsiung, Taiwan (2003), www.cs.wm.edu/~dsn/papers/icpp03.pdf
2. Banachowski, S.A., Brandt, S.A.: The BEST Scheduler for Integrated Processing of Best-Effort and Soft Real-Time Processes. In: Multimedia Computing and Networking (MMCN), January 2002, San Jose, CA (2002), www.cse.ucsc.edu/~sbanacho/papers/banachowski-mmcn02.ps
3. Becker, D., Wolf, F., Frings, W., Geimer, M., Wylie, B.J.N., Mohr, B.: Automatic trace-based performance analysis of metacomputing applications. In: 21st International Parallel and Distributed Processing Symposium (IPDPS), IEEE Computer Society, Los Alamitos (2007)

4. Berman, F., Casanova, H., Chien, A., Cooper, K., Dail, H., Dasgupta, A., Deng, W., Dongarra, J., Johnsson, L., Kennedy, K., Koelbel, C., Liu, B., Liu, X., Mandal, A., Marin, G., Mazina, M., Mellor-Crummey, J., Mendes, C., Olugbile, A., Patel, J.M., Reed, D., Shi, Z., Sievert, O., Xia, H., YarKhan, A.: New grid scheduling and rescheduling methods in the grads project. International Journal of Parallel Programming 33(2), 209–229 (2005)

5. Bucur, A.I.D., Epema, D.: Scheduling policies for processor co-allocation in multi-cluster systems. IEEE Transactions on Parallel and Distributed Systems 18, 958–972 (2007)

6. Bulpin, J.R., Pratt, I.A.: Multiprogramming performance of the Pentium 4 with hyper-threading. In: Second Annual Workshop on Duplicating, Deconstruction and Debunking (WDDD), pp. 53–62, Munchen, Germany (June 2004), www.ece.wisc.edu/~wddd/2004/06_bulpin.pdf

7. Chase, J.S., Anderson, D.C., Thakar, P.N., Vahdat, A.M., Doyle, R.P.: Managing energy and server resources in hosting centers. SIGOPS Operating Systems Review 35(5), 103–116 (2001)

8. Dean, J., Ghemawat, S.: Mapreduce: simplified data processing on large clusters. In: Symposium on Operating Systems Design and Implementation (OSDI), p. 10, Berkeley, CA, USA, USENIX Association (2004)

9. Ernemann, C., Hamscher, V., Schwiegelshohn, U., Streit, A., Yahyapour, R.: Enhanced algorithms for multi-site scheduling. In: Parashar, M. (ed.) GRID 2002. LNCS, vol. 2536, pp. 219–231. Springer, Heidelberg (2002)

10. Ernemann, C., Song, B., Yahyapour, R.: Scaling of workload traces. In: Feitelson, D.G., Rudolph, L., Schwiegelshohn, U. (eds.) JSSPP 2003. LNCS, vol. 2862, pp. 166–182. Springer, Heidelberg (2003), www.cs.huji.ac.il/~feit/parsched/

11. Ernemann, C., Yahyapour, R.: Applying economic scheduling methods to grid environments. In: Nabrzyski, J., Schopf, J.M., Weglarz, J. (eds.) Grid Resource Management - State of the Art and Future Trends, pp. 491–506. Kluwer Academic Publishers, Dordrecht (2003)

12. Etsion, Y., Tsafrir, D., Feitelson, D.G.: Desktop scheduling: How can we know what the user wants. In: 14th ACM International Workshop on Network and Operating Systems Support for Digital Audio and Video (NOSSDAV), County Cork, Ireland, June 2004, pp. 110–115 (2004), www.cs.huji.ac.il/~feit/papers/HuCpri04NOSSDAV.pdf

13. Feitelson, D.G.: Metrics for parallel job scheduling and their convergence. In: Feitelson, D.G., Rudolph, L. (eds.) JSSPP 2001. LNCS, vol. 2221, pp. 188–1205. Springer, Heidelberg (2001), www.cs.huji.ac.il/~feit/parsched/

14. Feitelson, D.G., Rudolph, L.: Gang scheduling performance benefits for fine-grain synchronization. Journal of Parallel and Distributed Computing 16(4), 306–318 (1992), www.cs.huji.ac.il/~feit/papers/GangPerf92JPDC.ps.gz

15. Feitelson, D.G., Rudolph, L., Schwigelshohn, U.: Parallel job scheduling – A status report. In: Feitelson, D.G., Rudolph, L., Schwiegelshohn, U. (eds.) JSSPP 2004. LNCS, vol. 3277, pp. 1–16. Springer, Heidelberg (2005), www.cs.huji.ac.il/~feit/parsched/

16. Flautner, K., Uhlig, R., Reinhardt, S., Mudge, T.: Thread-level parallelism and interactive performance of desktop applications. In: Ninth International Conference on Architectural Support for Programming Languages and Operating Systems (ASPLOS), November 2000, pp. 129–138 (2000), www.eecs.umich.edu/~tnm/papers/asplos00.pdf

17. Foster, I.T.: The anatomy of the grid: Enabling scalable virtual organizations. In: Sakellariou, R., Keane, J.A., Gurd, J.R., Freeman, L. (eds.) Euro-Par 2001. LNCS, vol. 2150, pp. 1–4. Springer, Heidelberg (2001)
18. Foster, I.T., Kesselman, C. (eds.): The GRID: Blueprint for a New Computing Infrastructure. Morgan Kaufmann, San Francisco (1998)
19. Fox, G.C., Gannon, D.: Concurrency and Computation: Practice and Experience. Special issue: Workflow in grid systems: Editorials 18(10), 1009–1019 (2006)
20. Frachtenberg, E.: Process Scheduling for the Parallel Desktop. In: Proceedings of the International Symposium on Parallel Architectures, Algorithms, and Networks (I-SPAN 2005), December 2005, Las Vegas, NV (2005)
21. Frachtenberg, E., Etsion, Y.: Hardware parallelism: Are operating systems ready (case studies in mis-scheduling). In: Second Workshop on the Interaction between Operating Systems and Computer Architecture (WIOSCA 2006), In conjunction with ISCA-33, June 2006, Boston, MA (June 2006)
22. Frachtenberg, E., Feitelson, D.G.: Pitfalls in parallel job scheduling evaluation. In: Feitelson, D.G., Frachtenberg, E., Rudolph, L., Schwiegelshohn, U. (eds.) JSSPP 2005. LNCS, vol. 3834, pp. 257–282. Springer, Heidelberg (2005), www.cs.huji.ac.il/~etcs/pubs/
23. Frachtenberg, E., Feitelson, D.G, Petrini, F., Fernandez, J.: Flexible CoScheduling: Mitigating load imbalance and improving utilization of heterogeneous resources. In: 17th International Parallel and Distributed Processing Symposium (IPDPS), April 2003, Nice, France (2003), www.cs.huji.ac.il/~etcs/pubs/
24. Frachtenberg, E., Feitelson, D.G., Petrini, F., Fernandez, J.: Adaptive parallel job scheduling with flexible coscheduling. IEEE Transactions on Parallel and Distributed Systems 16(11), 1066–1077 (2005), www.cs.huji.ac.il/~etcs/pubs/
25. Franke, C., Lepping, J., Schwiegelshohn, U.: On advantages of scheduling using genetic fuzzy systems. In: Frachtenberg, E., Schwiegelshohn, U. (eds.) JSSPP 2006. LNCS, vol. 4376, pp. 68–93. Springer, Heidelberg (2007)
26. Goyal, B., Lawande, S.: Grid Revolution: An Introduction to Enterprise Grid Computing. The McGraw-Hill Companies, New York (2006)
27. Peter Hofstee, H.: Power efficient processor architecture and the Cell processor. In: 11th International Symposium on High-Performance Computer Architecture, February 2005, San Francisco, CA (2005), www.hpcaconf.org/hpca11/papers/25_hofstee-cellprocessor_final.pdf
28. Hotovy, S.: Workload evolution on the cornell theory center IBM SP2. In: Feitelson, D.G., Rudolph, L. (eds.) IPPS-WS 1996 and JSSPP 1996. LNCS, vol. 1162, pp. 27–40. Springer, Heidelberg (1996)
29. Huedo, E., Montero, R.S., Llorente, I.M.: Evaluating the reliability of computational grids from the end user's point of view. Journal of Systems Architecture 52(12), 727–736 (2006)
30. Jones, T., Tuel, W., Brenner, L., Fier, J., Caffrey, P., Dawson, S., Neely, R., Blackmore, R., Maskell, B., Tomlinson, P., Roberts, M.: Improving the scalability of parallel jobs by adding parallel awareness to the operating system. In: 15th IEEE/ACM Supercomputing, Phoenix, AZ, November 2003, ACM Press and IEEE Computer Society Press (2003), www.sc-conference.org/sc2003/paperpdfs/pap136.pdf
31. Kanellos, M.: Designer puts 96 cores on single chip (October 2004), http://news.com.com/2100-1006_3-5399128.html
32. Li, J., Yahyapour, R.: Learning-based negotiation strategies for grid scheduling. In: IEEE International Symposium on Cluster Computing and the Grid (CCGrid 2006), Singapore, pp. 567–583. IEEE Press, Los Alamitos (2006)

33. Lu, Y.-H., Benini, L., De Micheli, G.: Low-power task scheduling for multiple devices. In: Proceedings of the Eighth International Workshop on Hardware/software codesign (CODES 2000), pp. 39–43. ACM, New York, NY, USA (2000)

34. MacLaren, J., Sakellariou, R., Garibaldi, J., Ouelhadj, D., Krishnakumar, K.T.: Towards service level agreement based scheduling on the grid. In: Proceedings of the Workshop on Planning and Scheduling for Web and Grid Services, July 2004, pp. 100–102, Whistler, BC, Canada (2004)

35. Medernach, E.: Workload analysis of a cluster in a grid environment (JSSPP-page). In: Feitelson, D.G., Frachtenberg, E., Rudolph, L., Schwiegelshohn, U. (eds.) JSSPP 2005. LNCS, vol. 3834, pp. 36–61. Springer, Heidelberg (2005), www.cs.huji.ac.il/~feit/parsched/

36. Nieh, J., Hanko, J.G., Northcutt, J.D., Wall, G.A.: SVR4 UNIX scheduler unacceptable for multimedia applications. In: Fourth ACM International Workshop on Network and Operating Systems Support for Digital Audio and Video (NOSS-DAV), November 1993 (1993), citeseer.ist.psu.edu/443381.html

37. Ousterhout, J.K.: Scheduling techniques for concurrent systems. In: Third International Conference on Distributed Computing Systems, October 1982, Miami, FL, pp. 22–30 (1982)

38. Parallel workload archive, http://www.cs.huji.ac.il/labs/parallel/workload

39. Pinedo, M.: Scheduling: Theory, Algorithms, and Systems, 2nd edn. Prentice-Hall, New Jersey (2002)

40. Piro, R.M., Guarise, A., Werbrouck, A.: An economy-based accounting infrastructure for the datagrid. In: Proceedings of the Fourth International Workshop on Grid Computing (GRID 2003), p. 202. IEEE Computer Society Press, Washington, DC, USA (2003)

41. Reinders, J.: Intel Threading Building Blocks. O'Reilly and Associates (July 2007)

42. Robertazzi, T.G., Yu, D.: Multi-Source Grid Scheduling for Divisible Loads. In: Proceedings of the 40th Annual Conference on Information Sciences and Systems, March 2006, pp. 188–191 (2006)

43. Sabin, G., Sadayappan, P.: Unfairness metrics for space-sharing parallel job schedulers. In: Feitelson, D.G., Frachtenberg, E., Rudolph, L., Schwiegelshohn, U. (eds.) JSSPP 2005. LNCS, vol. 3834, pp. 238–256. Springer, Heidelberg (2005), www.cs.huji.ac.il/~feit/parsched/

44. Schwiegelshohn, U., Yahyapour, R.: Fairness in parallel job scheduling. Journal of Scheduling 3(5), 297–320 (2000)

45. Schwiegelshohn, U., Yahyapour, R.: Attributes for communication between grid scheduling instances. In: Nabrzyski, J., Schopf, J.M., Weglarz, J. (eds.) Grid Resource Management – State of the Art and Future Trends, pp. 41–52. Kluwer Academic Publishers, Dordrecht (2003)

46. Shankland, S.: Azul's first-generation Java servers go on sale (April 2005), http://news.com.com/2100-1010_3-5673193.html?tag=nl

47. Shin, Y., Choi, K.: Power conscious fixed priority scheduling for hard real-time systems. In: Proceedings of the 36th ACM/IEEE conference on Design automation (DAC 1999), pp. 134–139. ACM, New York, NY, USA (1999)

48. Siddiqui, M., Villazón, A., Fahringer, T.: Grid capacity planning with negotiation-based advance reservation for optimized qos. In: Löwe, W., Südholt, M. (eds.) SC 2006. LNCS, vol. 4089, p. 103. Springer, Heidelberg (2006)

49. Snavely, A., Tullsen, D.M.: Symbiotic jobscheduling for a simultaneous multi-threading processor. In: Ninth International Conference on Architectural Support for Programming Languages and Operating Systems (ASPLOS), November 2000, Cambridge, MA, pp. 234–244 (2000),
http://citeseer.ist.psu.edu/338334.html

50. Sodan, A.C., Lan, L.: LOMARC—Lookahead matchmaking for multi-resource coscheduling. In: Feitelson, D.G., Rudolph, L., Schwiegelshohn, U. (eds.) JSSPP 2004. LNCS, vol. 3277, pp. 288–315. Springer, Heidelberg (2005),
www.cs.huji.ac.il/~feit/parsched/

51. Tchernykh, A., Ramírez, J.M., Avetisyan, A., Kuzjurin, N., Grushin, D., Zhuk, S.: Two level job-scheduling strategies for a computational grid. In: Wyrzykowski, R., Dongarra, J., Meyer, N., Waśniewski, J. (eds.) PPAM 2005. LNCS, vol. 3911, pp. 774–781. Springer, Heidelberg (2006)

52. Terstyanszky, G., Kiss, T., Delaitre, T., Winter, S., Kacsuk, P.: Service-oriented production grids and user support. In: Gannon, D., Badia, R.M. (eds.) Proceedings of the Seventh IEEE/ACM international conference on Grid computing, Barcelona, pp. 323–324 (2006)

53. Venugopal, S., Buyya, R., Winton, L.: A grid service broker for scheduling distributed data-oriented applications on global grids. In: Proceedings of the Second Workshop on Middleware for grid computing (MGC 2004), pp. 75–80. ACM, New York, NY, USA (2004)

54. Williams, S., Shalf, J., Oliker, L., Kamil, S., Husbands, P., Yelick, K.: The potential of the cell processor for scientific computing. In: Proceedings of the Third Conference on Computing frontiers (CF 2006), pp. 9–20. ACM, New York, NY, USA (2006)

55. Wiseman, Y., Feitelson, D.G.: Paired gang scheduling. IEEE Transactions on Parallel and Distributed Systems 14(6), 581–592 (2003)

56. Xie, T., Qin, X.: Enhancing security of real-time applications on grids through dynamic scheduling. In: Feitelson, D.G., Frachtenberg, E., Rudolph, L., Schwiegelshohn, U. (eds.) JSSPP 2005. LNCS, vol. 3834, pp. 219–237. Springer, Heidelberg (2005), www.cs.huji.ac.il/~feit/parsched/

57. Ye, G., Rao, R., Li, M.: A multiobjective resources scheduling approach based on genetic algorithms in grid environment. In: Proceedings of the Fifth International Conference on Grid and Cooperative Computing Workshops (GCCW 2006), pp. 504–509. IEEE Computer Society, Los Alamitos (2006)

58. Yoshimoto, K., Kovatch, P., Andrews, P.: Co-scheduling with user-settable reservations. In: Feitelson, D.G., Frachtenberg, E., Rudolph, L., Schwiegelshohn, U. (eds.) JSSPP 2005. LNCS, vol. 3834, pp. 146–156. Springer, Heidelberg (2005),
www.cs.huji.ac.il/~feit/parsched/

59. Zhou, D., Lo, V.: Wave scheduler: Scheduling for faster turnaround time in peer-based desktop grid systems. In: Feitelson, D.G., Frachtenberg, E., Rudolph, L., Schwiegelshohn, U. (eds.) JSSPP 2005. LNCS, vol. 3834, pp. 194–218. Springer, Heidelberg (2005), www.cs.huji.ac.il/~feit/parsched/

Group-Wise Performance Evaluation of Processor Co-allocation in Multi-cluster Systems

John Ngubiri and Mario van Vliet

Nijmegen Institute for Informatics and Information Science
Radboud University Nijmegen
Toernooiveld 1, 6525 ED, Nijmegen,
The Netherlands
{ngubiri, mario}@cs.ru.nl

Abstract. Performance evaluation in multi-cluster processor co-allocation - like in many other parallel job scheduling problems- is mostly done by computing the average metric value for the entire job stream. This does not give a comprehensive understanding of the relative performance of the different jobs grouped by their characteristics. It is however the characteristics that affect how easy/hard jobs are to schedule. We, therefore, do not get to understand scheduler performance at job type level. In this paper, we study the performance of multi-cluster processor co-allocation for different job groups grouped by their size, components and widest component. We study their relative performance, sensitivity to parameters and how their performance is affected by the heuristics used to break them up into components. We show that the widest component us characteristic that most affects job schedulability. We also show that to get better performance, jobs should be broken up in such a way that the width of the widest component is minimized.

1 Introduction

Most research on parallel job scheduling had been focused on single Shared Memory computers, Distributed Memory Multiprocessors and clusters [10][23]. Recently, research work has been extended to computational and data grids [13][27] as well as multi-cluster systems [4][15]. A multi-cluster system is set up by connecting multiple clusters (possibly in different locations) into a bigger computational infrastructure. This is advantageous since it brings together a higher computational power at a lower cost. Jobs submitted to the system can be processed by any of the clusters or a combination of clusters. If multiple clusters are to process a job, the job is broken up into components and co-allocated [7]. The relatively slower inter-cluster communication speed, however, leads to an extended execution time of the co-allocated jobs. This leads to a lower effective utilization of the multi-cluster system. Studies [4] have shown that despite the drawbacks of the slower wide area network, co-allocation is a viable option.

While evaluating performance in parallel job scheduling, the mean value of the measurement metric is mostly used. Previous studies have shown that evaluation

E. Frachtenberg and U. Schwiegelshohn (Eds.): JSSPP 2007, LNCS 4942, pp. 24–36, 2008.

using job groups is beneficial. Srinivassan et al. [22] demonstrates how a deeper understanding of robustness for moldable jobs' schedulers can be obtained using size based groups. Job groups were also used in [24] [25] when comparing performance of Conservative and Aggressive backfilling. More studies by Feitelson [12] employed group-wise analysis for different job streams and measurement metrics to show underlying performance implications.

We use job groups to study the performance of Fit Processor First Served (FPFS) algorithm when scheduling jobs on a multi-cluster system with co-allocation. The jobs are grouped using size, number of components and width of the widest component. We deduce the most influential job characteristic that determines its schedulability. We also compare two heuristics for breaking up large jobs into components as they are being prepared for co-allocation. We also study the sensitivity of the groups' performance on the scheduler and job stream parameters.

We observe that there is a remarkable performance difference among the groups when FPFS scheduler is used. The difference is very small for the FCFS scheduler. We also observe that the width of the widest component is the strongest (of the three) factor that affects the performance (hence schedulability) of a certain job. Finally, we observe that performance can be improved by changing scheduler parameters (within a certain range) and by partitioning the jobs in such a way that the width of the widest component is minimized.

The rest of the paper is organized as follows: We describe our research model in Section 2. In Section 3, we describe the scheduling algorithm and placement policy used. In Section 4, we describe the set up of our experiments. In Section 5, we study the relative performance of the groups and how their performance varies with the parameters of FPFS scheduler. We compare the effect of the component generation heuristics on scheduler performance in Section 6. In Section 7, we study how the proportion of the jobs broken into components affects performance. We discuss related work in Section 8 and make conclusion and suggestions for future work in Section 9.

2   The Research Model

2.1   Multi-cluster Set Up

We consider a system made up of five homogeneous clusters. The system is served by one queue and one scheduler. The system processes jobs by pure space slicing and is non-preemptive. In case a job has multiple components, the components are co-allocated.

2.2   Job Stream

Many supercomputer workloads have been archived [29] and analyzed. Most of them are for single supercomputers not multi-cluster systems which we consider in this study. Logs from the Distributed ASCI Supercomputer [26] were archived in [29] and analyzed in [17]. Co-allocation details however were not included in the study and the jobs on the different clusters of DAS were archived separately.

In this work therefore, we use synthetic workloads. The jobs are online and have exponentially distributed inter-arrival and execution times. These distributions have also been used in previous related work [4][15]. A job's execution time is unknown before it finishes execution. This is because we assume that the user is unable to accurately estimate the duration of his jobs [16].

Job Size Distribution :
The size of a job is defined by a distribution $D(q)$ where the probability p_i that a job has size i is given by

$$p_i = \begin{cases} \frac{3q^i}{Q} & \text{if } i \text{ is a power of 2} \\ \frac{q^i}{Q} & \text{if } i \text{ is not a power of 2} \end{cases} \tag{1}$$

$D(q)$ $(q < 1)$ is defined over an interval $[n_1,\ n_2]$ $(0 < n_1 < n_2)$. The parameter q is used to vary the mean job size while Q is in such a way that p_i sums up to 1. It favors small jobs and those whose size is a power of 2 which is known to be a realistic choice [11].

Components Generation
Broadly, jobs are divided into two - small and large jobs. Large jobs are broken into components and co-allocated. We define a parameter *thres* to be the size of the largest small job. Any job whose size is bigger than *thres* is broken into components. Multi-component jobs are evenly distributed among the large jobs. If the maximum components a job can have is k, then $2, 3, \cdots k$ component jobs have a proportion $\frac{1}{k-1}$ of the large jobs. To break a job of size s into n components, we make the first $n-1$ components to have width $\lfloor \frac{s}{n} \rfloor$ each while the nth component has width of $s - (n-1)\lfloor \frac{s}{n} \rfloor$. We use two approaches to determine the number of components a certain job will be broken into. We refer to them as *random* and *phased* approach.

a. *Random Approach*
   In random approach, we randomly chose the number of components a large job will be broken into. If for example large jobs can have $2, 3, \cdots k$ components, then every large job has a probability of $\frac{1}{k-1}$ of being broken into any of the possible number of components. This is used to represent a situation where the user decides how many components his job should be broken into.
b. *Phased Approach*
   In phased approach, the number of components a job has is determined by its size. If large jobs can have $2, 3, \cdots k$ components, we identify job bounds $b_1, b_2, \cdots b_{k-1}$ in such a way that the number of jobs with size range $(thres + 1, b_1), (b_1 + 1, b_2) \cdots (b_{k-2} + 1, b_{k-1}), (b_{k-1} + 1, s_{max})$ (s_{max} is the largest job size possible) make up $\frac{1}{k-1}$ of the large jobs. Jobs in the size range $(thres + 1, b_1)$ are broken into 2 components, those in a size range $(b_1 + 1, b_2)$ are broken in 3 components and so on. This is used to represent a situation where the system determines the number of components a job should have.

3   The Scheduling Algorithm

We now describe the FPFS scheduling algorithm used in our research.

In FPFS, jobs are queued in their arrival order. When searching for the next job to process, the scheduler starts from the head of the queue and searches deeper into the queue for the first job that fits into the system. In case one is found, it jumps all jobs ahead of it in the queue, gets allocated to the clusters and starts execution. If none is found, the scheduler waits for a job to finish execution or a job to arrive and the search is done again. This may however lead to starvation of some jobs as they are continuously jumped by other jobs from deep inside the queue. This is avoided by limiting the number of times (to $maxJumps$) a job can be jumped while at the head of the queue. After being jumped $maxJumps$ times, no other job is allowed to jump it (and get allocated to clusters) until enough processors has been freed (by terminating jobs) to have it start processing. In this paper, we use FPFS(x) to represent FPFS when $maxJumps = x$.

To map components to clusters, we use the Worst Fit (WFit) placement policy. In this policy, the widest component is placed in the freest cluster (and the smallest component in the busiest cluster). It tends to balance the load among the clusters as well as leaving the free processors as evenly distributed as possible among the clusters.

4   Experimental Set Up

4.1   Parameters Used

We use clusters with 20 nodes. The job stream is generated by $D(0.85)$ on the interval $[1, 38]$. This generates jobs with average size 5.03. Our jobs can be broken into up to 4 components. We consider a case where $thres = 11$ (the effect of the value of $thres$ is studied in Section 7). The jobs have a mean execution time of 10 and mean inter arrival time of 0.64. This leads to a load of 0.786. We chose this load since scheduler performance is more distinct at high loads. We do not model inter-cluster communication.

4.2   Performance Evaluation

We use the Average Response Time (ART) as the measurement metric. ART is measured for the entire job stream as well as job groups with in the job stream. Readings are taken at a maximum relative error of 0.05 at 95% confidence interval.

Jobs are grouped by the number of components, size and width of the widest component.

Component wise, jobs are grouped into C_1, C_2, C_3 and C_4 groups. These groups are made up of $1, 2, 3$ and 4 component jobs. At $thres = 11$, C_1 constitutes 89.6% of the jobs and the largest 10% of the jobs are broken into components. The details of the jobs in C_2, C_3 and C_4 depends on the partitioning approach used.

Size wise, jobs are grouped in four groups S_1, S_2, S_3 and S_4 which are size-based quartiles. S_1 consists of jobs with $size = 1$. S_2, S_3 and S_4 groups are made up of jobs in the size range $[2, 3], [4, 7]$ and $[8, 38]$ respectively. S_1, S_2, S_3 and S_4 constitute of $24\%, 26\%, 26\%$ and 24% of the job stream respectively.

Using width of the widest component, we generate groups W_1, W_2, W_3 and W_4 which are widest component based quartiles. The details of the jobs in the widest component based groups are dependent on the partitioning approach. When using the random approach (at $thres = 11$), W_1 and W_2 consist of jobs whose widest component is 1 and 2 while W_3 and W_4 consists of jobs whose width of the widest component is in the ranges $[3, 4]$ and $[5, 19]$. W_1, W_2, W_3 and W_4 jobs constitute $24\%, 26\%, 38\%$ and 12% of the job stream respectively.

5   Job Groups Performance

In this section, we investigate the (relative) performance of the different job groups scheduled by FPFS(0) and FPFS(10). We consider a randomly partitioned job stream ($thres = 11$). Practically, FPFS(0) is the same as FCFS since no job is allowed to jump another. We investigate the variation of performance of job groups with the $maxJumps$ value and deduce the practical implication of the (relative) performance trend.

5.1   Relative Performance of Job Groups

The relative performance of the groups for FPFS(0)/FCFS and FPFS(10) is summarized in Figure 1.

From Figure 1, we observe that (i) FPFS(10) performs better than FCFS for all job groups, (ii) there is a negligible difference in the different groups' performance for FCFS, (iii) there are big performance differences among the job groups when FPFS(10) scheduler is used and (iv) big jobs perform poorly.

The improvement in performance as the $maxJumps$ value increase from 0 (FCFS) to 10 can be explained by the global effect of allowing some jobs to jump others and get scheduled. This can be looked at positively and negatively. On the negative side, the jobs that jump may delay the time at which the jobs they jump start execution. This is because the criteria used to allow them jump does not put the execution time into consideration. On the positive side, the jobs that jump actually execute on processors that would be idle. Fishing these jobs from the queue makes it shorter hence lowering the waiting time for the jobs initially behind the jumping job. Since these jobs are used to fill the small remaining gaps, cases of small jobs fragmenting clusters are reduced. The net effect of shortening the queue gives advantage to jobs that have not yet been submitted since they find a shorter queue. Studies by Chiang et al. [6] show that in aggressive backfilling, rarely does a backfilled job delay jobs deep into the queue. This implies that while the disadvantage affects a few jobs at the head of the queue, the advantages go beyond the queue. The advantages outweigh the disadvantages hence a net gain.

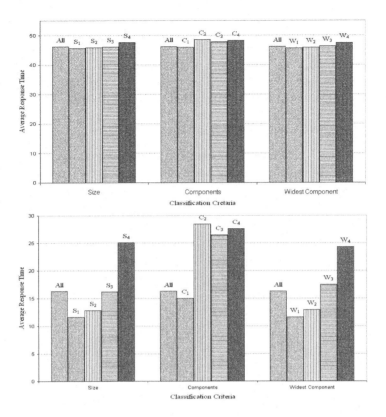

Fig. 1. Performance of different groups for FCFS (top) and FPFS(10) (bottom)

Since FCFS does not allow jobs to jump others, a job at the head of the queue blocks all others behind it until there are enough free processors in the system. There is therefore minimal performance difference. The slightly better performance of small jobs can be attributed to the fact that they are less likely to wait for long while at the head of the queue. Since FPFS allows mostly small jobs to jump and get scheduled before others ahead of it, there is a good performance for small jobs and a poor performance for large ones. We observe a direct relationship between performance and size and performance and width of the widest component. Jobs in C_2, C_3 and C_4 basically belong to S_4. The poor performance of C_2 shows the effect of size and widest component affects the performance trend in component based trends.

The system cannot alter the size of the job since we assume they are rigid. However, depending on the partition decisions made, the width of the widest component can be altered. This implies that a user who is interested in improving performance should concentrate on the partition approach and should aim at having jobs with narrow components.

The effect of the width of the widest component is caused by the way free processors are distributed in the clusters as dictated by the placement policy. Since

WFit places the widest component in the freest cluster, it distributes the free processors among the clusters as evenly as possible. It is therefore hard to get a big block of free processors in a single cluster to process a wide component. Since FPFS allows jobs that can fit to jump those which cannot fit, the terminating jobs do not necessarily create the required processors as the jumping jobs reduce them further. This causes relative starvation for jobs with wide components.

5.2   Performance Variations with $MaxJumps$

We now investigate the variation of performance with $maxJumps$ for the different job groups. We use the size and width of the widest component partitions to illustrate our results (components follow the same trend) and summarize the results in Figure 2.

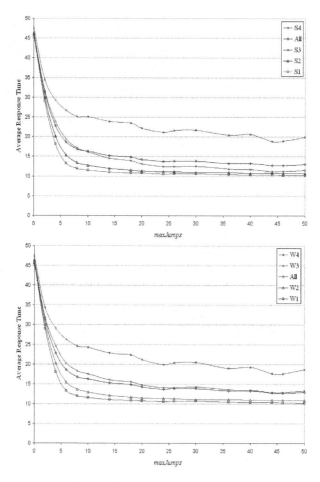

Fig. 2. Performance variations with $maxJumps$ for job groups grouped by size (top) and widest component (bottom)

From Figure 2, we observe that the different job groups have a similar performance trend. Increasing $maxJumps$ leads to an improvement in performance. The rate of improvement is high at low $maxJumps$ values. At high $maxJumps$ values $(maxJumps \geq 10)$, there is a minimal improvement in performance. Large jobs perform poorer compared to small jobs.

Increasing $maxJumps$ gives more jumping opportunities for small jobs. At very high $maxJumps$ values, small jobs are processed immediately they arrive (mean execution time is 10, therefore, the minimum mean response time is 10).

5.3   Load-Wise Implication

We now investigate the implication of the deviation in performance for the different groups. We do this by comparing amount of the load in each group. We summarize the comparative numerical and load composition in Table 1.

Table 1. Numerical and load contribution of the different groups (partition approach - random, $thres = 11$)

Criteria					
Size			Widest component		
Group	Number(%)	Load(%)	Group	Number(%)	Load(%)
S_1	24.88	5.08	W_1	24.88	5.08
S_2	25.64	11.49	W_2	25.64	11.49
S_3	25.20	24.13	W_3	22.98	23.45
S_4	24.28	59.30	W_4	26.50	59.98

From Table 1, we observe that there is a skewed relationship between the numerical and load wise contribution of the different job groups. This is in agreement with previous studies on workload characteristics [19]. Groups S_4 and W_4 register worst performance and constitute more than half of the load in the system. This implies that a big portion of the workload actually perform worse than the average. Since a job's contribution to the average response time is independent of its load, the numerical minority of poor performing jobs is not adequately implied by the ART metric.

6   The Effect of the Partitioning Format

In Section 5, we only used the random partitioning approach. We observed that the width of the widest component highly influence performance and can be altered by the partitioning scheme. In this section, we compare the random and phased partitioning approaches at $thres = 11$. We summarize the performance trend in Figure 3. We use only size based groups when making performance evaluation. This is because the partitioning approach does not influence the distribution of jobs in S_1, S_2, S_3 and S_4. Component based groups, for phased partitioning, are analogous to size based groups with different job proportion. We only show S_1 and S_4 which are the extremes. S_2 and follow the same trend.

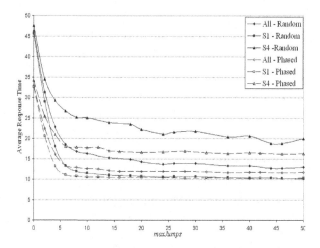

Fig. 3. Performance variations of selected groups with *maxJumps* for job streams partitioned using the random and phased approach(*thres* = 11)

From Figure 3, we observe that there is an improvement in performance for jobs in S_1 and S_4. There is also a reduction in the difference between S_4 and S_1 jobs. The improvement is also registered in for FCFS.

The improvement in performance can be explained by the change in widest component width distribution. Since phased partition approach breaks bigger jobs into more components, the widest components gets lower hence easier to pack.

This implies that performance can be improved by improving the scheduling approach as well as improving the partitioning approach. Since the difference between S_1 and S_4 is smaller in a phased partitioned job stream, it shows us that the improvement in performance comes with the improvement in fairness.

7 The Effect of *thres*

From Section 6, we observe that it is actually necessary to break up large jobs and co-allocate them. We took a case where $thres - 11$. We investigate the effect of *thres* value on scheduler performance. We show the trend in Figure 4.

From Figure 4, we observe that increasing *thres* leads to poor performance. the deterioration of performance is higher for large jobs than for small jobs.

Small jobs can easily be fished from the queue by the scheduler. This implies that whether *thres* is low or high, they have high chances of being scheduled. Having a high *thres* however leads to poor component placement and adversely impacts on the entire job stream. Lowering *thres* is therefore beneficial to the entire job stream but mostly to the large jobs. At high *thres* values, the scheduler is more unfair. The value of *thres* therefore needs to be kept low in th interest of performance and fairness.

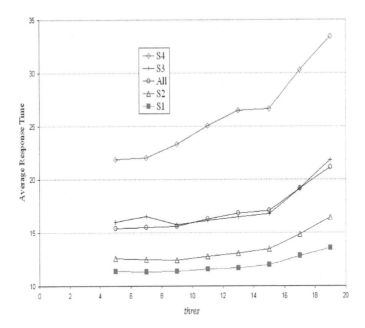

Fig. 4. Performance variations of FPFS(10) with *thres* for a randomly partitioned job stream

8   Related Work

Multi-cluster systems have attracted a sizeable amount of research of recent. Some multi-cluster systems have also been set up for research in performance analysis, co-allocation and the general field of parallel processing. These include the Distributed ASCI Supercomputer (DAS) [26] located in The Netherlands. Earlier work on DAS was reported by Bal et al [1]. Specific work on co-allocation on DAS was done by Jones [15], Bucur [4] and Bucur and Epema [5], [2], [3].

Many schedulers have been proposed for parallel job scheduling [10]. For space slicing cases like the one we are considering in this research, backfilling has been the most popular. Backfilling seeks to allow small jobs to be processed before they reach the head of the queue. This is under a condition that they do not pose a disadvantage to the jobs they jump. This is therefore catered for in the conditions the job has to satisfy to be allowed to jump. Conservative backfilling [18] allows the job to jump others if it will not delay the reservation time of any job in the queue. Aggressive backfilling [20] on the other hand allows a job to jump if it will not affect the reservation time of the job at the head of the queue. Backfilling basically allows jobs to jump and get processed without giving a setback to the jumped jobs. Work by Shmueli and Feitelson [21] employs backfilling but by ensuring that the job picked is the one which can offer the best utilization of the processor hole available. It however brings in an extra consideration of determining how far deep in the queue the scheduler should go while searching for the job that offers best results. This is only possible if enough information about the jobs (execution time in this case) is known; in some cases, they are not known [8]. Lack of knowledge of some parameters restricts what the scheduler can do. Backfilling cannot be employed in cases where the runtime of the jobs is unknown. This because the scheduler lacks the basis on which reservations can be made. Lack of runtime knowledge can be caused by the inability of the user to accurately estimate the job runtime [16]. In such a case, a job can be allowed to jump so long as it can fit in the available processor hole. This is done in the FPFS scheduler. Starvation is controlled by limiting the number of times a job at the head of the queue is jumped.

The choice of the measurement metric for parallel job scheduling evaluation has to be taken with a lot of care [14]. Some metrics may have different implications depending on the circumstance. While average waiting time and average response time can have a similar performance for dedicated processing, they don't in a time sliced / preemptive cases.

Grouping jobs by their characteristics and evaluate how they perform helps in getting a deeper understanding of the scheduler performance [12]. Srinivasan et al. [22] use job groups to get a deeper understanding of scheduler robustness while scheduling moldable jobs. Deeper comparative studies between Conservative and Aggressive backfilling were studied in [25][24] by studying performance of job groups in the job stream.

In multi cluster systems, studies have been done to study and improve scheduler performance. Jones [15] focused on scheduling techniques and how they are affected by network characteristics like latencies. Bucur and Epema investigated the performance of co-allocation in different scenarios. This involved queue prioritization [5], job structures [2] and scheduling policies [3].

9   Conclusions and Future Work

We have investigated the group-wise performance of processor co-allocation in multi-cluster systems. We use the FPFS scheduler. We have observed that increasing *maxJumps* improves performance for the jobs that jump and those which are jumped. There is however a higher level of unfairness as *maxJumps* is increased. We have also observed that the performance can be improved by using a superior scheduler, a batter partitioning strategy as well as breaking up a bigger proportion of jobs. When partitioning, the aim should be put at having a low width of the widest component.

Our work also opens up more avenues for research. Phased partitioning has shown an improvement in performance. There is a need to investigate a possibility of a better partitioning heuristic. This is due to the fact that the widest component is actually reducible. There is also a need to investigate the how the job characteristics like average size and moldability affect scheduler performance.Breaking up jobs into components creates a packing benefit but also comes with a communication overhead. Communication leads to an increase in the execution time of the job. Different jobs have different intensity of communication and different multi-cluster systems have different local area and wide area communication speeds. There is therefore need for detailed study of communication based effects and the extent of their effects on scheduler performance. Finally, there is a need to investigate performance behavior using smaller partitions (beyond the quartiles used here) in order to get a deeper understanding of the inter-job performance behavior.

References

1. Bal, et al.: The Distributed ASCI Supercomputer Project. Operating Systems Review 34(4), 76–96 (2000)
2. Bucur, A.I.D., Epema, D.H.J.: The Influence of the Structure and Sizes of Jobs on the Performance of Co-allocation. In: Feitelson, D.G., Rudolph, L. (eds.) IPDPS-WS 2000 and JSSPP 2000. LNCS, vol. 1911, pp. 154–173. Springer, Heidelberg (2000)
3. Bucur, A.I.D., Epema, D.H.J.: The Performance of Processor Co-allocation in Multicluster Systems. In: proceedings of the 3rd IEEE/ ACM International Symposium on Cluster Computing and the Grid (CCGrid 2003), pp. 302–309 (2003)
4. Bucur, A.I.D.: Performance Analysis of Processor Co-allocation in Multicluster Systems. PhD Thesis, Delft University of Technology, Delft, The Netherlands (2004)
5. Bucur, A.I.D., Epema, D.H.J.: Local versus Global Schedulers with Processor Co-allocation in Multicluster Systems. In: Feitelson, D.G., Rudolph, L., Schwiegelshohn, U. (eds.) JSSPP 2002. LNCS, vol. 2537, pp. 184–204. Springer, Heidelberg (2002)
6. Chiang, S.H., Arpaci-Dusseau, A., Vernon, M.K.: The Impact of More Accurate Requested Runtimes on Production Job Scheduling Performance. In: Feitelson, D.G., Rudolph, L., Schwiegelshohn, U. (eds.) JSSPP 2002. LNCS, vol. 2537, pp. 103–127. Springer, Heidelberg (2002)
7. Czajkowski, K., Foster, I.T., Kasselman, C.: Resource Co-allocation in Computational Grids. In: Proceedings of the 8th IEEE International Symposium on High Performance and Distributed Computing, California, USA, pp. 37–47 (1999)
8. Edmonds, J.: Scheduling in the Dark. In: Proceedings of the 31st Annual ACM Symposium on Theory of Computing, pp. 179–188 (1999)
9. Feitelson, D.G., Rudolph, L., Schwiegelshohn, U., Sevcik, K., Wong, P.: Theory and Practice in Parallel Job Scheduling. In: Feitelson, D.G., Rudolph, L. (eds.) IPPS-WS 1997 and JSSPP 1997. LNCS, vol. 1291, pp. 1–34. Springer, Heidelberg (1997)
10. Feitelson, D.G., Rudolph, L., Schwiegelshohn, U.: Parallel Job Scheduling - A Status Report. In: Feitelson, D.G., Rudolph, L., Schwiegelshohn, U. (eds.) JSSPP 2004. LNCS, vol. 3277, pp. 1–16. Springer, Heidelberg (2005)
11. Feitelson, D.G., Rudolph, L.: Towards Convergence of Job Schedulers for Parallel Supercomputers. In: Feitelson, D.G., Rudolph, L. (eds.) IPPS-WS 1996 and JSSPP 1996. LNCS, vol. 1162, pp. 1–26. Springer, Heidelberg (1996)
12. Feitelson, D.G.: Metric and Workload Effects on Computer Systems Evaluation. Computers 18, 18–25 (2003)
13. Foster, I., Kasselman, C.: The Grid: Blue Print for a New Computing Infrastructure. Morgan Kaufmann, San Francisco, CA, USA (1999)

14. Frachtenberg, E., Feitelson, D.G.: Pitfalls in Parallel Job Scheduling Evaluation. In: Feitelson, D.G., Frachtenberg, E., Rudolph, L., Schwiegelshohn, U. (eds.) JSSPP 2005. LNCS, vol. 3834, pp. 257–282. Springer, Heidelberg (2005)
15. Jones, W.M.: Improving Parallel Job Scheduling Performance in Multi-clusters Through Selective Job Co-allocation, PhD dissertation, Clemson University, Clemson, South Carolina, USA (2005)
16. Lee, C.B., Schwartzman, Y., Hardy, J., Snavely, A.: Are User Runtime Estimates Inherently Inaccurate? In: Feitelson, D.G., Rudolph, L., Schwiegelshohn, U. (eds.) JSSPP 2004. LNCS, vol. 3277, pp. 253–263. Springer, Heidelberg (2005)
17. Li, H., Groep, D., Walters, L.: Workload Characteristics of a Multi-cluster Supercomputer. In: Feitelson, D.G., Rudolph, L., Schwiegelshohn, U. (eds.) JSSPP 2004. LNCS, vol. 3277, pp. 176–193. Springer, Heidelberg (2005)
18. Lifka, L.: The ANL/IBM SP Scheduling System. In: Feitelson, D.G., Rudolph, L. (eds.) IPPS-WS 1995 and JSSPP 1995. LNCS, vol. 949, pp. 295–303. Springer, Heidelberg (1995)
19. Moreira, J., Pattnaik, P., Franke, H., Jann, J.: An Evaluation of Parallel Job Scheduling for ASCI Blue-Pacific. In: Proceedings of the IEEE/ACM Supercomputing Conference SC 1999. Portland, Oregon, USA (1999)
20. Mualem, A.W., Feitelson, D.G.: Utilization, Predictability, Workloads and User Runtime Estimates in Scheduling the IBM SP2 with Backfilling. IEEE Transactions in Parallel and Distributed Systems 12(6), 529–543 (2001)
21. Shmueli, E., Feitelson, D.G.: Backfilling with Lookahead to Optimize the Performance of Parallel Job Scheduling. In: Feitelson, D.G., Rudolph, L., Schwiegelshohn, U. (eds.) JSSPP 2003. LNCS, vol. 2862, pp. 228–251. Springer, Heidelberg (2003)
22. Srinivasan, S., Krishnamoorthy, S., Sadayappan, P.: A Robust Scheduling Technology for Moldable Scheduling of Parallel Jobs. In: Proceedings of the IEEE International Conference on Cluster Computing, pp. 92–99 (2003)
23. Strohmaier, E., Dongarra, J.J., Meuer, H.W., Simon, D.: Recent Trends in the Marketplace of High Performance Computing. Journal of Parallel Computing 31, 261–273 (2005)
24. Srinivasan, S., Kettimuthu, R., Subramani, V., Sadayappan, P.: Selective Reservation Strategies for Backfill Job Scheduling. In: Feitelson, D.G., Rudolph, L., Schwiegelshohn, U. (eds.) JSSPP 2002. LNCS, vol. 2537, pp. 55–71. Springer, Heidelberg (2002)
25. Srinivasan, S., Kettimuthu, R., Subramani, V., Sadayappan, P.: Characterization of backfilling Strategies for Parallel Job Scheduling. In: Proceedings of the 2002 International Conference on Parallel Processing Workshops, pp. 514–520 (2002)
26. The Distributed ASCI Supercomputer, http://www.cs.vu.nl/das2
27. The Global Grid Forum, http://www.gridforum.com
28. The Mesquite Software inc: The CSIM 18 Simulation Engine Users Guide
29. The Parallel Workloads Archive, http://www.cs.huji.ac.il/labs/parallel/workload/logs.html

Enhancing an Open Source Resource Manager with Multi-core/Multi-threaded Support

Susanne M. Balle and Daniel J. Palermo

Hewlett-Packard Corp.
High Performance Computing Division
Susanne.Balle@hp.com, Dan.Palermo@hp.com

Abstract. Current resource managers do not have adequate node allocation and distribution strategies to efficiently schedule jobs on multi-core multi-threaded systems. Clusters composed of multiple cores per processor as well as multiple processors per node are presenting new challenges to users when trying to run their program efficiently on this class of machines. New allocation algorithms and their respective user interfaces need to be devised to ensure minimum contention for cache and memory, reduced on-chip contention, etc. as well as evaluate trade-offs between resource contentions.

1 Introduction

Multi-core processing is a growing industry trend as single-core processors rapidly reach the physical limits of possible complexity and speed. Both AMD and Intel are currently marketing dual-core processors. Quad cores are currently available and CPUs with larger core count will be available in 2008.

In a clustered environment, an important factor contributing to an application's performance is the layout of its processes onto the nodes, i.e. workload balancing. Developers currently worry about finding the optimal layout for their application on CPUs and nodes. With the introduction of multi-core and hyper-threaded processors, the level of complexity increases considerably. A common problem with today's resource managers e.g. LSF [3], PBSpro [1], etc. is that they consider cores to be "normal" CPUs without taking into consideration locality between cores and memory, resources shared between cores, or other architectural features of the system. For users using the default node allocation scheme, the lack of extra support in the resource managers can result in a performance degradation and variability.

The goals of this paper are to illustrate the problems that developers encounter when running their applications in a multi-socket multi-core clustered environment and to present solutions to these problems. We discuss how we enhanced an open-source resource manager, SLURM, to better support multi-core computing environments. SLURM is an integral part of HP's XC Cluster offering. The development of SLURM is a joint effort between Lawrence Livermore National Laboratory (LLNL), Hewlett-Packard, Bull, and LinuxNetworX. The HP

E. Frachtenberg and U. Schwiegelshohn (Eds.): JSSPP 2007, LNCS 4942, pp. 37–50, 2008.

XC cluster [5] is a scalable, Linux-based Supercomputing Utility, enabling high system utilization. It leverages industry-leading technology from open source, HP and its partners.

The paper starts with a brief description of multi-core architectures. We then introduce the SLURM resource manager and describe the current state of multi-core support in resource managers. We show the problems users encounter when using multi-core systems and present our solutions to these problems. We show performance data illustrating that both a standard benchmark (HPLinpack) and an ISV application (LSDyna) achieve sizeable performance improvements using the features available in the new multi-core aware SLURM.

2 Multi-core Architectures

To achieve higher processor density and higher performance per watt, processor architectures are focusing on multi-core designs. CPU vendors have exploited the traditional methods to increase performance, such as higher clock speeds and improved internal parallelism, to the fullest and must now rely on providing resources for explicit parallelism. Several multi-core processor architectures that are becoming available in HP systems are discussed below.

The dual-core AMD Opteron provides two 64-bit Opteron cores on a single die. Each core within a dual-core Opteron has two levels of cache with none of the levels shared between cores. L1 is a split 64KB/64KB instruction/data cache, and L2 is a unified 1MB cache. In 2007, AMD plans to offer a 4-core version of the Opteron which will also likely have a shared level 3 cache.

The dual-core Intel Xeon provides two 64-bit Xeon Extended Memory 64 Technology (EM64T) cores on a single die. Each core has two levels of cache with none of the levels shared between cores. L1 is a split 64KB/64KB instruction/data cache, and L2 is a unified 2MB cache. The Intel Xeon EM64T also supports 2-way Hyperthreading within each core resulting in one chip providing 4 logical processors to the operating system. In 2007, Intel released a 4-core version of the Xeon which, with Hyperthreading, would provide 8 logical processors in a single package.

The Intel Itanium Processor Family (IPF) incorporates a dual-core design in the next major revision of the processor code named Montecito. Compared with earlier releases, the Montecito release of IPF will provide two Itanium 2 cores on a single die, a separate L2 I-cache, increased cache capacity, extra functional units for shifting and population count, and Hyperthreading. Hyperthreading in Montecito provides hardware support for 2 logical threads per physical core providing a total of 4 logical processors to the operating system.

3 SLURM: Simple Linux Utility for Resource Management

A resource manager is a tool that dispatches jobs to resources according to specified policies and constrained by specific criteria. SLURM is an open-source

resource manager designed for Linux clusters of all sizes. The overview of the
SLURM architecture presented in this section is an edited excerpt of the doc-
umentation available on the SLURM website [2] and the paper by Jette and
Grondona [4].

SLURM provides three key functions: First, it allocates exclusive and/or non-
exclusive access to resources (compute nodes) to users for some duration of
time so they can perform work. Second, it provides a framework for starting,
executing, and monitoring work (typically a parallel job) on a set of allocated
nodes. Finally, it arbitrates conflicting requests for resources by managing a
queue of pending work.

SLURM consists of a slurmd daemon running on each compute node, a central
slurmctld daemon running on a management node and six command line utilities:
srun, scancel, sinfo, squeue, scontrol, and smap which can run anywhere in the
cluster.

The six SLURM commands have the following functionalities:

- srun is used to submit a job for execution, allocate resources, attach to an
  existing allocation, or initiate job steps.
- scancel is used to cancel a pending or running job or job step. It can also be
  used to send an arbitrary signal to all processes associated with a running
  job or job step.
- scontrol is the administrative tool used to view and/or modify SLURM state.
- sinfo reports the state of partitions and nodes managed by SLURM. It has
  a wide variety of filtering, sorting, and formatting options.
- squeue reports the state of jobs or job steps. It has a wide variety of filtering,
  sorting, and formatting options. By default, it reports the running jobs in
  priority order and then the pending jobs in priority order.
- smap reports state information for jobs, partitions, and nodes managed
  by SLURM, but graphically displays the information to reflect network
  topology.

SLURM uses a general purpose plug-in mechanism to select various features
such as scheduling policies and node allocation mechanisms which allows it to be
flexible and utilize custom as well as default methods. When a SLURM daemon
is initiated, it reads a configuration file to determine which of the available plug-
ins should be used.

4   Current State of multi-core/multi-threaded Support

In early 2006, we investigated current resource managers to understand if they
had the adequate scheduling and node allocation strategies to efficiently schedule jobs on multi-core/multi-threaded systems. At the time of the investigation,
we were not aware of any resource manager which has multi-core multi-
threaded support. We investigated PBSpro 7 [1] and concluded that it allocates

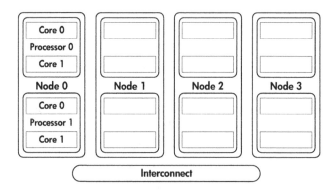

Fig. 1. Four-node dual-core dual-processor cluster

processors as its finest granularity. The latest version of LSF 6.2 [3] has an option
which allows it to allocate resources at the core level but without taking into
consideration the existing characteristics between cores. In versions of SLURM
prior to v1.2 [2], the lack of multi-core support meant that it viewed cores as
CPUs and did not make a distinction at the processor level.

Below we illustrate the problem that users typically encountered when using
the default block distribution in SLURM (prior to v1.2) on a four-node dual-
socket dual-core cluster.

Figure 1 shows a four-node cluster (Nodes 0 to 3) with dual-socket dual-core
nodes. SLURM allocates resources at the node/CPU granularity level which
means that for this example it would view each node as having four CPUs. An
8-process job is initiated using SLURM by typing: "srun -n 8 a.out". If the above
system contained single- core sockets, the default layout would result in having
processes 0 and 1 on Node 0, processes 2 and 3 on Node 1, processes 4 and 5
on Node 2 and processes 6 and 7 on Node 3. In a dual-core environment, the
default node allocation would be processes 0 and 1 as well as processes 2 and 3
on Node 0 and processes 4, 5, 6, and 7 on Node 1 leaving Node 2 and Node 3
unallocated for this job. The latter allocation is not the expected default layout
for the non-expert user and can result in detrimental performance for certain
types of applications such a memory bound applications. The two processes on
the cores within the same processor have to share hardware resources which
could result in resource contention.

The existing pre-defined distributions, namely block and cyclic, are not adequate in a multi-core multi-threaded environment since they do not make a
distinction between sockets and cores/threads. The extra levels of logical processors (cores and threads) in the CPU/socket should allow the job scheduler to
create more elaborate distribution schemes.

In the next section, we present the features we are currently adding to SLURM
as part of the multi-core support.

5   Identified Problems

We interviewed users with experience running applications on multi-core and multi-threaded systems to understand the problems they experience as well as the features they seek. We researched prior and ongoing work in the Linux kernel community to allow the Linux kernel users to take better advantage of the new architectures. We were especially interested in the different level of affinities in the Linux kernel and its schedulers.

There are three major features which have been introduced in the Linux 2.6 kernel that are of interest when discussing multi-core support and CPU affinity. These features include:

- The new "O(1)" job scheduler
- Kernel support for both process and memory affinity
- On-going work in page migration

At the end of our investigation phase, we identified three major enhancements that would make SLURM more attractive to users by increasing its usefulness in a multi-core environment.

The enhancements are:

- Need for a flag or feature allowing users to "pin" processes to logical processors (node, socket, core or thread). HPLinpack and LSDyna experiments, carried out on a four node dual-core Opteron cluster, confirm the interviewees' conclusions that pinning the processes to the cores does give better as well as repeatable timing results. For the non-expert users, we need to provide higher-level flags and have the pinning happen automatically.
- Need for new node allocation and distribution strategies for clusters of multi-core systems. This includes being able to specify a block or a cyclic distribution at the core level and at the thread level as well as adequate default distributions for the cores and the threads.
- Need for an adequate multi-core user interface which support the new multi-core enhancements. The user interface consists of low-level expert flags as well as high-level flags. The latter allows users to take advantage of the lower level logical processors (core or thread) without having to understand the system architecture in detail.

6   Pinning Processes to Cores

Process affinity is at the heart of the SLURM multi-core support since the Linux kernel job scheduler is not able to optimally assign processes to cores for high-performance technical computing applications. OS job schedulers, originally designed to achieve maximum throughput for oversubscribed workloads in single-core systems, when used for perfectly subscribed jobs in multi-core systems typically try to distribute load across available processors sometimes migrating processes to temporarily idle cores instead of staying where the cache is hot. Users have observed that by pinning processes to cores, performance can be increased. This is a result of avoiding the overhead of migrating processes to cores with cold caches, thereby staying close to the caches that already contain the data a process is accessing. This is true even on systems comprised of multiple single-core processors.

Linux provides several affinity controls to pin or bind processes to cores. We have selected the sched_setaffinity(...) and the sched_getaffinity(...) interfaces provided in the Linux 2.6 kernel to implement our pinning feature. These interfaces allow users, or in our case SLURM on behalf of a user, to set and get a process's CPU affinity mask. Setting a process's CPU affinity allows SLURM to specify which scheduling queues are allowed for a given process thereby providing them with the ability to bind a process to a specific core or set of cores. One of sched_setaffinity(...)'s parameter is the affinity bit mask where a 1 indicates that a process may use the core (ID represented by the bit position). A mask of all 1's indicates the process may use any core (at the discretion of the OS). A mask containing a single 1 indicates a process is bound to a specific core.

We have added the ability to SLURM for users to bind their tasks to particular logical processor (sockets, cores per socket, and threads per core) as well as sets of logical processors using high-level flags as well as an expert low-level flag (see Section 9). We developed the SLURM affinity task plug-in using the task plug-in infrastructure. The former encompasses all the CPU affinity pieces needed, including automatic mask generation when using the high-level flags, to support the process to core pinning functionality in SLURM. We allow users to take advantage of this new feature in two ways. They can either provide the affinity mask directly to SLURM via the –cpu_bind flag or by using high-level flags (see Section 9).

One complication that arises when binding processes to cores is that different combinations of hardware, BIOS, and operating systems result in different core numbering schemes. Given, the fact that the core indexing varies among different systems, it is not possible to devise a single set of masks that would achieve the same results on all systems. When specifying masks directly with –cpu_bind users must be aware of the core mapping in order to achieve a desired placement across the processors and cores. The higher-level switches use an abstraction layer which will make the logical processor to physical core mapping transparent to users (see Section 10).

7   Node Selection and Allocation

SLURM uses a general purpose plug-in mechanism for selecting various features. The node selection plug-in also called select plug-in determines the set of nodes to be used for a given job based on the user's specified requirements. This type of plug-in is accessed within the slurmctld daemon.

SLURM currently supports two platform-independent node-selection plug-ins:

- select/linear – The default plug-in selects nodes assuming a one-dimensional array of nodes utilizing a best-fit algorithm. This plug-in does not allocate individual processors, memory, etc. and is recommended for systems without shared nodes.

- select/cons_res – A plug-in that can allocate individual processors, memory, etc. within nodes. This plug-in is recommended for systems with programs sharing nodes.

It is important to notice that only one select plug-in can be specified for a given configuration and that the choice of select plug-in is done on SLURM start-up.

We researched the different SLURM components related to node allocation to figure out how to integrate the multi-core support. The conclusion of our investigation phase is that because the multi-core support should become an inherent part of SLURM it shouldn't be implemented as a separate node-selection plug-in.

We updated the select/linear plug-in, the select/cons_res plug-in as well as the node-selection infrastructure module with a mechanism that allows selection of logical processors at a finer granularity. The updated mechanism continues to support node level allocation and will support finer grained distributions within the allocated nodes. Users will be able to specify the number of nodes, sockets, cores and threads. Their applications should be distributed across a specified number of logical processors and the enhanced node allocation mechanisms will grant the requested layout if the resources are available.

8   New multi-core Process Distributions

The introduction of multi-core processors allows for more advanced distributions. Our first new approach is to create planes of cores. We plan to divide the cluster into planes (including a number of cores on each node) and then schedule first within each plane and then across planes. This approach results in new useful layouts. On a dual-socket node with quad-core sockets, this distribution could result in: as few as one plane (i.e. where the logical processors are scheduled by first filling up the nodes and then scheduling across the nodes) or as many as eight planes (always schedule across the nodes first). Two planes would provide better locality but potentially more contention for other resources. On the other hand, four planes (scheduling across the logical processors) would minimize contention for cache and memory.

We reused the srun "–distribution" flag to allow users to specify the new distribution methods (see Section 9):

"srun –distribution plane=<# of cores within a plane> <srun arguments>"

9   Enhanced User Interface

The increase in complexity of the processors and thereby of the systems makes it more difficult for users to specify a job's layout on the existing resources. Our goal is for SLURM to provide an intuitive user interface to help users allocate their jobs in this environment. We have enhanced the user interface such that it is powerful for expert users, easy to use for naïve users as well as satisfactory for intermediate users. We preserve the existing interface and functionality to ensure backward compatibility.

As described above, several features required for adequate multi-core support have been identified as absent from SLURM. Adding these new features to SLURM required enhancing the user interface to providing users with the necessary functionality.

The enhancements impacting the user interface are:

- A low-level flag allowing users to explicitly "pin" processes to cores.
- High-level flags to automatically generate masks to pin processes to logical processors in terms of sockets, cores, and threads.
- A new multi-core "aware" distribution to give users more control over distributing tasks.
- A finer grained node description method which allows users to specify the number of sockets, cores and threads in allocation requests and constraints, and as displayed by sinfo, scontrol, and squeue.

Overview of New Srun Flags

It is important to note that many of these flags are only meaningful if the processes' affinity is set. In order for the affinity to be set, the task/affinity plugin must be first enabled in slurm.conf:

```
TaskPlugin=task/affinity      # enable task affinity
```

In the case where we set the affinity at a higher level than the lowest level of logical processor (core or thread) we allow the processes to roam within a specific socket or core. We introduce the notion of fat masks to describe affinity masks which bind a process to more than one logical processor.

Several new flags have been defined to allow users to better take advantage of the new architecture by explicitly specifying the number of sockets, cores, and threads required by their application. Figure 2 summarizes the new multi-core flags.

10   Motivation behind High-Level Srun Flags

The motivation behind allowing users to use higher level srun flags instead of –cpu_bind is that the later can be difficult to use. The high-level flags are easier to use than the low-level explicit binding –cpu_bind flag because:

- Affinity mask generation happens automatically when using the high-level flags.

Low-level (explicit binding)	
–cpu_bind=map_cpu:<list>	Specify a CPU ID binding for each task
–cpu_bind=mask_cpu:<list>	Specify a CPU ID binding mask for each task
–cpu_bind=rank	Bind by task rank
High-level (automatic mask generation)	
–sockets-per-node=<S>	Number of sockets in a node to dedicate to a job (minimum or range)
–cores-per-socket=<C>	Number of cores in a socket to dedicate to a job (minimum or range)
–threads-per-core=<T>	Number of threads in a core to dedicate to a job (minimum or range)
-B <S>[:<C>[:<T>]]	Combined shortcut option for –sockets-per-node, –cores-per-socket, –threads-per-core
–cpu_bind=sockets	Auto-generated masks bind to sockets (implied -B level)
–cpu_bind=cores	Auto-generated masks bind to cores (implied -B level)
–cpu_bind=threads	Auto-generated masks bind to threads (implied -B level)
Application hints	
–hint=compute_bound	use all cores in each physical socket
–hint=memory_bound	use only one core in each physical socket
–hint=[no]multithread	[don't] use extra threads with in-core multi-threading
New Distributions	
-m / –distribution	Distributions of: block | cyclic | hostfile | **plane=x** | [**block|cyclic**]:[**block|cyclic**]
New Constraints	
–minsockets=<MinS>	Nodes must meet this minimum number of sockets
–mincores=<MinC>	Nodes must meet this minimum number of cores per socket
–minthreads=<MinT>	Nodes must meet this minimum number of threads per core
Task invocation control	
–ntasks-per-node=<N>	number of tasks to invoke on each node
–ntasks-per-socket=<N>	number of tasks to invoke on each socket
–ntasks-per-core=<N>	number of tasks to invoke on each core

Fig. 2. New srun flags to support the multi-core/multi-threaded environment

– The length and complexity of the –cpu_bind flag vs. the length of the combination of -B and –distribution flags make the high-level flags much easier to use.

Also as illustrated in the example below it is much simpler to specify a different layout using the high-level flags since users do not have to recalculate mask or logical processor IDs. The new approach is effortless compared to rearranging the mask or map.

Given a 32-process MPI job and a four quad-socket dual-core node cluster (8 cores per node), we want to use a block distribution across the four nodes and then a cyclic distribution within the node across the physical processors. We have had several requests from users that they would like this distribution to be the default distribution on multi-core clusters. Below we show how to obtain the wanted layout using 1) the new high-level flags and 2) –cpu_bind.

10.1   High-Level Flags

Using SLURM's new high-level flag, users can obtain the above described layout
on HP XC with:

mpirun -srun -n 32 -N 4 -B 1:1 –distribution=block:cyclic a.out

or

mpirun -srun -n 32 N 4 -B 1:1 a.out

(since –distribution=block:cyclic is the default distribution)

Where -N is the number of nodes to dedicate to a job. The -B 1:1 option
requests binding with at least socket per node (with no maximum specified) and
at least one core per socket (with no maximum specified). With cores shown as
c0 and c1 and processors shown as p0 through p3, the resulting task IDs in a
single node in the cluster are:

	c0	c1			c0	c1
p0	t0	t4		p1	t1	t5
p2	t2	t6		p3	t3	t7

The computation and assignment of the task IDs is transparent to the user.
Users don't have to worry about the core numbering (Section 6) or any setting
any CPU affinities. By default CPU affinity will be set when using multi-core
supporting flags.

10.2   Low-Level Flag –cpu_bind

Using SLURM's –cpu_bind flag, users must compute the logical processor IDs
or taskset masks as well as make sure they understand the core numbering on
their system. Another problem arises when core numbering is not the same on
all nodes. The –cpu_bind option only allows users to specify a single mask for all
the nodes. Using SLURM high-level flags remove this limitation since SLURM
will correctly generate the appropriate masks for each requested nodes.

**On a Four dual-socket dual-core node Cluster with Block Core Num-
bering** The cores are shown as c0 and c1 and the processors are shown as
p0 through p3. The CPU IDs within a node in the block numbering are: (this
information is available from the /proc/cpuinfo file on the system)

	c0	c1			c0	c1
p0	0	1		p1	2	3
p2	4	5		p3	6	7

resulting in the following taskset mapping for processor/cores and task IDs which
users need to calculate:

taskset mapping for processor/cores

	c0	c1		c0	c1
p0	0x01	0x02	p1	0x04	0x08
p2	0x10	0x20	p3	0x40	0x80

task ids

	c0	c1		c0	c1
p0	t0	t4	p1	t1	t5
p2	t2	t6	p3	t3	t7

The above maps and task IDs can be translated into the following mpirun command:

mpirun -srun -n 32 -N 4 –cpu_bind=mask_cpu:1,4,10,40,2,8,20,80 a.out

or

mpirun -srun -n 32 -N 4 –cpu_bind=map_cpu:0,2,4,6,1,3,5,7 a.out

On a four dual-socket dual-core node cluster with cyclic core numbering. On a system with cyclically numbered cores, the correct mask argument to the mpirun/srun command looks like: (this will achieve the same layout as the command above on a system with block core numbering.)

mpirun -srun -n 32 -N 4 –cpu_bind=map_cpu:0,1,2,3,4,5,6,7 a.out

Block map_cpu on a system with cyclic core numbering. If users do not check their system's core numbering before specifying the map_cpu list and thereby do not realize that the new system has cyclic core numbering instead of block numbering then they will not get the expected layout.. For example, if they decide to re-use their mpirun command from above:

mpirun -srun -n 32 -N 4 –cpu_bind=map_cpu:0,2,4,6,1,3,5,7 a.out

they get the following unintentional task ID layout:

	c0	c1		c0	c1
p0	t0	t2	p1	t4	t6
p2	t1	t3	p3	t5	t7

since the processor IDs within a node in the cyclic numbering are:

	c0	c1		c0	c1
p0	0	4	p1	1	5
p2	2	6	p3	3	7

The important conclusion is that using the –cpu_bind flag is not trivial and that it assumes that users are experts.

11   Performance Results

To evaluate the performance of binding processes to cores we examined the behavior of the HPLinpack benchmark using the HPL program as well as of an ISV application, LSDyna. The HPLinpack benchmark solves a dense system of linear equations and is used to rank the Top 500 supercomputer sites. LS- Dyna is a general-purpose, explicit and implicit finite element program used to analyze the nonlinear dynamic response of three-dimensional inelastic structures. Both benchmarks were run on a system with a 2.6 Linux kernel.

Table 1 shows the performance of HPLinpack measured with and without affinity controls. The taskset command uses the sched_get,setaffinity(...) interfaces hereby allowing processes to be bound to a specific core or to a set of cores.

Binding processes to sockets or cores using taskset improves the application's performance. The greatest benefit is seen when binding to specific cores (0x1, 0x2, 0x3, 0x4 versus 0xf). The underlying functionality provided by taskset (sched_setaffinity) is the same as used in both HP MPI and SLURM (activated via the –cpu_bind option). The SLURM process binding supports non-HP MPI programs as well. It is our goal that HP MPI will use the SLURM multi-core support including the process binding on platforms such as XC where SLURM is available.

We also evaluated the effects of CPU binding on a larger, long-running application by examining the performance of LSDyna using a data set simulating a 3-car collision. Without any CPU binding, the overall run-time of the application on a single 2GHz DL385 dual-socket dual-core (Opteron) system is roughly 2 days and 6 hours. In Table 2, the performance of LSDyna is shown using different numbers of cores and nodes and various bindings.

On a dual-processor dual-core node, running LSDyna without binding which allows the OS to schedule the job across the cores, is 5.16% faster than forcing the job to bind to cores on the same socket. Binding the job to cores on the separate sockets, however, only improved performance slightly at 0.36% which means that we are likely reproducing what the OS was doing automatically. This demonstrates how the memory bandwidth is shared between cores on the same socket. Separating the two processes onto separate sockets for a memory bound application, improves performance by increasing the overall memory bandwidth.

Table 1. HPLinpack with N=32381 run on 16 cores (4 nodes x 2 sockets x 2 cores)

Configuration	CPUs	Time (sec)	% Speedup
No affinity control used	16	467.16	
taskset 0xf	16	481.83	-3.04%
taskset 0x1; 0x2; 0x4; 0x8	16	430.44	8.53%
–cpu_bind=map_cpu:0,1,2,3 -B 1:1	16	430.36	8.55%

Table 2. Performance comparison of LSDyna with and without CPU binding

Cores	Nodes	Binding	CPU binding option low-level flag high-level flag	Time (sec)	Time (D:H:M:S)	Speedup	% Speedup vs. no binding
1	1	No		194,809	2:06:06:49	1.00	
1	1	Yes	–cpu_bind=map_cpu:0 -B 1:1	194,857	2:06:07:37	1.00	-0.02%
2	1	No		104,994	1:05:09:54	1.86	
2	1	Yes	–cpu_bind=map_cpu:0,1 -B 1:1	110,702	1:06:45:02	1.76	-5.16%
2	1	Sockets	–cpu_bind=map_cpu:0,2 -B 1:1-1	104,620	1:05:03:40	1.86	0.36%
2	2	No		102,336	1:04:25:36	1.90	
2	2	Yes	–cpu_bind=map_cpu:0 -B 1:1	100,266	1:03:51:06	1.94	4.72%
8	2	No		33,616	0:09:20:16	5.80	
8	2	Yes	–cpu_bind=map_cpu:0,1,2,3 -B 1:1	31,996	0:08:53:16	6.09	5.06%
8	4	No		28,815	0:08:00:15	6.76	
8	4	Yes	–cpu_bind=map_cpu:0,1 -B 1:1	28,532	0:07:55:32	6.83	0.99%
8	4	Sockets	–cpu_bind=map_cpu:0,2 -B 1:1-1	26,081	0:07:14:41	7.47	10.48%

Examining an "8 core 2 node" run (resulting in all 4 cores utilized on both nodes), we conclude that binding processes to cores runs 5.06% faster. Once a job's processes use all available cores, the additional OS processes result in a total number of "runable" processes than is greater than the number of cores. In this case, binding becomes necessary to avoid performance degradation.

When examining the placement of the processes on a loaded system, processes in the unbound run were seen to continually move between the cores which is due to the fact that OS processes cause the total number of runable processes to exceed the number of available cores. With binding, however, the processes stay on the selected core even when the system is fully utilized system.

On a less loaded system, unbound processes tend to stay on the core where they are initiated. This is the reason why the relative improvement of binding drops off with an "8-core 4-node" run (only two cores are utilized per node, leaving two cores idle). Compared to an "8-core 4-node" run with no binding, binding to cores on the same socket ran only 0.99% faster. We expect this run to represent the binding the OS did automatically. Since the system was only half utilized we saw very little migration between sockets. Binding to cores on separate sockets, however, ran 10.48% faster due to improved memory bandwidth since only one core was used in each of the two sockets.

12   Conclusion

The multi-core support we added to SLURM is available starting with SLURM version 1.2. It allows users to use SLURM's default settings on clusters of multi-core nodes without suffering any application performance degradation or large variation in application runtime from run to run. We considered different approaches as well as investigated several features which would help SLURM better support job launching and resource management in a multi-core environment. We decided to add support for all three types of users i.e. expert, intermediate, and naïve users rather than focusing on a single type. We believe that the high-level flags are easy to use and will allow even novice users to take close to full advantage of the new architecture. The process binding is generated automatically when users use the high-level switches thereby allowing users to access very sophisticated functionalities without having to understand the underlying hardware in detail.

Acknowledgment

The authors thank Chuck Schneider, John Eck, Teresa Kaltz, Dick Foster and Kirby Collins from the Solution Engineering group for input on the multi-core/hyperthreading support. We thank Ron Lieberman for many discussions on his experiences with multi-core support in HP MPI. We thank Dan Christians and Chris Holmes for sharing their discussions on the –procmask flag and finally we thank Moe Jette (SLURM project leader) and Danny Auble, Chris Morrone, and Mark Grondona from LLNL for their collaboration around SLURM integration and enhancements.

References

1. Altair pbs professional 7.0, http://www.altair.com/software/pbspro.htm
2. Slurm website (June 2007)
3. Platform, L.S.F.: Platform lsf administrator's primer v6.2 documentation (2006)
4. Yoo, A.B., Jette, M.A., Grondona, M.: Slurm: Simple linux utility for resource management. In: Feitelson, D.G., Rudolph, L., Schwiegelshohn, U. (eds.) JSSPP 2003. LNCS, vol. 2862, pp. 44–60. Springer, Heidelberg (2003)

A Job Self-scheduling Policy for HPC Infrastructures

Francesc Guim and Julita Corbalan*

Barcelona Supercomputing Center
{`francesc.guim,julita.corbalan`}@bsc.edu

Abstract. The number of distributed high performance computing architectures has increased exponentially these last years. Thus, systems composed by several computational resources provided by different Research centers and Universities have become very popular. Job scheduling policies have been adapted to these new scenarios in which several independent resources have to be managed. New policies have been designed to take into account issues like multi-cluster environments, heterogeneous systems and the geographical distribution of the resources.

Several centralized scheduling solutions have been proposed in the literature for these environments, such as centralized schedulers, centralized queues and global controllers. These approaches use a unique scheduling entity responsible for scheduling all the jobs that are submitted by the users.

In this paper we propose the usage of self-scheduling techniques for dispatching the jobs that are submitted to a set of distributed computational hosts that are managed by independent schedulers (such as MOAB or LoadLeveler). It is a non-centralized and job-guided scheduling policy whose main goal is to optimize the job wait time. Thus, the scheduling decisions are done independently for each job instead of using a global policy where all the jobs are considered. On top of this, as a part of the proposed solution, we also demonstrate how the usage of job wait time prediction techniques can substantially improve the performance obtained in the described architecture.

1   Introduction

The increasing complexity of the local systems has led to new distributed architectures. These forthcoming systems are composed of multiple computational resources with different characteristics and policies. In these new distributed scenarios, traditional scheduling techniques have evolved into more complex and sophisticated approaches where other factors, such the heterogeneity of the resources [22] or the geographical distribution [11], have been taken into account.

Distributed HPC architectures are usually composed of several centers containing many hosts. In the job scheduling strategies proposed in literature, jobs

---

* This paper has been supported by the Spanish Ministry of Science and Education under contract TIN2004-07739-C02-01.

E. Frachtenberg and U. Schwiegelshohn (Eds.): JSSPP 2007, LNCS 4942, pp. 51–75, 2008.

are submitted to one centralized scheduler that is responsible for scheduling all the submitted jobs to all the computational resources available in the system. Therefore, users submit jobs to this scheduler and it schedules them according to a global scheduling policy. It takes into account all the queued jobs and the resources available in the center to decide which jobs have to be submitted to, where and when.

Similar to the philosophy of the AppLeS project [2], in this paper we propose not to use a global scheduler or global structures for managing the jobs submitted in these scenarios. Rather, we propose using self-scheduling techniques for dispatch the jobs that users want to submit to the set of distributed hosts. In this architecture, the jobs are scheduled by their own dispatcher and there are no centralized scheduling decisions. The dispatcher is aware of the status of the different resources that are available for the job, but it is not aware of the rest of the jobs that other users have submitted to the system. Thus, the job itself decides which is the most appropriate resource for it to be executed. The target architectures of our work are distributed systems were each computational resource is managed by an independent scheduler (such as MOAB or SLURM). Different from AppLeS approach, we propose the interaction between the job dispatcher and the local schedulers. Thus, the presented work proposes the usage of two level of scheduling layers: at the top, the job is scheduled by the dispatcher (the schedule is based on the information provided by the local schedulers and their capabilities); and once the resource is selected and the job submitted, the job become scheduled by the local resource scheduler.

For this purpose, we have designed the ISIS-Dispatcher. It is a scheduling entity that is associated to one and only one job. Therefore, once the user wants to submit a job, a new dispatcher is instantiated. It is responsible for submitting the job to the computational resource that best satisfies the job requirements and that maximizes its response time. The ISIS-Dispatcher has been designed for deployment in large systems, for instance groups of HPC Research Centers or groups of universities. The core of the ISIS-Dispatcher algorithm is based on task selection policies. We also have described a new task selection policy (Less-WaitTime) based on the job wait time prediction. The main advantage of this is that it takes into account the capacity of the available resources while the others not (i.e: Less-WorkLeft, Less-Queued-Jobs etc.).

In this paper we have evaluated the different task assignment other policies proposed in the literature and the Less-WaitTime policy (LWT). The evaluation of the presented architecture shows how the self-scheduling policy can achieve good performance results (in terms of resource usage and job performance). Furthermore, we state how the usage of prediction techniques for the waiting time used in the new Less-WaitTime policy can substantially improve the overall performance. The main reason for this improvement is caused by the fact that it takes into account the status of the resource and its capacity (i.e: number of processors), while the original techniques only considered the status of the resources (i.e: number of queued jobs) and were designed for homogeneous architectures with resources having the same configurations.

The rest of the paper is organized as follows: in sections 2 and 3 we present the background of the presented work and our main contributions; in the section 4 we describe the proposed scheduling architecture, the task selection policies that have been evaluated in the dispatcher and a description of how the prediction of the wait time metric is computed in each center; next the simulation environment used is described, including the models and modules that it includes; in section 6 the experiments and their evaluation studied in this work are presented; and finally, in section 7 the conclusions are presented.

2   Motivation and Related Work

2.1   Backfilling Policies

Authors like Feitelson, Schwiegelshohn, Rudolph, Calzarossa, Downey or Tsafrir have modeled logs collected from large scale parallel production systems. They have provided inputs for the evaluation of different system behavior. Such studies have been fundamental since they have allowed an understanding how the HPC centers users behave and how the resources of such centers are being used. Feitelson has presented several works concerning this topic, among others, he has published papers on log analysis for specific centers [15][27], general job and workload modeling [12][17][14], and, together with Tsafrir, papers on detecting workload anomalies and flurries [38]. Calzarossa has also contributed with several workload modellization surveys [4][5]. Workload models for moldable jobs have been described in works of authors like Cirne et al. in [7][8], by Sevcik in [32] or by Downey in [9].

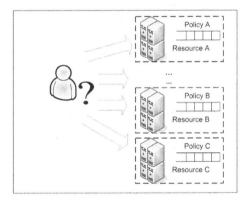

Fig. 1. Heterogeneous multi-host architectures

Concerning job scheduling policies, backfilling [34] policies have been the main goal of study in recent years. As with research in workload modeling, authors like S-H Chiang have provided the community with many quality works regarding this topic. In [18] general descriptions of the most commonly used backfilling variants and parallel scheduling policies are presented. Moreover, a deeper description of the conservative backfilling algorithm can be found in [37], where the authors present policy characterizations and how the priorities can be used when choosing the appropriate job to be scheduled. Other works are [19] and [6].

More complex approaches have been also been proposed by other researchers. For instance, in [28] the authors propose maintaining multiple job queues which separate jobs according to their estimated run time, and using a backfilling aggressive based policy. The objective is to reduce the slowdown by reducing the probability that short job is queued behind a long job. Another example is the optimization presented by Shmueli et al. in [33] which attempts to to maximize the utilization using dynamic programming to find the best packing possible given the system status.

2.2 Global Scheduling

The previously-discussed works have analyzed how local centers behave when jobs are submitted to a specific host managed by one scheduler. In such conditions jobs are executed in the host to which they were submitted. However, in the current HPC centers, they may have many hosts managed by one centralized scheduler, or even more than one host managed by independent schedulers. In these cases, there is the possibility that a job submitted to a Host A could start earlier in Host B of the same center, or even that it could achieve more performance (i.e.: improving the response time) in another Host C. In recent years, scheduling research activities have started to focus on these new scenarios where many computational resources are involved in the architectures.

In the coming large distributed systems, like grids, more global scheduling approaches are being considered. In these scenarios users can access a large number of resources that are potentially heterogeneous, with different characteristics and different access and scheduling policies (see Figure 1). Thus, in most cases the users do not have enough information or skills to decide where to submit their jobs. Several models have been proposed in the literature to solve the challenges open in these architectures. We will discuss the most referenced models:

1. Model 1: There are K independent systems with their own scheduling policies and queuing systems, and one or more external controllers. In this scenario users submit jobs to the specific host with a given policy, and a global scheduling entity tries to optimize the overall performance of the system and the service received by the users. For example, as is exemplified in figure 2a the controller may decide to backfill jobs among the different centers [39].
2. Model 2: There is a centralized global scheduler that manages the jobs at the global level and at local level schedulers and queuing systems are also installed. In this situation the users submit jobs to the centralized scheduling system that will later submit the job to the selected scheduling system of a given center. Jobs are queued at the two different levels: first at the global scheduler queue and second at the local scheduler queue (see Figure 2b). This is the typical brokering approach.

3. Model 3: There is a centralized dispatcher that schedules and manages all the jobs but no local schedulers are installed. The local computational nodes only carry out the resource allocation since all the scheduling decisions are taken by the centralized dispatcher. The jobs are queued only at the upper level. (see Figure 3a)
4. Model 4: There is one centralized global queue where all the jobs are queued. The local computational schedulers pull jobs from the global queue when there are enough available resource for run them. In this way the scheduling decisions are done independently at the local level. In this situation (see Figure 3b) the users submit jobs to this centralized queue.

In [39], Yue proposes to apply a global backfilling within a set of independent hosts where each of them is managed by an independent scheduler (Model 1, Figure 2a). The core idea of the presented algorithm is that the user submits the jobs to a specific system, managed by an independent scheduler. A global controller tries to find out if the job can be backfilled to another host of the center. In the case that the job can be backfilled in another host before it starts, the controller will migrate the job to the selected one. As the algorithm requires the job runtime estimation provided by the user, this optimization is only valid in very homogeneous architectures. This solution may not scale in systems with a high number of computational hosts. Furthermore, other administrative problems may arise, for instance it is not clear if the global *backfiller* presented could scan the queues of all the host involved in the system due to security reasons or VOs administration policies [21].

Sabin et al. studied in [22] the scheduling of parallel jobs in a heterogeneous multi-site environment (Model 2, Figure 2b). They propose carrying out a global scheduling within a set of different sites using a global meta-scheduler where the users submit the jobs. Two different resource selection algorithms are proposed: in the first one the jobs are processed in order of arrival to the meta-scheduler, each of them is assigned to the site with the least instantaneous load; in the second one when the job arrives it is submitted to K different sites (each site schedules according to a conservative backfilling policy), once the job is started in one site the rest of the submissions are canceled (this technique is called multiple requests, MR).

In [11] they analyze the impact of geographical distribution of Grid resources on machine utilization and the average response time. A centralized Grid dispatcher that controls all the resource allocations is used (Model 3, Figure 3a). The local schedulers are only responsible for starting the jobs after the resource selection is made by the Grid Scheduler. Thus, all the jobs are queued in the dispatcher while the size of the job wait queues of the local centers is zero. In this model, a unique global reservation table is used for all the Grid and the scheduling strategy used consists of finding the allocation that minimizes the job start time. A similar approach is the one presented by Schroeder et al. in [31], where they evaluate a set of task assignment policies using the same scenario (one central dispatcher).

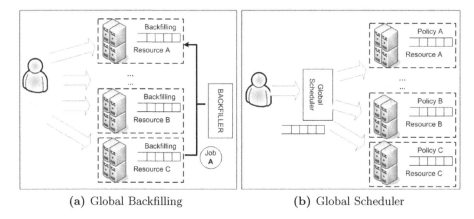

(a) Global Backfilling   (b) Global Scheduler

Fig. 2. Proposed solutions (I)

In [30] Pinchak et al. describe a metaqueue system to manage the jobs with explicit workflow dependencies (Model 3 , Figure 3b). In this case, a centralized scheduling system is also presented. However the submission approach is different from the one discussed before. Here the system is composed of a user-level metaqueue that interacts with the local schedulers. In this scenario, instead of the push model, in which jobs are submitted from the metaqueue to the schedulers, placeholding is based on the pull model in which jobs are dynamically bound to the local queues on demand.

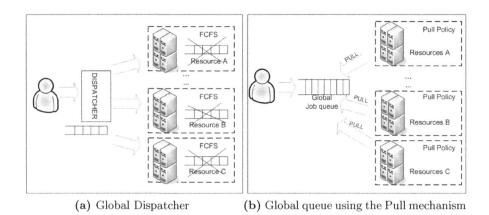

(a) Global Dispatcher   (b) Global queue using the Pull mechanism

Fig. 3. Proposed solutions (II)

In the previously discussed works, using the global policies, the utilization of the available computational resources have been increased. Furthermore, the service received by the users has also been improved. However, in very large domains these approaches may not scale. Therefore, implementing a centralized scheduling algorithms in these architectures is not appropriate.

In the AppLess project [2][3] Berman et al. introduced the concept of application-centric scheduling in which everything about the system is evaluated in terms of its impact on the application. Each application developer schedules their application so as to optimize their own performance criteria without regard to the performance goals of other applications which share the system. The goal is to promote the performance of an individual application rather than to optimize the use of system resources or to optimize the performance of a stream of jobs. In this scenario the applications are developed using the AppLess framework and they are scheduled by the Apples agents. These agents do not use the functionalities provide by the resource management systems. Therefore, they rely on systems such as Globus [20], Legion [23], and others to perform that function.

2.3 Task Assignment Policies

The scheduling policy presented in this paper uses task assignment policies to decide where the jobs should be submitted. The subject of job or task assignment policy has been studied in several works and several solutions have been proposed by the research community. Some of the task assignment policies that have been used in the literature are:

- The *Random* policy. The jobs are uniformly distributed among all the available clusters.
- The *Less-SubmittedJobs* policy. The job i is assigned to the host $i \bmod h$ (it generates a Round Robin submission).
- The *Shorts-Queue* policy. The jobs are submitted to the host with the least submitted jobs.
- The *Least-WorkLeft* policy. The jobs are submitted to the host with the least pending work. Where it is computed as $PW = \sum_{\forall jobs} RequestedTime_{job} * Processor_{job}$.
- The *Central-Queue* policy. The jobs are queued in a global queue. The hosts pull the jobs from the global queue when enough resources are available.
- The *SITA-E* policy (proposed in [26]). The jobs are assigned to the host based on their runtime length. Thus, *short* jobs would be submitted to **host 1**, *medium* jobs to **host 2** and so on. This policy uses the runtime estimation of the job. In this case the duration cutoffs are chosen so as to equalize load.
- The *SITA-U-opt* policy (proposed in [31]). It purposely unbalances load among the hosts, and the task assignment is chosen so as to minimize the mean slowdown.
- The *SITA-U-fair* policy (also proposed in [31]). Similar to the *opt*, they base the assignment to unbalance the host load. However, the goal for this policy is to maximize fairness. In this SITA variant, the objective is not only to minimize the mean slowdown, but also to balance the slowdown for large jobs equal to short jobs.

The evaluations presented in [31][26] concerning the performance of all these task assignment policies have shown that the SITA policies achieve better results. Schroeacher et al. stated that the Random policy performs acceptably for low loads, but for high loads, however, the average slowdown explodes. Furthermore, the SITA-E showed substantially better performance than Least-Work-Left and Random policies for high loads. However, the Least-Work-Left showed lower slowdown than the SITA-E. SITA-U policies showed better results than the SITE-E. SITA-U-fair improved the average slowdown by a factor of 10 and its variance by a factor of 10 to 100. Harchol presented similar work in [1], where the same situation is studied, however the presented task policy does not know the job duration. Although both SITA-U and SITA-E policies have shown promising performance results, they cannot be used for the Self-Scheduling policy described in this paper due to the fact that they assume having knowledge of the global workload.

3   Paper Contribution

To summarize, all the previous scenarios have two common characteristics:

- The scheduling policies are centralized. Thus, the users submit the jobs to a global scheduler.
- They assume that the local resources are homogeneous and are scheduled according the same policy.

Our proposal will be deployed in scenarios with the following conditions:

- The users can submit the jobs directly to the computational resources. Also, they should be able to submit the jobs using the described dispatching algorithm.
- The computational resources can be heterogeneous (with different number of processors, computational power etc.). Also, they can be scheduled by any run-to-completion policy.
- The local schedulers have to provide functionalities for access to information concerning their state (such as number of queued jobs).

In this paper we study the use of job-guided scheduling techniques in scenarios with distributed and heterogeneous resources. The main contributions of this work are:

- The scheduling policy is a job-guided policy. The users submit the job using the ISIS-Dispatcher (see figure 4). Each job is scheduled by an independent Dispatcher.
- Similar to AppLess, the ISIS-Dispatcher is focused on optimizing the job metrics with the scheduling decisions, for instance the job average slowdown, the job response time, the wait time or the cost of the used resources assigned to the job.

- The application has not to be modified for use the proposed architecture. The scheduling is totally transparent to the user and the application.
- The scheduling is done according the information and functionalities that the local schedulers provide (see *job X* of the figure 4). Thus, there is an interaction between the two scheduling layers.
- We keep the local scheduling policies without important modifications. Centers do not have to adapt their scheduling policies or schedulers to ISIS-Dispatcher. They have to provide dynamic information about the system status, for example: the number of queued jobs, when a job would start if it were submitted to the center or which is the remaining computational work in the center.
- In the simulation environment used in the evaluation, we modeled the different levels of the scheduling architecture. Consequently, not only were the dispatcher scheduling policy modeled, but also the local scheduling policies used in the experiments are modeled using an independent reservation table for each of them.
- We propose and evaluate the use of the Less-Waittime task assignment policy that is based on the wait time predictions for the submitted jobs. The evaluation for this policy is compared with the task assignment policies described above, which can be applied in the job-guided scheduling ISIS-Dispatcher policy (SITA policies cannot).

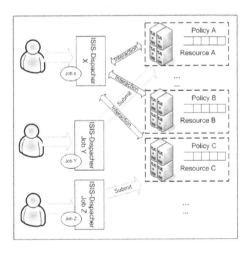

Fig. 4. ISIS-Dispacher architecture

4   The ISIS-Dispatcher

The main objective of this work is to provide a scheduling component that will be used by the user or any other component (e.g.: components that requires self-scheduling or self-orchestration) to decide where to submit their jobs. Figure 4 provides an example of a possible deployment of the proposed architecture. In this example, there are three different users that have access to several computational resources. Each computational resource has its own scheduling policy, different configurations and a particular state (queued jobs, running jobs etc.). When the user wants to submit the job to these resources an instance of the ISIS-Dispatcher is executed and associated to the job. It will decide which is the most appropriate center to submit the job to.

As we have already mentioned, the dispatcher chooses the resource based on a set of metrics provided by each of their schedulers. In this paper we evaluate two different sets of metrics: run time metrics concerning the status of the resource (like the number of queued jobs), and the estimated wait time metric. This prediction information could also be provided by an external prediction service.

In the rest of the section we describe the submission algorithm, the task assignment policies that have been evaluated in this paper, and finally, the prediction model that has been used for evaluated the *Less-WaitTime*.

4.1   The Submission Algorithm

When the user wants to submit a Job α to the system, he/she contacts the ISIS-Dispatcher which manages the job submision and provides the static description of the job $req_\alpha = \{\partial_1, .., \partial_n\}$. In this evaluation, the user provides the script/executable file, the number of requested processors and the requested runtime time. Once the dispatcher has accepted the submission, it carries out the following steps:

1. For each computational resource σ_i (with particular configuration, characteristics and managed by a given center) in all the resources $\{\sigma_1, .., \sigma_n\}$ available to the user:
   (a) The dispatcher checks that the static properties of σ_i match to the static description of the job $\{\partial_1, .., \partial_n\}$. For example, it would check that the computational resource has equal or more processors than that requested by the job[1].
   (b) In affirmative cases, the dispatcher contacts the predictor service and requests a prediction for the job runtime in the given resource.

   $$RTPred_\alpha(\{\partial_1, .., \partial_n\}, \sigma_i)$$

   In the evaluation presented in this paper, the prediction used was the user run time estimation provided in the original workloads. However, we are currently evaluating the use of datamining techniques to predict the run time in these distributed architectures.
   (c) Once the dispatcher receives the job runtime prediction for the given job in the given resource. For each metric γ_i that has to be optimized $(\{\gamma_1, .., \gamma_n\})$:

---

[1] In architecture with thousands of resources, it is not feasible to contact all the resources. Future versions will include heuristics to decide which hosts the dispatcher has to connect to, and which not.

    i. It contacts the scheduler that manages the resource and requests the value of the metric: $\alpha_{\gamma_i,\sigma_i} = LocalModule.Perf(RTPred_\alpha, Reqs_\alpha)$

    ii. It adds the performance metric returned to the list of metrics ($metrics_{\{\alpha,\sigma_i\}}$) for the job in the given resource.

2. Given all the list of retrieved metrics, $metrics_\alpha = \{\alpha_{\{\gamma_i,\sigma_1\}}, .., \alpha_{\{\gamma_m,\sigma_n\}}\}$, where a metric entry is composed of the metric value and the resource where the metric was requested. Using an optimization function, $\alpha_{\gamma_i,\sigma_j} = SelectBestResource(metrics_\alpha)$, the best resource is selected based on the metrics that have been collected.

3. The dispatcher will submit the job to the center that owns the resource.

The function *SelectBestMetric* used in the evaluation of this paper is a simplified version of the once presented above. In each of the evaluation experiments, in step (c) of the previous algorithm, only one metric per computational resource was used. ($\{\alpha_{\{\gamma_1,\sigma\}}, .., \alpha_{\{\gamma_n,\sigma\}}\}$).

4.2 Task Assignment Policies

For this paper we evaluated four different task assignment policies

- The Less-JobWaittime policy minimizes the wait time for the job. Given a static description of a job, the local resource will provide the estimated wait time for the job based on the current resource state. We implemented a prediction mechanism for different sets of scheduling policies (EASY-Backfilling, LXWF-Backfilling, SJF-Backfilled First and FCFS) that use a reservation table that simulates the possible scheduling outcome taking into account all the running and queued jobs at each point of time (see below).
- The Less-JobsInQueue policy submits the job to the computational resource with the least number of queued jobs. (The presented Shortest-Queue in the background).
- The Less-WorkLeft policy submits the job to the computational resource with the least amount of pending work.
- The Less-SubmittedJobs policy submits the jobs to the center with the least number of submitted jobs.

4.3 Job Wait Time Prediction

The Less-JobWaittime task assignment policy submits the job to the center that returns the lowest predicted wait time. The approach taken in this evaluation was that each center has to provide such predictions. However, other architectures can also be used, for instance having several prediction/model services. In that case no interactions with the local centers would be required.

How to predict the amount of time that a given job will wait in the queue of a system has been explored by other researchers in several works [10][35][36][29]. What we propose in this paper is the use of reservation tables. The reservation is used by the local scheduling policies to schedule the jobs and decide where and when the jobs will start.

In this paper the prediction mechanism uses the reservation table to estimate the possible scheduling outcome. It contains two different types of allocations: allocations for those jobs that are running; and pre-allocations for the queued jobs. The status of the reservation table in a given point of time is only one of all the possible scheduling outcomes and the current scheduling may change depending on the dynamicity of the scheduling policy. Also, the accuracy of the job runtime estimation or prediction has an impact on the dynamicity of the scheduling outcomes, mainly due to the job runtime overestimations.

The prediction of the wait time of a job α at time T_1, that requires α_{time} and α_{cpus}, in a given resource, will be computed with: the earliest allocation that the job would receive in the resource given the current outcome if it was submitted at time T_1. Obviously, this allocation will depend on the scheduling policy used in the center, and probably will vary in different time stamps. All the scheduling events are reflected on the status of the reservation table. The prediction technique presented in this work is mainly designed for FCFS and backfilling policies. The information that is used for allocating the job in the reservation table is: the number of required processors and its estimated runtime.

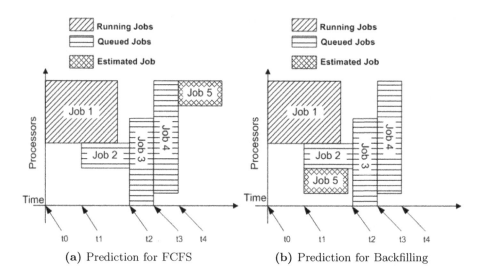

(a) Prediction for FCFS   (b) Prediction for Backfilling

Fig. 5. Scenario All SJF-Backfilled First

Figures 5 provide two examples of how a prediction for a new job would be computed in the two scheduling policies used in this paper. In both examples the current time is t_1, there is one job running (*Job 1*), and three more queued (*Job 2, Job 3* and *Job 4*). If a prediction for the wait time for the job *Job 5* was required by a given instance of the ISIS-Dispatcher, the center would return $t_4 - t_1$ in the case of FCFS (Figure 5a) and would return 0 in the case of Backfilling (Figure 5b).

5   Simulation Characteritzation

In this section we describe the simulation environment that was used to evaluate the presented policy and architecture: first we describe the C++ event-driven simulator that was used to simulate local and distributed High Performance Computing Architectures; and second, we characterize all the experiments that were designed to evaluate the current proposal.

5.1   The Alvio Simulator

All the experiments were conducted using the C++ event-driven Alvio simulator [24]. The simulator models the different components that interact in local and distributed architectures. Conceptually, it is divided into three main parts: the simulator engine, the scheduling polices model (including the resource selection policies), and the computational resource model. A simulation allows us to simulate a given policy with a given architecture. Currently, three different policies have been modeled: the First-Come-First-Served, the Backfilling policies can be used, and finally, the ISIS-Dispatcher scheduling policy. For the backfilling policies the different properties of the wait queue and backfilling queue are modeled (SJF, LXWF and FCFS) and different numbers of reservations can also be specified.

The architecture model allows us to specify different kind of architectures. Currently, cluster architectures can be modeled, where the host is composed of a set of computational nodes, where each node has a set of consumable resources (currently Memory Bandwidth, Ethernet Bandwidth and Network bandwidth). Although the use of these consumable resources can be simulated in a high level fashion, for the experiments presented in this paper it has not been used.

The local scheduling policies (all excluding the ISIS-Dispatcher) use a set of job queues and a reservation to schedule the jobs. The reservation table that is linked to a given architecture has the running jobs allocated to the different processors during the time. One allocation is composed of a set of buckets that indicate that a given job α is using the processors β from $\alpha_{startTime}$ until $\alpha_{endTime}$. Depending on the policy configuration, the scheduling policy will temporarily allocate the queued jobs (for instance, to estimate the wait time for the jobs). The distributed scheduling ISIS-Dispatcher policy does not have a reservation table because it does not allocate the jobs to the processors. Furthermore, the local scheduling policies must provide a functionality that allows querying metrics concerning the current state of the local system. This functionality will be used by the dispatcher to decide where to submit the jobs.

5.2   Experiments

In this section we present the workloads used in the simulations and the scenarios that were designed to evaluate the proposal.

5.3   Workloads

The design and evaluation of our experiments were contrasted and based on the analytical studies available for each of the workloads that we used in our simulations:

- The San Diego Supercomputer Center (SDSC) Blue Horizon log (144-node IBM SP, with 8 processors per node)
- The San Diego Supercomputer Center (SDSC-SP2) SP2 log (128-node IBM SP2)
- The Cornell Theory Center (CTC) SP2 log [16] (512-node IBM SP2).

For the simulation we used traces generated with the fusion of the first four months of each trace (FUSION). The following section describes the simulation: first we simulated the four months for each trace independently; second, using the unique fusion trace, different configurations of a distributed scenario composed by the three centers were simulated. We chose these workloads because they contain jobs with different levels of parallelism and with run times that vary substantially. More information about their properties and characteristics can be found in the workload archive of Dror Feitelson [13].

5.4   Simulation Scenarios

In all the scenarios presented below, all the metrics presented in section 4 were evaluated. In the second and third scenarios we also evaluated what happens when the characteristics of the underlying systems have different configurations, in terms of scheduling policies and computational resource configurations.

The characteristics of each of the evaluated scenarios are:

1. In the first scenario (ALL-SJF), all the centers used the same policy: Shortest Job Backfilled First. The number of processors and computational resources were configured in exactly the same way as the original.
2. In the second scenario (CTC/4), the SFJ-Backfilled first was also used for all the centers. However, in this case we emulated what would happen if the CTC center performed four times slower than the two others. In this case, all the jobs that ran to this center spent four times longer than the runtime specified in the runtime of the original workload[2]. The main goal is to evaluate the impact of having resources with different computational power.
3. In the last scenario (CTC-FCFS), the SDSC and SDSC-Blue also used the SJF-Backfilled First policy. However, the CTC center used the FCFS scheduling policy. As in the first scenario, the computational resource configuration was exactly the same as the original.

The first scenario evaluates situations where all the hosts available have the same scheduling policy. Thus, each computational host is managed by the same

---

[2] This is only a first approximation. Future studies may use more detailed models.

Table 1. Performance Variables for each workload

Center	Estimator	BSLD	SLD	WaitTime
SDSC	Mean	8,66	12,9	2471
	STDev	47,7	86,07	8412
	95_{th} Percentile	17,1	18,92	18101
SDSC-Blue	Mean	6,8	7,6	1331
	STDev	29	36	5207,2
	95_{th} Percentile	28,5	29	8777
CTC	Mean	2,8	3,03	1182
	STDev	23	27,1	4307,3
	95_{th} Percentile	2,3	2,5	6223
CTC/4	Mean	19,8	20,467	9664
	STDev	57,23	58,203	20216
	95_{th} Percentile	114,3	116,3	54450
CTC FCFS	Mean	12,833	14,04	3183,3
	STDev	66,54	77,03	9585
	95_{th} Percentile	32,403	32,65	32996,4

scheduling policy and each computational unit (the processors) of all the hosts has the same power. We defined the two other scenarios to evaluate how the presented scheduling policy behaves with heterogeneous computational resources and with different scheduling policies. In the second scenario we evaluated the impact of having heterogeneous resources. In this situation the CTC processors perform four times slower than the processors of the other two centers. In the last scenario we evaluated the impact of having different scheduling policies in the local hosts.

6   Evaluation

6.1   The Original Workloads

Table 1 presents the performance metrics for the simulation of the workloads used in this paper (CTC, SDSC and SDSC-Blue) with SJF Backfilling in each center. We also include the simulations for the CTC with the other two different configurations that were used in the experiments of the distributed scenarios: the first includes the CTC, and the second also includes the CTC simulation, but using the FCFS policy. As can be observed, the workload that has the best slowdown and wait time is the CTC. The SDSC and SDSC-Blue have a similar average bounded slowdown, however, the 95_{th} percentile of the SDSC-Blue is one order of magnitude greater than the SDSC. In terms of wait time, jobs remain longer in the wait queue in the workload of the SDSC than the other two. In terms of 95_{th} percentile the jobs spend three times longer in the SDSC than in the CTC.

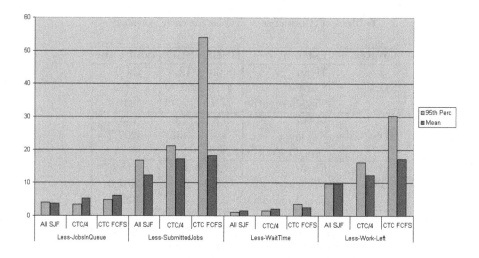

Fig. 6. Bounded Slowdown

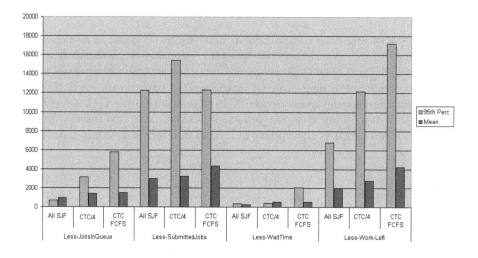

Fig. 7. Wait time

The performance obtained when reducing the computational power and the policy of the CTC center (Table 1) is not surprising. Using FCSC or reducing by four the computational power of the CTC significantly increases the slowdown and wait time for the CTC workload. The capacity of the resource of execute the same workload was reduced four times. Thus, the original scenario cannot cope with the same job stream. The main concern was to evaluate later this configuration in the distributed scenario.

Table 2. Ratio: Original Job Perf. / ISIS Less-WaitTime Job Perf.

Center	Estimator	Ratio BSLD	Ratio SLD	Ratio WaitTime
SDSC	Mean	5,44	7,5	10,98
	STDev	5,1	9,27	4,36
	95_{th} Percentile	14,1	14,92	53,2
SDSC-Blue	Mean	4,2	4,4	5,9
	STDev	3,1	3,6	2,7
	95_{th} Percentile	23,5	22	25,8
CTC	Mean	1,8	1,7	5,2
	STDev	2,5	2,9,1	2,3
	95_{th} Percentile	1,6	1,6	18

6.2 The First Scenario: All Centers with SJF-Backfilled First

Figure 6 presents the average and 95_{th} percentile for the average slowdown in the three presented scenarios and the different task assignment policies studied. In the *scenario 1* (all centers with SJF), the Less-JobQueuedJobs and Less-WaitTime policies showed the best performance. However, the first one obtains a slowdown (1,7) twice as small as the second one (3,9). The other two policies performed substantially worst. The average slowdown and the 95_{th} percentile are three or even ten times greater than in the others. For instance the average slowdown of the Less-Waitime is around two while the same slowdown for the Less-WorkLeft in the same scenario is around ten. The average wait time in this scenario (see Figure 7) presented similar behavior to the slowdown. However, the percentile shows that in the case of the Less-SubmittedJobs and Less-WorkLeft the wait time of the jobs has a high variance. This fact is also corroborated by the standard deviation that the wait time experiments in both policies (see Figure 11).

Table 3. Number of submitted jobs per host

Resource	Less-JobsInQueue	Less-WorkLeft
CTC	10788	10912
SDSC	1953	2560
SDSC-Blue	9550	8819

The Less-WorkLeft policy takes into account the amount of pending work and the Less-JobsInQueue not. Therefore, we expected that the first policy one would perform much better than the second one. However, the presented results showed the contrary. Analyzing both simulations we have stated that in some situations the Less-WorkLeft policy unbalances excessively the number of submitted jobs. As shown in table 3 it submits around 800 jobs more to the SDSC center than the Less-JobsInQueue. The figures 8 and 9 show that the amount of queued jobs in the SDSC is substantially bigger in the Less-WorkLeft policy in this specific interval of the simulation. This unbalance is caused by the characteristics of the stream of jobs that are submitted during this interval to the system. The initial part of this stream is composed by several jobs that requires from 256 processors until 800 processors and that have large runtime. Because of the capacity of the SDSC center (128 processors), these jobs can only be allocated to the CTC center (412 processors) and the SDSC-Blue (1152 processors). This causes that an important amount of smaller jobs (with less than 128 processors) have to be submitted to the SDSC center for accumulate the same amount of pending work that are assigned to the other two centers. Thus, as we state in [25], this stream of jobs composed by jobs that requires all the processors of the host and jobs that requires small number of processors causes an important fragmentation in the scheduling of the SDSC. These situations occurs several times in the simulation and they decrease substantially the performance achieved by the Less-WorkLeft policy.

Table 4. Average of processors used and running jobs per hour

Center	Variable	Original Workload	Less-WaitTime Scenario
SDSC	Running Jobs	5,1	6,02
	Number of used CPUs	52,3	58,3
SDSC-Blue	Running Jobs	4,5	4
	Number of used CPUs	492,8	435,2
CTC	Running Jobs	148,5	282,7
	Number of used CPUs	18,2	23,4

What the results suggest is that the Less-SubmittedJobs policy has the worst performance of all the assignment policies, since the choice of where the job is submitted does not depend on the static properties of the job (estimated runtime and processors). Regarding the other two policies, the Less-JobsInQueue policy performs substantially better than the Less-WorkLeft.

Table 2 provides the ratio for the job performance variables in the original scenario (where jobs where submitted to the independent centers) against the performance for the jobs in the ALL-SJF scenario using the Less-WaitTime policy. The results show that the jobs of all the centers obtained substantially better service in the new scenario. For instance, the average bounded slowdown in SDSC is 5.44 times greater than the average bounded slowdown for the jobs in the *original workloads*. On the other hand, the resource usage achieved by the Less-WaitTime policy has been improved. As the table 4 shows, the average of used processors per hour in the centers has been improved. Although the SDSC-Blue has experimented a soft drop in its processors usage, the CTC has experimented a notoriously increment in its processors usage. Also, as can be been seen in the number of running jobs per hour the packing of jobs has been improved.

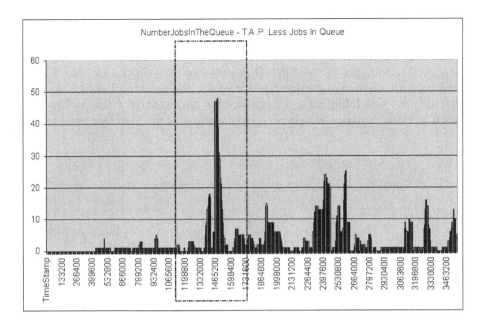

Fig. 8. Number of queued jobs in the SDSC

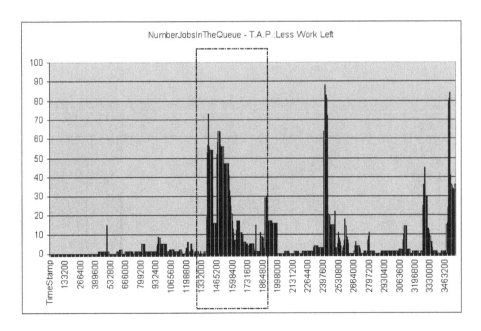

Fig. 9. Number of queued jobs in the SDSC

6.3   Second and Third Scenarios: CTC/4 and CTC with FCFSC

The other two scenarios analyzed in the paper show that the ISIS-Dispacher scheduling policy is able to react in heterogeneous environments where the computational capabilities of the different centers can vary (in the *scenario 2* with a resource with less computational power and in the *scenario 3* with a resource with different scheduling policy). Compared to the *scenario 1* the performance shown in both scenarios experienced only a small drop. Thus, the system was

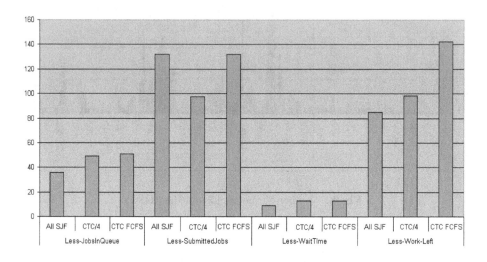

Fig. 10. Bounded Slowdown Standard Deviation

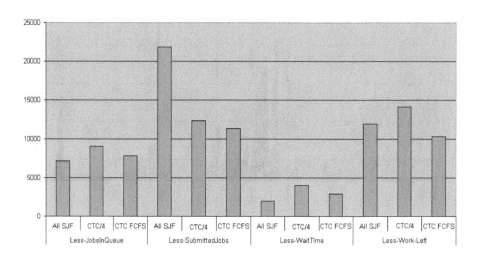

Fig. 11. Wait time Standard Deviation

able to schedule the jobs to the different resources adapting to the different capabilities of each of the available centers. This fact can be observed in figure 12 where the normalized amount of workload done by each center is described for *scenarios 1 and 2*. Clearly, in the situation where the CTC center used a scheduling policy with lower performance, the amount of workload was automatically balanced from this center to the SDSC-Blue and to the SDSC center (similar properties were found in the *scenario 3*). Regarding the performance achieved by each of the task assignment policies used in the experiments, the results show similar behaviors to those we observed in the first scenario.

Clearly, independently of the configuration used, using the Less-WaitTime assignment policy in the ISIS-Dispatcher scheduling policy obtained the best performance results in all the scenarios that were evaluated. It has demonstrated that it is better able to adapt to the difference configuration of the local centers, and to provide a similar service to all the jobs.

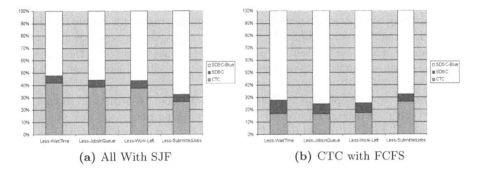

(a) All With SJF   (b) CTC with FCFS

Fig. 12. Work distribution in the ISIS-Scenarios

7   Conclusions and Future Work

In this paper we have presented the use of a job-guided scheduling technique designed to be deployed in distributed architectures composed of a set of computational resources with different architecture configurations and different scheduling policies. Similar to the AppLeS project, the main goal of the technique presented here is to provide the user with a scheduling entity that will decide the most appropriate computational resource to submit his/her jobs to. We support the interaction between the job dispatcher and the local schedulers. Thus, the presented work proposes the usage of two level of scheduling layers: at the top, the job is scheduled by the dispatcher (the schedule is based on the information provided by the local schedulers and their capabilities); and once the resource is selected and the job submitted, the job become scheduled by the local resource scheduler.

The scheduling policy presented here uses a set of task assignment policies to decide where the jobs are finally submitted. This paper has also evaluated how the most representative task assignment scheduling policies presented in the literature perform in the policy presented here (including the Less-WorkLeft, Less-Less-SubmittedJobs and Less-JobsInQueue policies). Furthermore, a task selection policy using the wait time prediction and focused on reducing the wait time for jobs has been proposed.

We have evaluated the proposal in three different scenarios using the workloads CTC, SDSC and SDSC-Blue from the Workload Log Archive. The first scenario was composed of a set of centers with the same scheduling policies and different computational resources (different numbers of processors); the second was composed of a set of centers with different scheduling policies (two with SJF-Backfilled First and one with FCFS) and different computational resources ; and finally, the last one was composed of centers with the same policies and different computational resources with different computational power (one of the centers performed four times slower than the other two). Although the scheduling proposal presented in this paper is non-centralized and the dispatcher does not store any information regarding the progress of the global scheduling, it has been shown that using the appropriate task assignment policy (in this analysis the Less-Waittime policy showed the most promising results) it is able to achieve good global performance, adapting to the underlying center resource characteristics and to the local scheduling policies. Furthermore, not only the job wait time has been improved, the resource usage and the job packing have been also improved.

In future work we plan to use prediction techniques to estimate job runtime rather than user estimates. We are currently working on prototypes where the run time of jobs is estimated using C45 algorithms and discretization techniques (and other datamining techniques). In such scenarios, users will only have to provide the number of requested processors and the static description of the job. We will have to evaluate the impact of prediction and user runtime estimation errors on such architectures.

We will extend the current submission algorithm including other negotiation mechanisms between the local centers and the dispatcher, for instance using Service Level Agreement negotiations or advanced reservations. Furthermore, the ISIS-Dispatcher will be alive during the complete job cycle of life monitoring the job evolution. It will be able to decide to migrate the job to other resources or to carry out other scheduling decisions to achieve better performance. In the current version the dispatching algorithm contacts to all the schedulers that matches the job requirements to gathering the scheduling information. Future version of this algorithm will include user and job heuristics for reduce the amount of schedulers to be queried. Thus, the number of communications will be reduced.

References

1. Bansal, N., Harchol-Balter, M.: Analysis of SRPT scheduling: investigating unfairness (2001)
2. Berman, F., Wolski, R.: The apples project: A status report (1997)

3. Berman, F., Wolski, R.: Scheduling from the perspective of the application. pp. 100–111 (1996)
4. Calzarossa, M., Haring, G., Kotsis, G., Merlo, A., Tessera, D.: A hierarchical approach to workload characterization for parallel systems. In: Hertzberger, B., Serazzi, G. (eds.) HPCN-Europe 1995. LNCS, vol. 919, pp. 102–109. Springer, Heidelberg (1995)
5. Calzarossa, M., Massari, L., Tessera, D.: Workload characterization issues and methodologies. In: Reiser, M., Haring, G., Lindemann, C. (eds.) Performance Evaluation: Origins and Directions. LNCS, vol. 1769, pp. 459–482. Springer, Heidelberg (2000)
6. Chiang, S.-H., Arpaci-Dusseau, A.C., Vernon, M.K.: The impact of more accurate requested runtimes on production job scheduling performance. In: Feitelson, D.G., Rudolph, L., Schwiegelshohn, U. (eds.) JSSPP 2002. LNCS, vol. 2537, pp. 103–127. Springer, Heidelberg (2002)
7. Cirne, W., Berman, F.: A comprehensive model of the supercomputer workload. In: 4th Ann. Workshop Workload Characterization (2001)
8. Cirne, W., Berman, F.: A model for moldable supercomputer jobs. In: 15th Intl. Parallel and Distributed Processing Symp. (2001)
9. Downey, A.B.: A parallel workload model and its implications for processor allocation. In: 6th Intl. Symp. High Performance Distributed Comput (August 1997)
10. Downey, A.B.: Using queue time predictions for processor allocation. In: Feitelson, D.G., Rudolph, L. (eds.) IPPS-WS 1997 and JSSPP 1997. LNCS, vol. 1291, pp. 35–57. Springer, Heidelberg (1997)
11. Ernemann, C., Hamscher, V., Yahyapour, R.: Benefits of global grid computing for job scheduling. In: 5th IEEE/ACM International Workshop on Grid Computing (2004)
12. Feitelson, D.G.: Packing schemes for gang scheduling. In: Feitelson, D.G., Rudolph, L. (eds.) IPPS-WS 1996 and JSSPP 1996. LNCS, vol. 1162, pp. 89–110. Springer, Heidelberg (1996)
13. Feitelson, D.D.G.: Parallel workload archive (2006)
14. Feitelson, D.G.: Workload modeling for performance evaluation. In: Calzarossa, M.C., Tucci, S. (eds.) Performance 2002. LNCS, vol. 2459, pp. 114–141. Springer, Heidelberg (2002)
15. Feitelson, D.G., Nitzberg, B.: Job characteristics of a production parallel scientific workload on the nasa ames ipsc/860. In: Feitelson, D.G., Rudolph, L. (eds.) IPPS-WS 1995 and JSSPP 1995. LNCS, vol. 949, pp. 337–360. Springer, Heidelberg (1995)
16. Feitelson, D.G., Rudolph, L.: Workload evolution on the cornell theory center ibm sp2. In: Feitelson, D.G., Rudolph, L. (eds.) IPPS-WS 1996 and JSSPP 1996. LNCS, vol. 1162, pp. 27–40. Springer, Heidelberg (1996)
17. Feitelson, D.G., Rudolph, L.: Metrics and benchmarking for parallel job scheduling. In: Feitelson, D.G., Rudolph, L. (eds.) IPPS-WS 1998, SPDP-WS 1998, and JSSPP 1998. LNCS, vol. 1459, pp. 1–24. Springer, Heidelberg (1998)
18. Feitelson, D.G., Rudolph, L., Schwiegelshohn, U.: Parallel job scheduling - a status report. In: Feitelson, D.G., Rudolph, L., Schwiegelshohn, U. (eds.) JSSPP 2004. LNCS, vol. 3277, p. 9. Springer, Heidelberg (2005)
19. Feitelson, D.G., Weil, A.: Utilization and predictability in scheduling the ibm sp2 with backfilling. In: Proceedings of the 12th International Parallel Processing Symposium, pp. 542–546 (1998)

20. Foster, I., Kesselman, C.: Globus: A metacomputing infrastructure toolkit. J Intl - International Journal of Supercomputer Applications (1997)
21. Foster, I., Kesselman, C., Tuecke, S.: The anatomy of the Grid: Enabling scalable virtual organizations. In: Sakellariou, R., Keane, J.A., Gurd, J.R., Freeman, L. (eds.) Euro-Par 2001. LNCS, vol. 2150, Springer, Heidelberg (2001)
22. Gerald, S., Rajkumar, K., Arun, R., Ponnuswamy, S.: Scheduling of parallel jobs in a heterogeneous multi-site environment. In: Feitelson, D.G., Rudolph, L., Schwiegelshohn, U. (eds.) JSSPP 2003. LNCS, vol. 2862, Springer, Heidelberg (2003)
23. Grimshaw, A.S., Wulf, W.A., French, J.C., Weaver, A.C., Reynolds Jr, P.F.: Legion: The next logical step toward a nationwide virtual computer (CS-94-21), 8 (1994)
24. Guim, F., Corbalan, J., Labarta, J.: The internals of the alvio-simulator: Simulator of hpc infraestructures (upc-dac-rr-cap-2007-2). Technical report, Architecture Computer Deparment - Technical University of Catalunya (2005)
25. Guim, F., Corbalan, J., Labarta, J.: Modeling the impact of resource sharing in backfilling policies using the alvio simulator. In: 15th Annual Meeting of the IEEE / ACM International Symposium on Modeling, Analysis, and Simulation of Computer and Telecommunication Systems (submitted, 2007)
26. Harchol-Balter, M., Crovella, M.E., Murta, C.D.: On choosing a task assignment policy for a distributed server system. Journal of Parallel and Distributed Computing 59(2), 204–228 (1999)
27. Windisch, V.L.K., Moore, R., Feitelson, D., Nitzberg, B.: A comparison of workload traces from two production parallel machines. In: 6th Symp. Frontiers Massively Parallel Comput, pp. 319–326 (1996)
28. Lawson, B.G., Smirni, E.: Multiple-Queue Backfilling Scheduling with Priorities and Reservations for Parallel Systems. In: Feitelson, D.G., Rudolph, L., Schwiegelshohn, U. (eds.) JSSPP 2002. LNCS, vol. 2537, pp. 72–87. Springer, Heidelberg (2002)
29. Li, H., Chen, J., Tao, Y., Groep, D., Wolters, L.: Improving a local learning technique for queue wait time predictions. Cluster and Grid computing (2006)
30. Pinchak, C., Lu, P., Goldenberg, M.: Practical heterogeneous placeholder scheduling in overlay metacomputers: Early experiences. In: Feitelson, D.G., Rudolph, L., Schwiegelshohn, U. (eds.) JSSPP 2002. LNCS, vol. 2537, pp. 205–228. Springer, Heidelberg (2002)
31. Schroeder, B., Harchol-Balter, M.: Evaluation of task assignment policies for supercomputing servers: The case for load unbalancing and fairness. Cluster Computing 2004 (2004)
32. Sevcik, K.C.: Application scheduling and processor allocation in multiprogrammed parallel processing systems. Performance Evaluation, 107–140 (1994)
33. Shmueli, E., Feitelson, D.G.: Backfilling with Lookahead to Optimize the Performance of Parallel Job Scheduling. In: Feitelson, D.G., Rudolph, L., Schwiegelshohn, U. (eds.) JSSPP 2003. LNCS, vol. 2862, pp. 228–251. Springer, Heidelberg (2003)
34. Skovira, J., Chan, W., Zhou, H., Lifka, D.A.: The EASY - LoadLeveler API Project. In: Feitelson, D.G., Rudolph, L. (eds.) IPPS-WS 1996 and JSSPP 1996. LNCS, vol. 1162, pp. 41–47. Springer, Heidelberg (1996)
35. Smith, W., Taylor, V.E., Foster, I.T.: Using run-time predictions to estimate queue wait times and improve scheduler performance. In: Feitelson, D.G., Rudolph, L. (eds.) JSSPP 1999, IPPS-WS 1999, and SPDP-WS 1999. LNCS, vol. 1659, pp. 202–219. Springer, Heidelberg (1999)

36. Smith, W., Wong, P.: Resource selection using execution and queue wait time. predictions, p. 7
37. Talby, D., Feitelson, D.: Supporting priorities and improving utilization of the ibm sp scheduler using slack-based backfilling. In: Parallel Processing Symposium, pp. 513–517 (1999)
38. Tsafrir, D., Feitelson, D.G.: Instability in parallel job scheduling simulation: the role of workload flurries. In: 20th Intl. Parallel and Distributed Processing Symp. (2006)
39. Yue, J.: Global Backfilling Scheduling in Multiclusters. In: Manandhar, S., Austin, J., Desai, U., Oyanagi, Y., Talukder, A.K. (eds.) AACC 2004. LNCS, vol. 3285, pp. 232–239. Springer, Heidelberg (2004)

QBETS: Queue Bounds Estimation from Time Series

Daniel Nurmi[1], John Brevik[2], and Rich Wolski[1]

[1] Computer Science Department
University of California, Santa Barbara
Santa Barbara, California
[2] Mathematics and Statistics Department
California State University, Long Beach
Long Beach, California[*]

Abstract. Most space-sharing parallel computers presently operated by high-performance computing centers use batch-queuing systems to manage processor allocation. Because these machines are typically "space-shared," each job must wait in a queue until sufficient processor resources become available to service it. In production computing settings, the queuing delay (experienced by users as the time between when the job is submitted and when it begins execution) is highly variable. Users often find this variability a drag on productivity as it makes planning difficult and intellectual continuity hard to maintain.

In this work, we introduce an on-line system for predicting batch-queue delay and show that it generates correct and accurate bounds for queuing delay for batch jobs from 11 machines over a 9-year period. Our system comprises 4 novel and interacting components: a predictor based on nonparametric inference; an automated change-point detector; machine-learned, model-based clustering of jobs having similar characteristics; and an automatic downtime detector to identify systemic failures that affect job queuing delay. We compare the correctness and accuracy of our system against various previously used prediction techniques and show that our new method outperforms them for all machines we have available for study.

1   Introduction

Typically, high-performance multi-processor compute resources are managed using *space sharing*, a scheduling strategy in which each program is allocated a dedicated set of processors for the duration of its execution. In production computing settings, users prefer space sharing to time sharing, since dedicated processor access isolates program execution performance from the effects of a competitive load. Because processes within a partition do not compete for CPU or memory resources, they avoid the cache and translation look-aside buffer (TLB) pollution

---

[*] The work was supported in part by NSF Grants Numbered CCF-0526005, CCF-0331654, and NGS-0305390, and by the San Diego Supercomputer Center.

E. Frachtenberg and U. Schwiegelshohn (Eds.): JSSPP 2007, LNCS 4942, pp. 76–101, 2008.

effects that time slicing can induce. Additionally, inter-process communication occurs with minimal overhead, since a receiving process can never be preempted by a competing program.

For similar reasons, resource owners and administrators prefer space sharing as well. As long as the time to allocate partitions to, and reclaim partitions from, parallel programs is small, no compute cycles are lost to time-sharing overheads, and resources are efficiently utilized. Thus, at present, almost all production high-performance computing (HPC) installations use some form of space sharing to manage their multi-processor and cluster machines.

Because each program in a space-shared environment runs in its own dedicated partition of the target machine, a program cannot be initiated until there are a sufficient number of processors available for it to use. When a program must wait before it can be initiated, it is queued as a "job" along with a description of any parameters and environmental inputs (*e.g.* input files, shell environment variables, *etc.*) it will require to run. However, because of the need both to assign different priorities to users and to improve the overall efficiency of the resource, most installations do not use a simple first-come-first-served (FCFS) queuing discipline to manage the queue of waiting jobs. Indeed, a number of queue management systems, including PBS [28], LoadLeveler [1], EASY [20], NQS/NQE [23], Maui [22] and GridEngine [16] each offer a rich and sophisticated set of configuration options that allow system administrators to implement highly customized priority mechanisms.

Unfortunately, while these mechanisms can be used to balance the need for high job throughput (in order to ensure machine efficiency) with the desires of end-users for rapid turnaround times, the interaction between offered workload and local queuing discipline makes the amount of time a given job will wait highly variable and difficult to predict. Users may wait a long time – considerably longer than the job's eventual execution time – for a job to begin executing. Many users often find this potential for unpredictable queuing delay particularly frustrating since, in production settings, they often *can* make reasonable predictions of how long a program will execute once it starts running. Without an ability to predict its queue waiting time, however, users cannot plan reliably to have results by a specific point in time.

In this paper, we present a method for automatically predicting bounds, with quantitative confidence levels, on the amount of time an individual job will wait in queue before it is initiated for execution on a production "batch scheduled" resource. The method consists of three interacting but essentially independent components: a percentile estimator, a change-point detector, and a clustering procedure. At a high level, clustering is used to identify jobs of similar characteristics. Within each cluster, job submissions are treated as a time series and the change-point detector delineates periods of stationarity. Finally, the percentile estimator computes a quantile that serves as a bound on future wait time based only on history from the most recent stationary region in each cluster. All three components can be implemented efficiently so that on-line, real-time predictions are possible. Thus, for each job submission, our method can generate a predicted bound on its delay using a stationary history of previous jobs having similar quantitative characteristics. In addition, as jobs complete their time in queue, new data becomes available. Our method automatically incorporates this information by adjusting its clustering and change-point estimates in response to the availability of new data.

The percentile estimation method we describe here is a product of our previous work in predicting the minimum time until resource failure [3,24,26]. In this work, we describe its application to the problem of predicting bounds on the delay experienced by individual jobs waiting for execution in batch-controlled parallel systems. To do so effectively, we have coupled this methodology with a new method for detecting change points in the submission history and a new clustering methodology that automatically groups jobs into service classes. This latter capability is necessary since many sites implement dynamically changing priority schemes that use "small" jobs to "backfill" [19] the machine as a way of ensuring high levels of resource utilization. Moreover, our quantile-based prediction method makes it possible to infer when the the machine may have crashed while the queuing system still accepts jobs (a common failure mode in these settings where jobs are submitted from one or more "head" nodes). Using this new system, we have found that it is possible to predict bounds on the delay of individual jobs that are tighter then parametric methods based on Maximum Likelihood Estimation (MLE) of Weibull, log-normal, and log-uniform distributions. To achieve these tighter bounds, however, all four components – non-parametric quantile estimation, change-point detection, clustering, and availability inference – must be integrated and employed in concert. Because the systems in inherently an adaptive time series forecasting methodology, we give it the name QBETS as an acronym for **Q**ueue **B**ounds **E**stimation from **T**ime **S**eries.

We compare QBETS with various parametric methods in terms of prediction correctness and accuracy. We also demonstrate how the combination of techniques that compose QBETS improves the predictive power for production systems.

Our evaluation uses job submission traces from 11 supercomputers (including 8 currently in operation) operated by the National Science Foundation and the Department of Energy over the past 10 years comprising approximately 1.4 million job submissions. By examining job arrival time, requested execution time, and requested node count, we simulate each queue in each trace and compute a prediction for each job. Our results indicate that QBETS (which is more effective than competitive parametric methods) achieves significantly tighter bounds on job wait time in most cases. Thus the system automatically "reverse engineers" the *effective* priority scheme that is in place at each site and determines what job sizes are receiving the fastest turn-around time.

Thus, this paper makes two significant new contributions with regard to predicting individual job queue delays.

– We present QBETS as an example of an accurate, non-parametric, and fully automatic method for predicting bounds (with specific levels of certainty) on the amount of queue delay each individual job will experience.

- We verify the efficacy of QBETS and detail its ability to automatically take into account job resource characteristics to improve prediction bounds using currently operating large-scale batch systems, and from archival logs for systems that are no longer in operation.
- We describe an implementation of QBETS that provides an on-line batch queue job delay prediction service to high performance computing users and how we have made available a number of programmatic interfaces to the system such that others may trivially integrate QBETS into their own projects.

We believe that these results constitute a new and important capability for users of batch-controlled resources. Using an on-line, web-based, real-time version of QBETS [27] that allows users to generate predictions on demand, these users are better able to decide on which machines to use, which queues on those machines to use, the maximum amount of run time to request, and the number of processors to request so as to minimize job turnaround time or maximize the utilization of their respective time allocations. In a related work, we show how QBETS has already been used to augment a real application workflow scheduler to achieve a 2x improvement in overall workflow completion time [25]. Our techniques are also useful as a scheduling policy diagnostic for site administrators. For example, our results indicate that the amount of requested execution time is a far more significant factor in determining queue delay than is requested processor count (presumably due to back-filling [19]). One site administrator at a large scale computer center expressed surprise at this result, since she believed she had set the scheduling policy at this site to favor jobs with large processor counts in an effort to encourage users to use the resource for "big" jobs. Because short jobs can be more readily scheduled when back-filling is used, users are circumventing the site policy and submitting small jobs to improve turn-around time. In addition, we have successfully explored the use of these types of predictions to construct a "virtual resource reservation" out of regular batch queue controlled resource (*Cf.* Section 5). These examples illustrate how QBETS is already having an impact on large-scale batch-controlled settings by improving application turnaround time, streamlining large scale scheduling policies, and providing a new service to the community which has been adopted by several projects.

This ability to make predictions for individual jobs distinguishes our work from other previous efforts. An extensive body of research [6,8,9,11,12,13,14,32] investigates the statistical properties of offered job workload for various HPC systems. In most of these efforts, the goal is to formulate a *model* of workload and/or scheduling policy and then to derive the resulting statistical properties associated with queuing delay through simulation. Our approach focuses strictly on the problem of *forecasting* future delay bounds; we do not claim to offer an explanatory, or even a descriptive, model of user, job, or system behavior. However, perhaps because of our narrower focus, our work is able to achieve predictions that are, in a very specific and quantifiable sense, more accurate and more meaningful than those reported in the previous literature.

In Section 2, we discuss related approaches further, followed by a detailed description of QBETS in Section 3. As mentioned previously, Section 4 discusses our predictor performance experiment, evaluation procedure and the specific results we have achieved. We briefly cover some of the ways in which the QBETS system is already impacting other existing research projects in Section 5. Finally, in Section 6 we recap and conclude.

2   Related Work

Previous work in this field can be categorized into two groups. The first group of work belongs under the general heading of the scheduling of jobs on parallel supercomputers. In works by Feitelson and Rudolph [12,13], the authors outline various scheduling techniques employed by different supercomputer architectures and point out strengths and deficiencies of each. The prevalence of distributed memory clusters as supercomputer architectures has led to most large scale sites using a form of "variable partitioning" as described in [12]. In this scheme, machines are space-shared and jobs are scheduled based on how many processors the user requests and how much time they specify as part of the job submission. As the authors point out, this scheme is effective for cluster-type architectures but leads to fragmentation as well as potentially long wait times for jobs in the queue.

The second field of previous work relevant to our work involves using various models of large-scale parallel-job scenarios to predict the amount of time jobs spend waiting in scheduler queues. These works attempt to show that batch-queue job wait times can be inferred under the conditions that one knows the length of time jobs actually execute and that the algorithm employed by the scheduler is known. Under the assumption that both of these conditions are met, Smith, Taylor and Foster introduce in [32] a prediction scheme for wait times. In this work, the authors use a template-based approach to categorize and then predict job execution times. From these execution-time predictions, they then derive mean queue delay predictions by simulating the future behavior of the batch scheduler in faster-than-real time. In practice, however even when their model fits the execution-time data well, the mean error ranges from 33% to 73%.

Downey [8,9] uses a similar set of assumptions for estimating queue wait times. In this work, he explores using a log-uniform distribution to model the remaining lifetimes of jobs executing in all machine partitions as a way of predicting when a "cluster" of a given size will become available and thus when the job waiting at the head of the queue will start. As a base case, Downey performs a simulation which has access to the exact execution times of jobs in the queue, plus knowledge of the scheduling algorithm, to provide deterministic wait time predictions for the job at the head of the queue. As a metric of success, Downey uses the correlation between the wait times of the head jobs during the base case simulation and the wait times experienced by head jobs if his execution time model is used.

Both of these approaches make the underlying assumption that the scheduler is employing a fairly straightforward scheduling algorithm (one which does not allow for special users or job queues with higher or lower priorities), and also that the resource pool is static for the duration of their experiments (no downtimes, administrator interference, or resource pool dynamism).

Our work differs from these approaches in two significant ways. First, instead of inferring from a job execution model the amount of time jobs will wait, we make job wait time inference from the actual job wait time data itself. The motivation for why this is desirable stems from research efforts [7,17], which suggest that modeling job execution time may be difficult for large-scale production computing centers. Further, making inference straight from the job wait time data, we avoid having to make underlying assumptions about scheduler algorithms or machine stability. We feel that in a real world scenario, where site scheduling algorithms are rarely published and are not typically simple enough to model with a straightforward procedure, it is unlikely that valid queue wait-time predictions can be made with these assumptions.

Second, our approach differs in the statistic we use as a prediction. Most often, researchers look for an estimator of the expected (mean) wait time for a particular job. Our approach instead uses bounds on the time an individual job will wait rather than a specific, single-valued prediction of its waiting time. We contend that the highly variable nature of observed queue delay is better represented to potential system users as quantified confidence bounds than as a specific prediction, since users can "know" the probability that their job will fall outside the range. For example, the information that the expected wait time for a particular job is 3 hours tells the user less about what delay his or her job will experience than the information that there is a 75% chance that the job will execute within 15 minutes.

3   Batch Queue Prediction

In this section, we describe our approach to the four related problems that we must solve to implement an effective predictor: quantile estimation[1], change-point detection, job clustering, and machine availability inference. The general approach we advocate is first to determine if the machine of interest is in a state where jobs are being serviced, next to cluster the observed job submission history according to jobs having similar quantitative characteristics (e.g. requested node count, requested maximum execution time, or requested node-hours), then to identify the most recent region of stationarity in each cluster (treated as a time series), and finally to estimate a specific quantile from that region to use as a statistical bound on the time a specific job will wait in queue. While logically the steps occur in this order, we describe them in reverse order, providing only a summarization of our quantile estimation and stationarity approaches, primarily

---

[1] We use the term "quantile" instead of the term "percentile" throughout the remainder of this paper.

due to space constraints but also because we have analyzed these extensively in other publications [4,25].

3.1   Quantile Prediction

Our goal is to determine an upper bound on a specific quantile at a fixed level of confidence, for a given population whose distribution is unknown. If the quantile were known with certainty, and the population were the one from which a given job's queue delay were to be drawn, this quantile would serve as a statistical bound on the job's waiting time. For example, the 0.95 quantile for the population will be greater than or equal to the delay experienced by all but 5% of the jobs. Colloquially, it can be said that the job has a "95% chance" of experiencing a delay that is less than the 0.95 quantile. We assume that the quantile of interest (0.95, 0.99, 0.50, etc.) is supplied to the method as a parameter by the site administrator depending on how conservative she believes the estimates need to be for a given user community.

However, since the quantiles cannot be known exactly and must be estimated, we use an upper confidence bound *on the quantile* that, in turn, serves as a conservative bound on the amount of delay that will be experienced by a job. To be precise, to say that a method produces an upper 95% confidence bound on a given quantile implies that the bound produced by this method will, over the long run, overestimate the true quantile 95% of the time. The degree of conservatism we assume is also supplied to the method as a confidence level. In practice, we find that while administrators do have opinions about what quantile to estimate, the confidence level for the upper bound is less meaningful to them. As a result, we typically recommend estimating what ever quantile is desired by the upper 95% confidence bound on that quantile.

In this work, we examine the performance of four quantile prediction techniques. The first three are somewhat traditional techniques, each based on fitting a statistical distribution to historical data and using the distribution quantile of interest as the predictor for the next observation. We rely on MLE model fitting of three distributions; log-normal, log-uniform, and Weibull. We note that for the log-uniform and Weibull method, there is no straight-forward way to place confidence bounds on population quantiles and thus we use the model quantile as the predictor. For the log-normal and binomial method predictors, we use the upper 95% confidence bound, but note that even when we use tighter confidence intervals, the resulting predictions are not significantly impacted. The fourth approach is a novel, non-parametric method which makes inference directly from the data, instead of assuming some pre-defined underlying distribution. Here we describe our novel method, which we term the *Binomial Method*, beginning with the following simple observation: If X is a random variable, and X_q is the q quantile of the distribution of X, then a single observation x from X will be greater than X_q with probability $(1 - q)$. (For our application, if we regard the wait time, in seconds, of a particular job submitted to a queue as a random variable X, the probability that it will wait for less than $X_{.95}$ seconds is exactly .95.)

Thus (provisionally under the typical assumptions of independence and identical distribution) we can regard all of the observations as a sequence of independent Bernoulli trials with probability of success equal to q, where an observation is regarded as a "success" if it is less than X_q. If there are n observations, the probability of exactly k "successes" is described by a Binomial distribution with parameters q and n. Therefore, the probability that more than k observations are greater than X_q is equal to

$$1 - \sum_{j=0}^{k} \binom{n}{j} \cdot (1-q)^j \cdot q^{n-j} \qquad (1)$$

Now, if we find the smallest value of k for which Equation 1 is larger than some specified confidence level C, then we can assert that we are confident at level C that the kth value in a sorted set of n observations will be greater than or equal to the X_q quantile of the underlying population – in other words, the kth sorted value provides an *upper level-C confidence bound* for X_q.

Clearly, as a practical matter, neither the assumption of independence nor that of identical distribution (stationarity as a time series) holds true for observed sequences of job wait times from the real systems, and these failures present distinct potential difficulties for our method.

Let us first (briefly) address the issue of independence, assuming for the moment that our series is stationary but that there may be some autocorrelation structure in the data. We hypothesize that the time-series process associated to our data is *ergodic*, which roughly amounts to saying that all the salient sample statistics asymptotically approach the corresponding population parameters. Ergodicity is a typical and standard assumption for real-world data sets; *cf., e.g.,*[15]. Under this hypothesis, a given sample-based method of inference will, *in the long run*, provide accurate confidence bounds.

Although our method is not invalidated by dependence, a separate issue from the *validity* of our method is that exploiting any autocorrelation structure in the time series should, *in principle*, produce more accurate predictions than a static binomial method which ignores these effects. Indeed, most time-series analysis and modeling techniques are primarily focused on using dependence between measurements to improve forecasting [2]. For the present application, however, there are a number of obfuscating factors that foil typical time-series methods. First of all, for a given job entering a queue, there are typically several jobs in the queue, so that the most recent available wait-time measurement is for several time-lags ahead. The correlation between the most recent measurement at the time a job enters the queue and that job's eventual wait time is typically modest, around 0.1, and does not reliably contribute to the accuracy of wait-time predictions. Another issue is the complexity of the underlying distribution of wait times: They typically have more weight in their tails than exponential distributions, and many queues exhibit bimodal or multimodal tendencies as well. All of this makes any linear analysis of data relationships (which is the basis of the "classical" time-series approach) very difficult. Thus while the data is not independent, it is also not amenable to standard time-series approaches for exploiting correlation.

3.2   History Trimming

Unlike the issue of independence and correlation, the issue of non-stationarity *does* place limitations on the applicability of quantile prediction methods. Clearly, for example, they will fail in the face of data with a "trend," say, a mean value that increases linearly with time. On the other hand, insisting that the data be stationary is too restrictive to be realistic: Large compute centers change their scheduling policies to meet new demands, new user communities migrate to or from a particular machine, *etc.* It seems to be generally true across the spectrum of traces we have examined that wait-time data is typically stationary for a relatively long period and then undergoes a "change-point" into another stationary regime with different population characteristics. We thus use the Binomial Method as a prediction method for data which are stationary for periods and for which the underlying distribution changes suddenly and relatively infrequently; we next discuss the problem of detecting change-points in this setting.

Given an independent sequence of data from a random variable X, we deem that the occurrence of three values in a row above $X_{.95}$ constitutes a "rare event" and one which should be taken to signify a change-point. Why three in a row? To borrow a well-known expression from Tukey , two is not enough and four is too many; this comes from consideration of "Type I" error. Under the hypothesis of identical distribution, a string of two consecutive high or low values occurs every 400 values in a time series, which is an unacceptable frequency for false positives. Three in a row will occur every 8000 values; this strikes a balance between sensitivity to a change in the underlying distribution of the population and certainty that a change is not being falsely reported.

Now, suppose that the data, regarded as a time series, exhibits some autocorrelation structure. If the lag-1 autocorrelation is fairly strong, three or even five measurements in a row above the .95 quantile might not be such a rare occurrence, since, for example, one unusually high value makes it more likely that the next value will also be high. In order to determine the number of consecutive high values (top 5% of the population) that constitute a "rare event" approximately in line with the criterion spelled out for independent sequences, we conducted a Monte Carlo simulation with various levels of lag-1 autocorrelation in $AR(1)$ time series [15], observed the frequencies of occurrences of consecutive high and low values, and generated a lookup table for rare-event thresholds. Thus, to determine if a change-point has occurred, we compute the autocorrelation of the most recent history, look up the maximum number of "rare" events that should normally occur with this level of autocorrelation, and determine whether we have surpassed this number. If so, our method assumes the underlying system has changed, and that the relevant history must be trimmed as much as possible to maximize the possibility that this history corresponds to a region of stationarity. Note that indiscriminate history-trimming will not allow our method to function properly, since the resulting small sample sizes will generate unnecessarily conservative confidence bounds.

The minimum useful history length depends on the quantile being estimated and the level of confidence specified for the estimate. For example, it follows from Equation 1 above that in order to produce an upper 95% confidence bound for the .95 quantile, the minimum history size that can be used is 59. (This reflects the fact that $.95^{59} < .05$, while $.95^{58} > .05$.)

3.3 Job Clustering

According to our observations and to anecdotal evidence provided by users and site administrators, there are differences among the wait times various jobs might expect to experience in the same queue, based purely on characteristics of the jobs such as the amount of time and the number of nodes requested. This is certainly easy to believe on an intuitive level; for example, if a particular queue employs backfilling [19], it is more likely that a shorter-running job requesting a smaller number of nodes will be processed during a time when the machine is being "drained." Thus, for a given job, we might hope to make a better prediction for its wait time if we took its characteristics into account rather than making one uniform prediction which ignores these characteristics.

On the other hand, the same difficulties arise in trying to produce regression models [32] as we encountered in the problem of trying to use autoregressive methods: In particular, the data are typically multimodal and do not admit the use of simple quantile prediction models. We therefore explore the idea of *clustering* the data into groups having similar attributes, so that we can use our parametric and non-parametric predictors on each cluster separately.

In fact, in [5], based on advice we received from several expert site administrators for currently operating systems, we employed a rather arbitrary partitioning of jobs in each queue by processor count, running separate predictors within each partition, which resulted in substantially better predictions. However, it would clearly be desirable to find a partition which is in some (statistical) sense "optimal" rather than relying on such arbitrary methods; for our purposes, it is also desirable to find a partitioning method that can be machine-learned and is therefore applicable across different queues with different policies and user characteristics without direct administrator intervention or tuning. Moreover, as a diagnostic tool, it would be advantageous to be able to compare the machine-determined clustering with that determined by site administrators to illuminate the effects of administrator-imposed scheduling policies. In this section, we describe our approach to this problem, which falls under the rubric of *model-based clustering* [18,30,35].

3.4 Model-Based Clustering

The problem of partitioning a heterogeneous data set into clusters is fairly old and well studied [18,21,30,35]. The simplest and most common clustering problems involve using the values of the data, relative to some notion of distance. Often, one postulates that the distribution within each cluster is Gaussian, and the clusters are formed using some well-known method, such as the so-called k-means algorithm [21] or one of various "hierarchical" or "partitional" methods [30,35]. If the number of clusters is also unknown, a model-selection criterion such as BIC [31], which we will discuss further below, is often used to balance goodness of fit with model complexity.

In fact, it is tempting, if for no other reason than that of simplicity, to form our clusters in this way, according to how they naturally group in terms of one or more job attributes. Note, however, that this method of clustering in no way takes into account the wait times experienced by jobs, which is ultimately the variable of interest; it is by no means clear that a clustering of jobs by how their requested wait times group will result in clusters whose wait-time distributions are relatively homogeneous. For example, it is possible that a subset of the requested job execution times form a nice Gaussian cluster between 8 and 12 minutes, but that due to some combination of administrative policy, backfilling, and various "random" characteristics of the system as a whole, jobs requesting less than 10 minutes experience substantially different wait times than those requesting more than 10 minutes, so this cluster is actually meaningless in terms of predicting wait times.

In our case, then, the situation is somewhat more complicated than ordinary clustering: We wish to cluster the data according to some characteristics which are *observable at the time the job is submitted* (explanatory variables), but using the actual wait times (response variable) as the basis for clustering. That is, we wish to use observed wait times to cluster jobs, but then to determine how each cluster is characterized by quantitative attributes that are available when each job is submitted so that an arriving job can be categorized before it begins to wait. In the discussion that follows, we will use the *requested execution time* (used to implement backfilling) as the explanatory characteristic, but this is only for the sake of ease of exposition.

The idea behind our method runs as follows: We postulate that the set of requested times can be partitioned into k clusters $C_1, \ldots, C_k$, which take the form of intervals on the positive time axis, such that within each C_j the wait times are governed by an exponential distribution with unspecified parameter λ_j.

The choice of exponential distributions is something of an oversimplification – in fact a Weibull, log-normal or hyperexponential would probably be a more accurate choice – but the fact that the clusters are relatively homogeneous makes the exponential model accurate enough with relatively little computational expense; moreover, in practice, exponentials are more than discerning enough to produce an adequate number of clusters. As a check, we generated an artificial trace using different log-normally distributed wait times corresponding to the intervals of requested times $[1, 100]$, $[101, 200]$, $[201, 300]$, $[301, 400]$, and $[401, 500]$ and fed this data to our clustering method. It recovered the following clusters for the data: $[1, 39]$, $[40, 40]$, $[41, 100]$, $[101, 197]$, $[198, 300]$, $[301, 398]$, $[399, 492]$, $[493, 493]$, $[494, 500]$. Since our method always clusters the ends together to ensure that these clusters contain at least 59 elements, the exponential clustering method recovers the original clusters almost exactly.

We assume that the appropriate clustering is into connected intervals along the time axis; this provides an intuitive model for the eventual users of our predictions. Given a desired value for the number k of clusters, then, we use a modified form of *hierarchical clustering*. According to this method, we start with each unique value for the requested time in its own cluster. We then merge the two adjacent (in the sense of adjacency on the time axis) clusters that give the largest value of the *log-likelihood function* $\log L$, calculated jointly across the clusters, according to the maximum-likelihood estimators for the exponential parameters λ_j, which are given by $\frac{\#(C_j)}{\sum_{x \in C_j} x}$. This process continues until the number of clusters is equal to k. Note that this is a well-accepted method for clustering [21,30,35]; however, it does not guarantee that the resulting clustering will maximize the log-likelihood over all possible choices of k clusters, even if we assume that the clusters are all intervals. This latter problem is prohibitively expensive computationally for an on-line, real-time application, even for moderately large data sets, and we are therefore forced to use some restricted method.

Each arriving job can then be categorized by identifying the cluster whose minimum and maximum requested time straddle the job's requested time.

Continuing, the question of which value of k to use is a problem in *model selection*, which recognizes the balance between modeling data accurately and model simplicity. The most generally accepted model-selection criterion is the *Bayes Information Criterion* (BIC) [31], the form of which is

$$\mathrm{BIC}(\theta) = \log L(\theta) - \frac{p}{2} \log n,$$

where θ stands for the (vector of) free parameters in the model, L is the joint likelihood function across the whole data set, calculated using the MLE for θ, p is the dimensionality of θ ($2k - 1$ in our case: the $k - 1$ break points on the time axis to define our clusters, and the k values for the λ_j, all of which are scalars), and n is the total sample size. The first term in the BIC formula should be seen as a measure of goodness of fit, while the second term is a "penalty" for model complexity (*i.e.* one with a large number of parameters). It is always true that for a less restricted model (in our case, one allowing a larger number of clusters), the $\log L$ term will be larger, so the penalty function is critical to avoid overparameterizing. Maximizing the BIC expression over a set of proposed models has good theoretical properties and generally produces good results in practice. Thus, our clustering strategy is to specify a range of acceptable k-values; perform the hierarchical clustering described above for each of these values of k; and then calculate the BIC expression for each resulting clustering and choose the one for which BIC is greatest.

3.5   Availability Inference

Curiously, it is common for a batch queuing system to continue to accept jobs even when some form of failure has disabled those jobs from being eligible for execution on a set of computation nodes. We know of no automatic detector for this condition that is part of the production batch-scheduling systems used by the machines in our study. Moreover, based on our discussion of this issue with various site administrators, one common solution to this problem seems to be to rely on the users to call when they observe that jobs are no longer being released for execution (even though they can still be queued) and enquire as to whether there is a "problem.". If a ubiquitous service for notification of machine unavailability becomes common, QBETS can trivially be augmented to use such a system. In the meantime, we have found an elegent method to infer machine failures directly from the job waittime data.

To avoid incorporating jobs with artificially lengthened queue delays (due to machine downtime) in the history used for forecasting, QBETS attempts to infer when the computational part of the machine may be down so that these delays can be filtered. Notice that the combination of Binomial-based quantile estimation and history trimming (sans clustering) provides a relatively general non-parametric method for estimating bounds in time series. QBETS uses this generality in two ways.

First, it counts the number of jobs that have arrived between the points in time when the scheduler releases jobs for execution. As each count is generated, it is incorporated into a time series from which the upper 0.95 quantile (with 95% confidence) is estimated using a Binomial estimator with history trimming. When a count exceeds this upper bound, the QBETS predictor declares the machine to be potentially down until the scheduler releases another job for execution. This functionality is intended to mimic user behavior in which a queue that has been observed to grow "too long" indicates that the computational nodes may be unavailable.

QBETS also maintains a second upper 0.95 quantile predictor to forecast the bounds on the delay between job releases by the scheduler, again using a trimming Binomial estimator. If the time between when jobs are released exceeds the prediction of the bounds, the machine is also marked down until the next job is released. This detector is intended to reflect a user's determination that it as been "too long" since a job was released for execution.

When QBETS temporarily marks a machine as "down", jobs submitted during the down periods are not forecast. Instead, the user is given a signal that can be interpreted to mean "it is possible that the machine is down at this moment so no prediction is available." Since there is no ground truth as to when the machines in this study were actually down (no failure detector were or are available) it is impossible to know the extent to which this method generates false positive predictions. In general, however, the number of jobs for which "no prediction" would have been returned is a small fraction (usually less than 1%) of the total job submission count.

4   Results

In this section, we describe our method for evaluating the performance of our chosen batch-queue wait-time prediction system, and we then detail a set of simulation experiments that take as input traces of job submission logs gathered at various supercomputing centers. We describe the details of the simulations and then report the prediction performance that users *would have* seen had the tested system been available at the time each job in each trace was submitted.

We investigate the problem in terms of estimating an upper bound on the 0.95 quantile of queuing delay; however, our approach can be similarly formulated to produce lower confidence bounds, or two-sided confidence intervals, at any desired level of confidence. It can also be used, of course, for any population quantile. For example, while we have focused in this paper on the relative certainty provided by the .95 quantile, our method also effectively produces confidence bounds for the median (*i.e.*, the point of "50-50" probability). We note that the quantiles at the tail of the distribution corresponding to rarely occurring but large values are more variable, hence more difficult to estimate, than those nearer the center of the distribution. Thus, for typical batch-queue data, which is right-skewed with a substantial tail, the upper quantiles provide the greatest challenge for a prediction method. By focusing on an upper bound for the .95 quantile, we are testing the limits of what can be predicted for queue delay.

Note also that our assertion of retroactive prediction correctness and accuracy assumes that users would not have changed the characteristics of the jobs they submitted in response to the availability of the quantile predictions we generate. Moreover, the on-line prototype we have developed, while operational, is in use by only a few users (in fact, we ourselves used QBETS to select which site to execute many of the simulations that generated the results reported here), making it difficult to analyze whether, and how, predictions affect workload characteristics. However, unless such feedback induces chaotic behavior, our approach is likely to continue to make correct and accurate predictions under the new conditions. We do plan to monitor the workloads experienced by various sites after the system is deployed for general use at various large-scale sites and report on the effects as part of our future work.

4.1   Data Sets

We obtained 11 archival batch-queue logs from different high-performance production computing settings covering different machine generations and time periods. From each log, we extracted data for the various queues implemented by each site. For all systems except the ASCI Blue Pacific system at Lawrence Livermore National Laboratory (LLNL), each queue determines, in part, the priority of the jobs submitted to it.

The job logs come from three machines operated by the San Diego Supercomputer Center during three different periods: the Intel Itanium 2 based TeraGrid cluster (**sdscteragrid**), The SDSC "Blue Horizon" (**sdscblue**) and the IBM Power-4 system (**datastar**). We also use traces from the Cornell Theory

Center (**ctc**), Lawrence Livermore National Laboratory's SP-2 (**llnl**), the Cray-Dell cluster operated by the Texas Advanced Computing Center (**lonestar**), the National Center for Supercomputing Applications TeraGrid cluster (**ncsateragrid**), the California NanoSystems Institute Dell cluster (**cnsidell**), the Tokyo Tech Tsubame Supercomputer (**tsubame**), the Renaissance Computing Center (Renci) research cluster (**dante**) and the Argonne National Labs/University of Chicago TeraGrid (**ucteragrid**). The **ctc** and **sdscblue** logs we obtained from Feitelson's workload web site [10], the **llnl** data appears courtesy of Brent Gorda at LLNL, and we gathered the rest of the traces using our own infrastructure for real-time predictions. Collectively, the data comprises over one million job submissions spanning approximately a 9-year period.

4.2   Simulation

Our simulator takes as input a file containing historical batch-queue job wait times from a variety of machine/queue combinations and parameters directing the behavior of our models. For each machine/queue for which we have historical information, we were able to create parsed data files each of which contains one job entry per line comprising the UNIX time stamp when the job was submitted, the duration of time the job stayed in the queue before executing, the amount of requested execution time, and the node count.

The steady-state operation of the simulation reads in a line from the data file, makes a prediction (using one of the four prediction methodologies covered in Section 3) and stores the job in a "pending queue". The simulation then reads the next job arrival from the input file and, before making a prediction, potentially performs a number of tasks.

First, the simulator checks whether any jobs that had been previously queued have exited the queue since the last job arrived, in which case each such job is simply added to a growing list of historical job wait times stored in memory. Although the waiting time for the new job is carried in the trace, the predictor is not entitled to "see" the waiting time in the history until it stops waiting in queue and is released for execution. When the historical record changes, the predictor is given the new record so that it can update its internal state, if necessary.

After the queue has been updated, the current prediction value is used to make a prediction for the new job entering the queue, the simulation determines whether the predicted time for that job is greater than or equal to the actual time the job will spend in the pending queue (success), or the predicted time was less than the actual job wait time (failure). The success or failure is recorded, and the job is placed on the pending queue. Note that in a "live" setting this success or failure could only be determined after the job completed its waiting period.

In our first set of experiments, we use only the above simulator features to make predictions for each of the jobs in our traces, varying the predictor used (binomial method, log-normal, log-uniform, and Weibull). For our second set of experiments, we add history trimming, automatic job clustering, and availability inference, as described in Section 3, in the following ways.

When a job arrives, the predictor makes a prediction using its current historical window as before and in addition updates the availability inference engine with the current state of the queue, which potentially changes the state of the machine to 'unavailable'. When a job in the pending queue moves into the historical window, it is passed to the predictor, which may then trim the history as previously described. Every time a pre-determined number (1000 in our study) of simulated jobs are processed, automatic clustering is performed on the entire job history.

The code implementing the simulator is modularized so that any individual component of the system (predictor, history trimming system, clustering algorithm, availability inference algorithm) can be toggled on/off or replaced at

Table 1. Correctness and accuracy results of four predictors without QBETS. Under **Correctness**, values $>= 0.95$ indicate a correct result. Under **Accuracy**, highest RMS error ratio indicates most accurate method.

Machine/Queue	Correctness				Accuracy			
	BM	LogN	LogU	Weib	BM	LogN	LogU	Weib
cnsidell/ALL	0.92	0.97	0.97	0.81	1.00	**0.21**	**0.48**	2.14
dante/dque	0.82	0.75	0.96	0.40	1.00	1.28	**0.48**	8.82
datastar/TGnormal	0.91	0.83	0.98	0.84	1.00	4.16	**0.25**	3.51
datastar/express	0.93	0.88	1.00	0.84	1.00	3.16	**0.11**	3.90
datastar/high	0.90	0.92	0.97	0.85	1.00	0.74	**0.27**	1.48
datastar/normal	0.91	0.91	0.99	0.88	1.00	0.90	**0.17**	1.37
ucteragrid/dque	0.89	0.88	1.00	0.94	1.00	11.28	**0.00**	12.30
lonestar/development	0.92	0.92	1.00	0.92	1.00	3.30	**0.00**	4.40
lonestar/high	0.96	0.98	1.00	0.94	**1.00**	**0.61**	0.22	1.54
lonestar/normal	0.92	0.84	1.00	0.84	1.00	4.00	**0.04**	4.74
lonestar/serial	0.97	0.95	1.00	0.94	**1.00**	**2.77**	0.03	4.54
ncsateragrid/debug	0.93	0.88	0.99	0.91	1.00	2.02	**0.14**	0.59
ncsateragrid/dque	0.93	0.89	1.00	0.91	1.00	1.06	**0.06**	0.51
ncsateragrid/gpfs-wan	0.99	1.00	1.00	0.93	**1.00**	**0.16**	0.55	0.66
sdscteragrid/dque	0.93	0.86	0.98	0.90	1.00	2.44	**0.23**	0.26
tsubame/B	0.93	0.94	1.00	0.94	1.00	11.38	**0.00**	4.22
tsubame/default	0.93	0.84	1.00	0.84	1.00	13.16	**0.01**	6.22
tsubame/gaussian	0.96	0.94	1.00	0.95	**1.00**	137.71	**0.08**	**23.15**
tsubame/high	1.00	0.97	1.00	0.97	**1.00**	210.66	**0.14**	37.95
ctc/ALL	0.94	0.97	1.00	0.92	1.00	**0.48**	**0.04**	0.49
llnl/ALL	0.96	0.99	1.00	0.94	**1.00**	**0.29**	**0.08**	0.63
sdscblue/high	0.90	0.90	1.00	0.79	1.00	0.53	**0.15**	1.51
sdscblue/low	0.90	0.99	1.00	0.89	1.00	**0.36**	**0.11**	1.09
sdscblue/normal	0.89	0.94	1.00	0.85	1.00	0.44	**0.09**	1.13
sdscblue/express	0.92	0.90	0.99	0.84	1.00	1.12	**0.17**	2.20

runtime. In addition, the nature of the prediction employed methodologies allow the simulator to provide an "on-line" service; meaning it can be executed in a mode where it waits in an idle state until a new job datum arrives, at which point it will update its history and refresh its predictor.

4.3   Correct and Accurate Predictions

We define a *correct* prediction to be one that is greater than or equal to a job's eventual queuing delay, and a *correct predictor* to be one for which the total fraction of correct predictions is greater than or equal to the success probability specified by the target quantile. For example, a correct predictor of the 0.95 quantile generates correct predictions for at least 95% of the jobs that are submitted.

Table 2. Correctness and accuracy results of four predictors using QBETS. Under **Correctness**, values >= 0.95 indicate a correct result. Under **Accuracy**, highest RMS error ratio indicates most accurate method.

Machine/Queue	Correctness				Accuracy			
	BM	LogN	LogU	Weib	BM	LogN	LogU	Weib
cnsidell/ALL	0.96	0.93	0.93	0.97	**1.00**	0.05	1.55	**0.51**
dante/dque	0.80	0.69	0.87	0.72	1.00	0.05	0.71	0.40
datastar/TGnormal	0.97	0.90	0.97	0.96	**1.00**	0.46	**0.85**	**0.70**
datastar/express	0.97	0.87	0.99	0.93	**1.00**	0.78	**0.59**	1.28
datastar/high	0.96	0.95	0.98	0.95	**1.00**	**0.31**	**0.78**	**0.75**
datastar/normal	0.95	0.92	0.97	0.93	**1.00**	0.23	**0.65**	1.00
ucteragrid/dque	0.96	0.94	1.00	0.96	**1.00**	0.25	**0.19**	**0.78**
lonestar/development	0.98	0.92	1.00	0.96	**1.00**	2.12	**0.07**	**2.85**
lonestar/high	0.98	0.95	1.00	0.96	**1.00**	**0.34**	**0.29**	**0.81**
lonestar/normal	0.96	0.89	0.99	0.94	**1.00**	0.07	**0.50**	0.66
lonestar/serial	0.97	0.81	1.00	0.92	**1.00**	1.17	**0.21**	0.49
ncsateragrid/debug	0.96	0.86	0.98	0.91	**1.00**	1.37	**0.55**	2.02
ncsateragrid/dque	0.93	0.91	0.97	0.93	1.00	0.17	**0.46**	1.06
ncsateragrid/gpfs-wan	0.92	0.98	1.00	0.93	1.00	**0.38**	**0.66**	0.96
sdscteragrid/dque	0.96	0.88	0.98	0.93	**1.00**	0.12	**0.89**	0.50
tsubame/B	0.98	0.91	1.00	0.97	**1.00**	2.45	**0.29**	**1.27**
tsubame/default	0.97	0.94	1.00	0.96	**1.00**	0.05	**0.18**	**0.73**
tsubame/gaussian	0.98	0.95	1.00	0.97	**1.00**	**177.20**	**0.08**	**8.37**
tsubame/high	0.99	0.97	1.00	0.98	**1.00**	**70.46**	**0.17**	**18.76**
ctc/ALL	0.96	0.93	0.99	0.93	**1.00**	0.48	**0.18**	1.66
llnl/ALL	0.97	0.95	0.99	0.95	**1.00**	**0.65**	**0.57**	1.58
sdscblue/high	0.96	0.96	0.97	0.94	**1.00**	**0.24**	**0.87**	0.97
sdscblue/low	0.96	0.96	0.99	0.95	**1.00**	**0.26**	**0.38**	1.08
sdscblue/normal	0.97	0.95	0.97	0.95	**1.00**	**0.24**	**0.55**	1.03
sdscblue/express	0.97	0.91	0.98	0.94	**1.00**	0.17	**0.50**	0.55

Notice that it is trivial to specify a correct predictor under this definition. For example, to achieve a correct prediction percentage of 95%, a predictor could return an extremely large prediction (*e.g.*, a predicted delay of several years) for 19 of every 20 jobs, and a prediction of 0 for the 20th. To distinguish among correct predictors, we compare their *accuracy* in terms of the error they generate, where error is some measure of the difference between predicted value and the value it predicts.

In this work, we will use Root Mean Square (RMS) error for the over-predictions as a measure of accuracy for correct predictors. We consider only over-prediction error, as we believe that the error generated for the percentage of jobs that are incorrectly predicted is relatively unimportant to the user. For example, among predictors that are 95% correct, it is our contention that users would prefer one that achieves lower over-prediction error for the 95% of the jobs it predicts correctly over one that achieves a lower error rate on the 5% that are incorrectly predicted at the expense of greater overall error in the correct predictions.

Note that one cannot compare predictors strictly in terms of their error without taking into consideration their correctness. For example, a predictor that estimates the mean of each stationary region will generate a lower RMS than one that estimates the 0.95 quantile, but the mean predictor will not provide the user with a meaningful delay bound (*i.e.*, one having a probability value attached to it). Thus, for a given job workload, we only compare predictor accuracy among those predictors that are correct.

Note also that, while RMS error is used widely as a measure of accuracy for predictions of expected values (*e.g.* in time series), its meaning is less clear in the context of quantile prediction. In this paper, we are focusing on estimating a time value which is greater than the wait time of a specific job with probability .95. Therefore, if the distribution of wait times is highly right-skewed, a predictor may be working quite well and still have a very high RMS error. Thus, the actual *value* of the RMS error is not particularly meaningful; however, it is still useful as a means of *comparison*: For a particular set of jobs, if one correct prediction method has a lower RMS than another, then the first method, at least by this measure, produces tighter, less conservative upper bounds than the second.

4.4 Experiments

We perform two experiments in order to show the effectiveness of our prediction methods. The first experiment compares the correctness and accuracy of four different predictors for all data sets without the use of history trimming, job clustering or availability inference features. The results of this experiment are shown in Table 1. From the table, we first note that while each of the predictors is correct for some subset of the traces, the only predictor that is correct for all traces is the one based on the log-uniform distribution. Thus it might appear that the log-uniform-based method is the obvious winner for batch-queue prediction; however, upon closer inspection it becomes clear that the only reason this method is getting 95 percent or more of the predictions correct for any given trace is due to its extremely conservative individual predictions. This fact is reflected in the extremely low RMS ratios for the log-uniform method shown in Table 1 under **Accuracy**, which clearly indicates that the distance between the log-uniform predictions and the actual values is much greater than, say, the distance between the binomial method predictions and actual values for the same set of jobs. Note that in the table, bold values indicate that the shown method also was correct for that machine/queue/predictor tuple. The over-conservativeness of the log-uniform predictions is also borne out by the fact that, in general, its fraction of correct predictions is well above the target value of .95.

From the first set of experiments, we learned that there is no method that is both more correct and more accurate than the others. Our second experiment uses a combination of all of the features we have developed to improve both the correctness and the accuracy of each of the techniques. In Table 2, we show the results of the QBETS system on the same traces, varying only the predictor used during the simulation. Again, values in bold indicate machine/queue/predictor tuples which were correct. From these results, we can begin to see that the binomial method clearly stands apart from the rest in terms of both correctness and accuracy. Out of 25 traces, the binomial method was correct 22 times, which is more often than all others except for the log-uniform. Further, note that out of the 21 traces for which both the binomial and log-uniform methods were correct, the binomial was more accurate for every one of them. Additionally, overall, the binomial method was both correct and more accurate than any of the other predictors in 15 out of 25 traces; this number far exceeds the performance of any other predictor (log-normal 2/25, log-uniform 2/25, Weibull 5/25).

4.5   Correctness Analysis

Table 2 shows that when we use QBETS with the binomial-method predictor, we are able to predict bounds correctly for 95% or more individual job wait times for almost all of our traces. In this section, we explore the reasons for the effectiveness of QBETS and suggest that, for these reasons, the non-parametric approach should perform well when applied to other traces in the future.

In previous work [4], we showed that using history trimming is essential to ensure that a predictor not suffer from an inability to adjust to drastic infrequent increases in overall job queue wait times. In Figure 1, we can see the effect such drastic regime shifts have on a predictor without history trimming, and observe how trimming positively effects correctness on an example trace, the CNSI Dell cluster default queue (cnsidell/ALL). On the y-axis we show delay measured in seconds. Along the x-axis are Unix time stamps. The relatively straight line of values near the bottom of the graph depicts .95 quantile predictions made by the binomial method, but without QBETS enhancements, during a short time period. We can see that although a large number of observations lie above these predictions in the right half of the graph, there are enough relatively low values in the history that the inferred .95 quantile rises only very slowly. The other set of predictions, represented on the graph by a number of near-horizontal short segments, were made by the binomial method with QBETS over the same time period, is able to react to the shift toward longer wait times and is therefore able

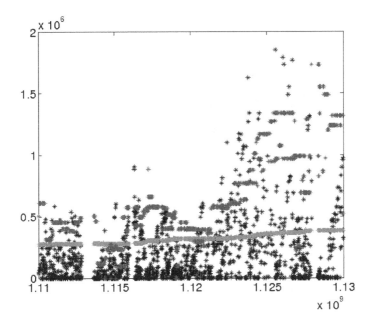

Fig. 1. Job queue delay times and predictions made with and without QBETS on the CNSI Dell cluster. Dark features (black) indicate actual job wait times, the medium shaded (cyan on color displays) linear features depict predictions made without QBETS, and the light colored features (red) depict predictions made with QBETS.

to produce more correct predictions. In general, this adaptivity greatly improves a predictor's ability to achieve its desired correctness, because such shifts are common in almost all of our traces. We note that while history trimming is an effective enhancement for all of the predictors, it works especially well with the binomial predictor; we posit that this is due to the fact that the binomial predictor is set up to make accurate inferences about quantiles, so that it is able to find changepoints in those quantiles reliably. In essence, the accuracy of the method (*Cf.* Section 4.6) feeds its correctness.

Although QBETS allows the predictor to react to drastic wait-time shifts, there are still traces for which it fails to meet the target percentage of correct predictions. In the cases where QBETS fails, we observe that in general, the reason is due to frequent drastic upward trends in wait times, which appear as 'spikes' in the trace graphs. Figure 2 shows such spikes in the middle of the Dante default queue trace. As we can see from this graph, if a large number of jobs is queued in a relatively short amount of time, and all of them experience wait times that are greater than the current quantile prediction, our method will fail to correctly make predictions for most of them, due to the fact that a wait time is not added to the predictor's available history until it comes out of the queue. Although the availability inference method attempts to discover these degenerate data cases, it cannot discover them all. In the traces for which

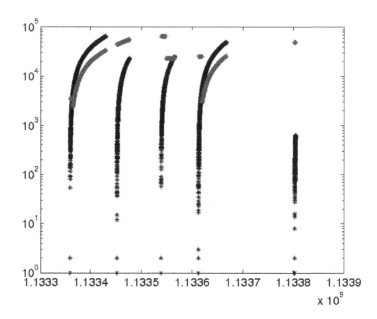

Fig. 2. Actual queue delay times and QBETS binomial method predictions illustrating how frequent, drastic linear delay increases on the Dante cluster cause the method to fail. Dark features (black) show actual observed job wait times, while the light features (red on color displays) depict QBETS predictions.

QBETS with binomial predictor is unable to succeed, such as the dante default queue trace shown here, there are many spikes that the availability inference method does not eliminate; their negative impact on the overall correctness measure outweighs the number of jobs the method does correctly capture.

While one might be tempted to use an extremely conservative method in order to combat this eventuality, this strategy may require such extreme measures as to make the method unreasonable for non-degenerate cases. We note that even the log-uniform method, which is the most conservative method we evaluate, fails to be correct in the face of the dante default queue trace.

4.6 Accuracy Analysis

In terms of accuracy, the results presented above support two assertions. First, QBETS is the most accurate of the methods we have tested. Second, the non-parametric binomial quantile estimator is more effective than the corresponding parametric approaches. That is, when the change-point detection, clustering, and machine downtime detection features of QBETS are omitted, and we are simply applying the binomial prediction method to all jobs using the entire history, the binomial method still provides more accurate over-predictions than the other methods.

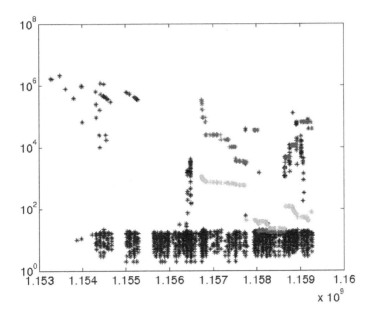

Fig. 3. Trace from the Tsubame machine, Gaussian submission queue indicating large difference between log-normal and binomial method QBETS predictions after the training period. Dark features (black) show actual observed job wait times, medium shaded features (cyan on color displays) depict less conservative predictions using the log-normal, and light features (red) show predictions when the binomial method was used.

This greater accuracy, we believe, is because the binomial technique estimates directly only a specific quantile and not the entire distribution. In contrast, parametric approaches using MLE attempt to "fit" the data to all quantiles and in so doing may not estimate the specific quantile of interest as accurately. In particular a log-normal or Weibull model such as we have chosen to evaluate in this experiment (and typically used for such highly right-skewed data as in our traces) suffers from the fact that quantiles out in the tail of the distribution are very sensitive to the estimated population parameters. For the same reason, using a estimation technique such as MLE, the estimated parameters are sensitive to a few very high values in the data set. Thus an estimated quantile for such a distribution is highly dependent on the model's ability, typically based on a small number of high values in the data, to fill in its right tail. In practice, the end result of this phenomenon is usually that the quantile estimates produced by these parametric models are much more conservative than the ones that can be made using the binomial method, which does not need to take into account the relationship between high and (irrelevant for our purposes) low values in the way that curve fitting does.

One fundamental reason for the superior accuracy of predictions generated using QBETS stems from the automatic job-clustering feature, which allows the predictor to only consider "like jobs" when making its prediction instead of all jobs, which may be only loosely related to the job of interest in terms of experienced wait time. During the experiment, we observed that QBETS automatically grouped jobs into three to five clusters, never choosing only one group for all jobs. Additionally, we observe that not only is QBETS more correct in general, but that QBETS with the binomial method predictor outperforms the other predictors in most of the traces. Again, the reason this is true is due to the fact that in general the binomial method is making more accurate predictions, as we see from Table 2 and Table 1; this amounts to heightened sensitivity to change-points in the data, thus allowing the history-trimming feature to activate more often than it does for other predictors.

This being said, there are a few cases where the parametric models were in fact **more** accurate than the binomial method. In these cases, most notably the tsubame/guassian and tsubame/high traces, we observe that the primary reason why the log-normal is achieving so much better RMS errors stems from the fact that in those traces, the training period data included a disproportionate number of very large wait times relative to the experimental set. The training set can be seen in Figure 3 as the period of observations before any predictions are being made; notice that the binomial method starts out making very conservative predictions based on the large number of high values in the training set, while there are enough low values to bring down the MLE log-normal parameters, making these predictions less conservative. In this case, data for the training period was bimodal, with about 10% of the wait times in an extremely high mode, orders of magnitude higher than the bulk of the wait times in the lower mode. This higher mode, which would have caused the log-normal predictions to be incorrect, disappeared at the end of the training period, leaving the binomial method with an unrepresentative data set to begin with and also rendering the log-normal predictions both correct and accurate. We note two things, however: First, the experimental set was only slightly larger than the training set, so that there was not time to balance the anomalies in the training data, and so may not have been reflective of long-term performance; second, by the middle of the experimental set, the binomial method predictor was able both to make more accurate predictions than the log-normal predictor for the relatively short wait times and also to maintain correctness when the wait times suddenly became longer again at the end of the trace.

5   QBETS Impact

Currently, QBETS is providing predictions to a growing base of HPC researchers and users around the world. Our batch queue monitoring sensors are gathering real-time batch queue delay data from 16 super-computers, 24 hours a day. From this database of job delay information, the QBETS prediction software is able to constantly generate up-to-date quantile predictions through a number of interfaces. Over the past several months, our records indicate that the QBETS system has been accessed over 50000 times from approximately 600 unique, non-searchbot Internet hosts. This level of activity indicates that users interested in integrating real-time QBETS predictions into their projects are using a number of interfaces, including a C API (in the form of a UNIX library), UNIX command line tools (for curious users and administrative scripting), a dedicated QBETS Web Service (for integration into existing Web Service based projects), and our own custom QBETS web site [27]. Using these interfaces, researchers have been able to use QBETS to accomplish a number of tasks, including the provision of HPC site selection hints for users (TeraGrid User Portal [33]), in-advance workflow scheduling for disaster recovery applications (LEAD Project [29]), redundant batch queue resource provisioning for fault-tolerant systems (LEAD/VGrADS [34]). Finally, we ourselves are building on the availability of QBETS by implementing a new system for making virtual advance reservations. Recently, we have run experimental trials that show our system is capable of providing users the ability to request an advance reservation, and probabilistically servicing such requests using regular batch controlled resources, without modification to the underlying batch queue software or administrative policies. As the popularity of QBETS continues to grow, we expect to add more systems to the infrastructure and possibly even integrate our work into existing batch queue resource managers to make QBETS part of many default HPC software installations.

6   Conclusions

Space-shared parallel computers use queuing systems for scheduling parallel jobs to processor partitions in such a way that each job runs exclusively on the processors it is given. In previous work [4,5] we've proposed a method for estimating bounds on the queuing delay experienced by each job and show that this non-parametric method (Binomial Method) outperforms competitive approaches.

Still, while working with traces comprising some 1.4 million jobs from 11 supercomputer sites, we observed several features of the data that have a negative effect on the performance of all of our prediction methods. First, the data can be described in the long-term as non-stationary, in that there are infrequent events (changes in policy or other fundamental operational subsystems) that have a substantial and lasting effect on queueing delays. Second, we observe that while some jobs request small allocations, other allocations are much larger. Such a situation leads to a predictor making very conservative estimates for the small jobs since we are concerned with upper bound quantile predictions. It seems that jobs may fall into "groups" of like jobs that one might expect to experience roughly similar queue wait-time delays. Finally, we note that in several of our traces, we notice sudden "spikes" in wait time delay, expressed by a drastic increase in job delay experienced in a very short time, likely indicating that the machine of interest is experiencing a period of unavailability.

We therefore introduce QBETS , which combines history trimming, automatic job clustering, availability inference, and various prediction methodologies to provide a batch queue job wait time prediction system which is shown to perform better than more naive approaches for almost all of the data we have access to. Additionally, we show that QBETS , with the non-parametric binomial method quantile predictor invented in our previous work, is both more correct and more accurate than any other tested technique and prediction method.

In the future, we intend to continue to improve both the correctness and accuracy of QBETS by exploring alternative clustering and prediction techniques and applying them experimentally to our ever-growing set of machine traces. Additionally, we intend to continue to provide real-time batch-queue wait-time predictions to the HPC user community through continued involvment in a wide variety of projects, and through our own batch queue prediction service oriented web site. Finally, we intend to use many of the techniques presented in this work towards defining a functionally static resource definition out of highly dynamic, heterogeneous underlying compute resources.

References

1. IBM LoadLeveler User's Guide. Technical report, International Business Machines Corporation (1993)
2. Box, G., Jenkins, G., Reinsel, G.: Time Series Analysis, Forecasting, and Control, 3rd edn. Prentice-Hall, Englewood Cliffs (1994)
3. Brevik, J., Nurmi, D., Wolski, R.: Quantifying machine availability in networked and desktop grid systems. In: Proceedings of CCGrid 2004 (April 2004)
4. Brevik, J., Nurmi, D., Wolski, R.: Predicting bounds on queuing delay for batch-scheduled parallel machines. In: Proceedings of PPoPP 2006 (March 2006)
5. Brevik, J., Nurmi, D., Wolski, R.: Predicting bounds on queuing delay in space-shared computing environments. In: Proceedings of IEEE International Symposium on Workload Characterization 2006 (October 2006)
6. Chiang, S.-H., Vernon, M.K.: Dynamic vs. static quantum-based processor allocation. In: Feitelson, D.G., Rudolph, L. (eds.) IPPS-WS 1996 and JSSPP 1996. LNCS, vol. 1162, Springer, Heidelberg (1996)
7. Clearwater, S., Kleban, S.: Heavy-tailed distributions in supercomputer jobs. Technical Report SAND2002-2378C, Sandia National Labs (2002)
8. Downey, A.: Predicting queue times on space-sharing parallel computers. In: Proceedings of the 11th International Parallel Processing Symposium (April 1997)
9. Downey, A.: Using queue time predictions for processor allocation. In: Proceedings of the 3rd Workshop on Job Scheduling Strategies for Parallel Processing (April 1997)
10. The Dror Feitelson's Parallel Workload Page,
    http://www.cs.huji.ac.il/labs/parallel/workload
11. Feitelson, D.G., Nitzberg, B.: Job characteristics of a production parallel scientific workload on the nasa ames ipsc/860. In: Feitelson, D.G., Rudolph, L. (eds.) IPPS-WS 1996 and JSSPP 1996. LNCS, vol. 1162, Springer, Heidelberg (1996)
12. Feitelson, D.G., Rudolph, L.: Parallel job scheduling: Issues and approaches. In: Feitelson, D.G., Rudolph, L. (eds.) IPPS-WS 1995 and JSSPP 1995. LNCS, vol. 949, Springer, Heidelberg (1995)
13. Feitelson, D.G., Rudolph, L.: Towards convergence in job schedulers for parallel supercomputers. In: Feitelson, D.G., Rudolph, L. (eds.) IPPS-WS 1996 and JSSPP 1996. LNCS, vol. 1162, Springer, Heidelberg (1996)

14. Frachtenberg, E., Feitelson, D.G., Fernandez, J., Petrini, F.: Parallel job scheduling under dynamic workloads. In: Feitelson, D.G., Rudolph, L., Schwiegelshohn, U. (eds.) JSSPP 2003. LNCS, vol. 2862, Springer, Heidelberg (2003)

15. Granger, C.W.P., Newbold, P.: Forecasting Economic Time Series. Academic Press, London (1986)

16. Gridengine home page, http://gridengine.sunsource.net/

17. Harchol-Balter, M.: The effect of heavy-tailed job size distributions on computer system design. In: Proceedings of ASA-IMS Conference on Applications of Heavy Tailed Distributions in Economics, Engineering and Statistics (June 1999)

18. Jain, A.K., Dubes, R.C.: Algorithms for clustering data. Prentice-Hall, Inc, Upper Saddle River, NJ, USA (1988)

19. Lifka, D.: The anl/ibm sp scheduling system. In: Feitelson, D.G., Rudolph, L. (eds.) IPPS-WS 1995 and JSSPP 1995. LNCS, vol. 949, pp. 295–303. Springer, Heidelberg (1995)

20. Lifka, D., Henderson, M., Rayl, K.: Users guide to the argonne SP scheduling system. Technical Report TM-201, Argonne National Laboratory, Mathematics and Computer Science Division (May 1995)

21. MacQueen, J.: Some methods for classification and analysis of multivariate observations. pp. 281–297 (1967)

22. Maui scheduler home page, http://www.clusterresources.com/products/maui/

23. Cray NQE User's Guide,
    http://docs.cray.com/books/2148_3.3/html-2148_3.3

24. Nurmi, D., Brevik, J., Wolski, R.: Modeling machine availability in enterprise and wide-area distributed computing environments. In: Proceedings of Europar 2005 (August 2005)

25. Nurmi, D., Mandal, A., Brevik, J., Koelbel, C., Wolski, R., Kennedy, K.: Evaluation of a workflow scheduler using integrated performance modelling and batch queue wait time prediction. In: Löwe, W., Südholt, M. (eds.) SC 2006. LNCS, vol. 4089, Springer, Heidelberg (2006)

26. Nurmi, D., Wolski, R., Brevik, J.: Model-based checkpoint scheduling for volatile resource environments. In: Proceedings of Cluster 2004 (September 2004)

27. NWS Batch Queue Pprediction web interface,
    http://nws.cs.ucsb.edu/ewiki/nws.php?id=Batch+Queue+Prediction

28. Pbspro home page, http://www.altair.com/software/pbspro.htm

29. Plale, B., Gannon, D., Brotzge, J., Droegemeier, K., Kurose, J., Mclaughlin, D., Wilhelmson, R., Graves, S., Ramamurhty, M., Clark, R.D., Yalda, S., Reed, D.A., Joseph, E., Chandraeskar, V.: CASA and LEAD: Adaptive Cyberinfrastructure for Real-Time Multiscale Weather Forecasting. IEEE Computer 39, 56–64 (2006)

30. Posse, C.: Hierarchical model-based clustering for large datasets. Journal of Computational and Graphical Statistics 10(3), 464 (2001)

31. Schwartz, G.: Estimating the dimension of a model. In: Ann. of Statistics, pp. 461–464 (1979)

32. Smith, W., Taylor, V.E., Foster, I.T.: Using run-time predictions to estimate queue wait times and improve scheduler performance. In: IPPS/SPDP 1999/JSSPP 1999: Proceedings of the Job Scheduling Strategies for Parallel Processing, pp. 202–219. Springer, London, UK (1999)

33. TeraGrid user portal, http://portal.teragrid.org

34. The virtual grid application development software (vgrads),
    http://vgrads.rice.edu/

35. Zhong, S.Z.: A unified framework for model-based clustering. Journal of Machine Learning Research 4, 1001–1037 (2003)

Probabilistic Backfilling

Avi Nissimov and Dror G. Feitelson

Department of Computer Science
The Hebrew University of Jerusalem

Abstract. Backfilling is a scheduling optimization that requires information about job runtimes to be known. Such information can come from either of two sources: estimates provided by users when the jobs are submitted, or predictions made by the system based on historical data regarding previous executions of jobs. In both cases, each job is assigned a precise prediction of how long it will run. We suggest that instead the whole distribution of the historical data be used. As a result, the whole backfilling framework shifts from a concrete plan for the future schedule to a probabilistic plan where jobs are backfilled based on the probability that they will terminate in time.

1 Introduction

Scheduling parallel jobs for execution is similar to bin packing: each job needs a certain number of processors for a certain time, and the scheduler has to pack these jobs together so that most of the processors will be utilized most of the time. To perform such packing effectively, the scheduler needs to know how many nodes each job needs, and for how long. The number of processors needed is typically specified by the user when the job is submitted. The main question is how to estimate how long each job will run.

The simplest solution to this question is to require the user to provide a runtime estimate [1]. However, logs of jobs that have run on large scale parallel supercomputers reveal that user runtime estimates are very inaccurate [2]. The reason for this is that systems typically kill jobs that exceed their estimate, giving users a strong incentive to over-estimate the runtimes of their jobs.

The alternative to user-provided estimates is system-generated predictions. Practically all systems collect information about jobs that have run in the past. This information can then be mined to generate predictions about the runtimes of newly submitted jobs. Algorithms for generating such predictions are described in Section 2.

Prediction algorithms typically work in two steps. Given a newly submitted job, they first scan the available historical data and look for "similar" jobs that have executed in the past. For example, similar jobs may be defined as all the jobs that were executed on behalf of the same user on the same number of processors. They then apply some function to the runtimes of this set of jobs. For example, the function can be to compute the distribution of runtimes, and

E. Frachtenberg and U. Schwiegelshohn (Eds.): JSSPP 2007, LNCS 4942, pp. 102–115, 2008.

extract the 90th percentile. This value is then used as the runtime prediction for the new job.

Our starting point is to observe that this prediction-generation process loses information: we have information about the runtimes of many previous similar jobs, but we reduce this into the single number — the prediction. Why not use all the available information instead? This means that scheduling decisions will be made based on assumed distributions of runtimes, rather than based on predictions of specific runtimes.

The advantage of making a specific prediction is that the scheduling becomes deterministic: when we want to know whether a job can run or not, we assume it will run for the predicted time, and then check whether we have enough processors that are free for this duration. But if we use a distribution, we are reduced to probabilistic arguments. For example, we may find that there is an 87% chance that the processors will be free for the required time. But this is actually a more accurate representation of the situation at hand, so it has the potential to lead to better decisions.

We apply the above ideas in the context of backfilling schedulers. Backfilling is an optimization usually applied to FCFS scheduling that allows small and short jobs to run ahead of their time provided they fit into holes that were left in the schedule. In our new approach, this fit becomes a probabilistic prediction; jobs will be backfilled provided there is a high probability that they will fit. In other words, we define a threshold τ and perform the backfilling provided that the probability that the job will not terminate in time is less than τ.

In keeping with the spirit of backfilling, the meaning of "will not terminate in time" is that the backfilled job will delay the first queued job. The algorithm for calculating this is described in detail in Section 4. The results of simulations that assess how well this performs are then shown in Section 5.

2   Algorithms That Use Predictions

There are many different algorithms that require predictions or user estimates of job runtimes, including EASY backfilling and shortest-job-first. In EASY backfilling, jobs are backfilled provided they do not delay the first queued job [1]. One of the conditions used to verify this is that the backfilled job will terminate before the time when enough processors for the first queued job will become available. This requires knowing the runtimes of currently executing jobs (in order to find out when they will free their processors), and the runtime of the potential backfill job (to find out if it will terminate in time). Shortest job first requires runtime knowledge in order to sort the jobs.

There has been some debate in the literature on whether accurate runtime predictions are actually important. Somewhat surprisingly, the first papers on this issue indicated that *inaccurate* predictions lead to improved performance [3,4]. However, more recent research has shown that accurate estimates are indeed beneficial [5,6,7], thus providing added motivation for the quest for more accurate predictions.

Several algorithms have been suggested to enable runtime predictions based on historical data. Gibbons first partitions the historical data into classes based on the user and the executable. Importantly, executions on different numbers of processors are included in the same class. He then finds a quadratic least-squares fit of the runtime as a function of the number of processors used. This is used to compute a prediction for the requested number of processors [8]. Smith et al. also divide jobs into classes, but use various job attributes in addition to the user and executable. They then use the mean runtime of all previous executions in the class as the prediction [9]. Mu'alem and Feitelson suggest using the mean runtime in the class plus 1.5 standard deviations, to reduce the danger of under-prediction [2]. Tsafrir et al. use the simplest scheme of all: they just use the average runtime of the last two terminated job that have been submitted by the same user [7].

The problem with using runtime predictions other than user estimates with backfilling is the fact that the jobs may be under-predicted. Killing the jobs in this situation is highly undesirable, since the users have neither tools to avoid it nor indication that this is going to happen. Therefore, the only reasonable way to solve under-prediction is to violate the reservation for the first job in the queue and delay it until the processors become available [7]. But there is no promise such delays will ever stop, unless we forbid future backfilling, because the backfilled jobs may in their turn also be under-predicted.

The same question arises when the predictions are initially set too large, like when using doubling (or tripling, quadrupling and so on) [7]. If the system were a single-user system, then this strategy would probably be good — it pushes forward the jobs with less requirements (on average), so the average waiting time is expected to decrease. However, since we are dealing with multi-user systems, such an approach is insufficient, and may appear extremely unfair.

In this work, however, we use EASY-backfilling as the base algorithm. According to [7], when the predictions are correct, the overall performance of EASY-backfilling usually improves.

3   Predicting Job Runtime Distributions

Both backfilling-based schedulers and SJF use single-value predictions due to their simplicity. But in fact predicting a job's runtime cannot usually be done deterministically. A job's runtime depends on many factors, that include not only system internal conditions such as the network load, but also terminations due to errors and user cancellations. These last factors are external to the system, and they greatly complicate runtime prediction. Errors usually show incorrect behavior pretty soon after a job starts, and many faults may be discovered long before a job would have terminated without the error. Users also know this, and they tend to test partial output soundness soon after their jobs start. Therefore, in cases of errors the job is usually terminated or canceled almost immediately. For instance, 2613 out of 5275 (~50%) canceled jobs in the SDSC-SP2 trace whose user estimates were set for at least 200 minutes were canceled within 20 minutes after their start times (this and other traces we use come from the Parallel Workloads Archive [10]; see Table 1). Modeling these scenarios is impossible with single-value predictions: a single value can give either a mean or a quantile of the job's runtime distribution, but cannot model a multi-modal distribution.

Another problem with single-value predictions is the fact that they should contain all the information upon which scheduling decisions are made. Different deviations from the real runtime cause different and possibly incomparable damage. This leads to prediction policies that are scheduler-dependent. An extreme example is backfilling, which kills jobs whose runtimes are longer than the user estimates. Thus, over-predictions are much less damaging than under-predictions. Therefore the user estimates tend to be biased upwards, as users tend to give high estimates fearing their jobs will be killed.

Predicting the distribution of a job's runtime is based on the concept of locality of sampling [11]. This makes a distinction between the global distribution of runtimes, when looking at a long time span, and the local distribution of runtimes that is observed at a certain instant. The idea is that runtimes — like other workload attributes — exhibit locality, so the local distribution is much more predictable than the global one.

To utilize this observation, we divide time into short slices, and characterize the runtime distribution in each one using binning. In particular, the model groups jobs arriving within each 15-minute slice of time together. The runtime distribution was modeled for each slice individually. The modeling is done by defining a set of discrete bins, and counting how many job runtimes fall in each bin. The bin sizes used were logarithmic, with ranges that grow by a factor of 1.8; this gives a better resolution for short jobs, which are more numerous. The values 15 minutes and 1.8 were selected empirically so as to maximize the observed locality in several different workload traces [12].

To reduce complexity it is desirable to track only a limited number of distinct distributions. The tradeoff here is that using more distributions increases accuracy, but also increases the complexity of the modeling. Therefore we want to find the number that provides good accuracy at an acceptable cost. In most cases it turned out that 16 distinct distributions provide reasonable results.

Coming up with representative distributions involves a learning process. Once enough data is available (we use one week's worth of activity) a set of 16 representative distributions is learned using an iterative process. The learnt distributions are then used in the HMM model described below as predictions for the different jobs. Typically only 2–3 iterations are needed to converge to an acceptable set; using more typically results in overfitting. The criterion for convergence is that the distance from the previous model, multiplied by the square root of the number of samples (all the jobs observed so far) is smaller than a given threshold. Later, as more data is accumulated, this will grow again beyond the threshold, and the learning process is repeated using all the additional data accumulated so far. Thus the quality of the model is expected to improve the longer the system is in use.

The final stage of the modeling is to create a Hidden Markov Model (HMM) to describe transitions and see how things change. The model has 16 states, corresponding to the different runtime distributions. States may have self-loops to account for situations where the local distribution stays the same for more than 15 minutes. Checking the observed distributions of how long each state is in effect indeed revealed that in the vast majority of cases this is geometrically distributed.

The distributions and model are learned on-line as more jobs are submitted and terminate. Thus when running the algorithm on a job trace, initially it is impossible to provide good predictions. when enough information accumulates, the model tracks the state that the system is in, and uses the distribution that characterizes this state as the prediction for newly submitted jobs.

4   Using Distributions in the Scheduling Algorithm

Given historical data regarding previous job executions, one can fit a model of the distribution of runtimes or just use the empirical distribution. This section discusses the ways how this information can be practically used by a scheduler. In particular, we base our work on the EASY backfilling scheme.

Given that runtimes are continuous, keeping historical data about multiple jobs can burden the system and increase the complexity of the scheduling algorithm. For that reason we will assume the distribution is discretized by dividing the runtimes into N bins. The sizes of the bins will be logarithmic: there will be many bins for short runtimes, and the top bins each represent a large range of runtimes.

EASY backfilling maintains a queue of waiting jobs (ones that have been submitted but have not yet started) ordered by their submission times. The steps of the EASY backfilling scheduling procedure, which is executed each time a job arrives or terminates, are as follows:

1. As long as there are enough idle processors to start the first job in the wait queue, remove this job from the queue and start it.
2. Given the first job in the queue that cannot start because of insufficient idle processors, find when the required number will become free and make the reservation for this job.
3. Continue scanning the queue, and start (backfill) jobs if they don't violate this reservation.

However, the idea of the algorithm can be expressed more concisely. In fact, Step 2 is more of an implementation issue than part of the core of the algorithm. Thus steps 2 and 3 can be united as follows: "Continue scanning the queue, and start jobs if this doesn't delay the start time of the first job in the queue". This is independent of how the condition of not delaying the first job is verified. And we can also relax the condition, and replace it with a condition that it will not be delayed with a high probability.

In EASY backfilling each job is assigned a single value for its predicted runtime, and this prediction is used as the exact runtime in a very deterministic way. But if we don't have a single-value prediction, but rather a distribution, it is not possible to make such a decision in a deterministic way. Instead, there are many cases with different probabilities that may contradict each other. Therefore we need to summarize all these possibilities. To do so, we define a single parameter that is the confidence probability τ. Our new condition for backfilling will be that *the probability that the backfilling postpones the start of the first job in the queue is less than τ*.

Let us now formalize this idea. For simplicity, it is assumed that the job runtimes are independent; thus, for each two jobs with runtimes R_1, R_2, we have that $\Pr(R_1, R_2) = \Pr(R_1)\Pr(R_2)$ (as usual, here and everywhere, $\Pr(R_1)$ denotes the probability of random variable R_1 to have its value). In particular, this means that the event of the availability of processors at different times due to terminations of the currently running jobs and the distribution of the backfilled job's runtime are independent.

The following notation will be useful. Suppose the current time is t_0. Assuming that the job we are considering is indeed backfilled, we denote its (unknown) true termination time by t_e. For each time t, $t_0 \leq t < \infty$, we denote by $c(t)$ the number of processors that are released by the currently running jobs before and including time t. Also, let c_q be the number of processors that must be released to start the first job in the queue, and c the number needed to start both the first job and the backfill job together. Armed with these notations, we can say that the algorithm should backfill iff

$$\Pr(\exists t \in (t_0, t_e) : c_q \leq c(t) < c) < \tau.$$

In words: the probability that there exists some time t before the termination of the backfilled job when the number of released processor's is enough to start the first job in the queue but not enough to run both jobs — so the backfilling postpones the start of the first job in the queue — is smaller than τ.

However, the termination time t_e is not known. Instead, we have a distribution. Integrating over all the possible termination times of the backfilled job we then receive the condition

$$\int_{t_0}^{\infty} \Pr(t_e, \exists t \in (t_0, t_e) : c_q \leq c(t) < c)\, dt_e < \tau.$$

Since by assumption of job runtimes independence t_e and $c(t)$ are independent, this probability is

$$\int_{t_0}^{\infty} \Pr(t_e)\Pr(\exists t \in (t_0, t_e) : c_q \leq c(t) < c)\, dt_e < \tau.$$

The first factor in the integrand is modeled by the predictor — it is exactly the predicted distribution of the job's runtime. As noted above these probabilities are typically modeled discretely, by dividing the runtime into bins and predicting the probability to fall into each bin. The second factor is much harder to calculate.

Algorithm 1. Runtime bin probability recalculation

```
 1 double[] recalculate(Job job)
 2     // old model
 3     double old_p[N] = job.model;
 4     // new distribution model
 5     double new_p[N];
 6     double upperBound = job.userEstimate;
 7     double lowerBound = currentTime-job.startTime;
 8     for each runtime bin j do {
 9         double newBinStart =
10             max{bin[j].start, min{lowerBound, bin[j].end}};
11         double newBinEnd =
12             min{bin[j].end, max{upperBound, bin[j].start}};
13         new_p[j] = old_p[j]*
14             (log(newBinEnd )-log(newBinStart )) /
15             (log(bin[j].end)-log(bin[j].start));
16     }
17     normalize(new_p);
18     return new_p;
19 }
```

First of all, in order to calculate the second factor, we must calculate the probability $\Pr(c(t) \geq c)$ for any given time t and any given requirement c. The probability of processor availability given termination probabilities at time t of the currently running jobs is calculated using Dynamic Programming. The matrix cell $M_t[n][c]$ denotes the probability that at time t, the jobs $1..n$ have released at least c processors. This is calculated recursively as

$$M_t[n][c] = M_t[n-1][c] + \\ (M_t[n-1][c-c_n] - M_t[n-1][c]) \cdot P_t[n].$$

The first term denotes the case when enough processors are already idle without termination of job number n. The second term is the probability that only the termination of job n freed the required processors. This is the product of two factors: that jobs $1..n-1$ freed at least $c-c_n$ but not c processors, and that the last job terminated in time (c_n is number of processor used by job number n, and $P_t[n]$ is the probability that job number n terminates not later than t). The initialization of the dynamic programing sets the obvious values: $M_t[*][0] = 1$ (we are sure that the jobs have released at least 0 processors), and $M_t[0][*] = 0$ (zero jobs do not release any number processors). In the algorithm implementation, these values may be calculated on-the-fly; for instance, if $c < c_n$ (the number of required processors is smaller than the number of processors used by job number n), then $M_t[n-1][c-c_n]$ doesn't exist in the real matrix, because the index is negative, but can easily be substituted by 1, so that $M_t[n][c] = M_t[n-1][c] + (1 - M_t[n-1][c]) \cdot P_t[n]$. If n is the number of running jobs, then $\Pr(c(t) \geq c) = M_t[n][c]$.

The above requires calculating the probabilities of running job terminations before or at the time t (denoted above as $P_t[]$). Each time the scheduler is called, a larger part of the distributions becomes irrelevant, because the jobs have already run longer than the times represented by the lower bins. Therefore the distributions needs to be recalculated. Because our data is discretized, the job runtime probabilities are estimated only at the ends of the runtime bins. The upper and lower bounds of job runtimes are the user estimate (since the job is killed after it; this is used even before the job starts) and the current runtime of the job (currentTime-job.startTime). Log-Uniform intra-bin interpolation is used. Algorithm 1 presents the recalculation procedure for the runtime bin probabilities. **Line 3** receives the job distribution model as proposed by the predictor (reminder: N is the number of the runtime bins, and $j = 1..N$ is the index of a runtime bin). **Lines 9-12** ensure that the new runtime bin boundaries satisfy the old bin boundaries and global boundaries. If the runtime bin doesn't intersect the global boundaries then newBinStart==newBinEnd and therefore new_p[j]=0. **Lines 13-15** recalculate the probability measure remainders after log-uniform interpolation.

After all the events representing the possible termination of a job are inserted into a list and sorted by the time, one can easily calculate the vector of termination probabilities at time t.

Let $A(t)$ be the event that t is the real start time of Q[0] (the first job in the queue) without backfilling, and that backfilling of the job delays the first job beyond this time. This means that

$$A(t) = (t \in (t_0, t_e)) \land (\forall s < t, c(s) < c_q) \land (c_q \le c(t) < c)$$

In words, t is before the end time of backfilled job and t is the first time when the first job in the queue can start but only if this job isn't backfilled. Therefore, according to our probabilistic backfilling condition, the backfilling should happen iff

$$\Pr(\exists t \in (t_0, t_e) : A(t)) < \tau$$

But the events are disjoint, therefore the total probability is the integral of probabilities:

$$\int_{t_0}^{t_e} \Pr(A(t)) dt < \tau \tag{1}$$

The problem is to calculate $\Pr(A(t))$.

Suppose $t \in (t_0, t_e)$. Let us change the definition of t to be discrete time (in any units). Due to the monotonicity of $c(t)$, $\Pr(A(t)) = \Pr(c(t-1) < c_q \land c_q \le c(t) < c)$. If $c(t) \ge c$ or $c(t-1) \ge c$, then $c(t) \ge c_q$, since $c > c_q$ and $c(t)$ is monotonous (see Venn diagram in Figure 1). Therefore,

$$\Pr(A(t)) = \Pr(c(t) \ge c_q) - \Pr(c(t-1) \ge c_q \lor c(t) \ge c)$$
$$= M_t[n][c_q] - \Pr(c(t-1) \ge c_q \lor c(t) \ge c).$$

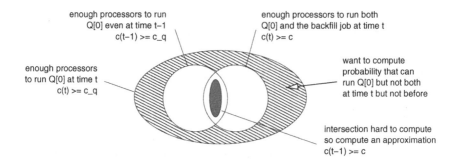

Fig. 1. Explanation of the $\Pr(A(t))$ formula

But in the second term, the two events in the disjunction don't imply each other, so

$$\Pr(\, c(t-1) \geq c_q \ \vee \ c(t) \geq c\,) =$$
$$= \Pr(c(t-1) \geq c_q) \ + \ \Pr(c(t) \geq c) \ - \ \Pr(c(t-1) \geq c_q \wedge c(t) \geq c)$$
$$= M_{t-1}[n][c_q] \ + \ M_t[n][c] \ - \ \Pr(c(t-1) \geq c_q \wedge c(t) \geq c)$$

The last term is pretty hard to calculate. However, it has a lower bound of $M_{t-1}[n][c]$ — the probability that before the last event there were enough processors to run both jobs (which implies $c(t-1) \geq c_q$ and $c(t) \geq c$). Using all the above considerations leads to the bound

$$\Pr(A(t)) \ \geq \ (M_t[n][c_q] - M_t[n][c]) \ - \ (M_{t-1}[n][c_q] - M_{t-1}[n][c]) \qquad (2)$$

The integral over t of $\Pr(A(t))$ in Equation (1) turns into a sum when time is discretized. Replacing $\Pr(A(t))$ with the lower bounds from Equation (2) leads to a telescoping series. Since the first item equals 0 (because initially the number of processors is less than c_q), the total sum is $M_{t_e-1}[n][c_q] - M_{t_e-1}[n][c]$. But although each of $M_t[n][c_q], M_t[n][c]$ is monotonically growing as a function of t, their difference is not monotonous; while all $\Pr(A(t)) \geq 0$, and their sum is monotonous. This means we have a tighter bound of

$$\sum_{t \in (t_0,t_e)} \Pr(A(t)) \geq \max_{t \in (t_0,t_e)} \{M_t[n][c_q] - M_t[n][c]\}$$

To summarize, the version of EASY backfilling that uses runtime distributions rather than point predictions will backfill a job if the following condition holds

$$\sum_{t_e} \Pr(t_e) \max_{t \in (t_0,t_e)} \{M_t[n][c_q] - M_t[n][c]\} \ < \ \tau$$

That is, if the probability that such a time exists is less than the threshold. Algorithm 2 presents the simplified pseudo-code of this backfilling scheduler. Some

Algorithm 2. The distribution-based condition for backfilling.

```
bool shouldBackfill(Job job) {
    List events = <list of job terminations sorted by time>
    int n = <# of running jobs>
    double P[n];
    // max(t){M[n][c]-M[n][c0]}
    double pMax = 0;
    double result = 0;
    int c0 = <# of processors needed to run Q[0]>
    int c =  <# of processors needed to run both jobs>
    for each j=runtime bin do {
        for each e in events before bin[j].end do {
            P[e.job] += e.probability;
            <calculate M using Dynamic Programming, given P>
            pMax = max{pMax, M[n][c0]-M[n][c]};
        }
        result += job.model[j]*pMax;
    }
    return result < THRESHOLD;
}
```

notes on the implementation: The `result` variable is monotonously growing, so once it is bigger than the threshold the total result is false for sure, so no further calculations are run. The `pMax` variable is also monotonously growing. This means that if the remaining runtime bin probability multiplied with the current `pMax` together with the current `result` are bigger than the threshold, it is also enough to stop calculating and return false. These improvements are very important, since the scheduler runs on-line. Our simulations (reported in the next section) indicate that indeed the overhead of the scheduler is very low: simulating a full year of activity, with order of 100,000 calls to the scheduler, takes about half an hour.

If the predictor returns no runtime prediction (which might happen if no historical data is available), then the single probability event is inserted, which is the user estimate with probability of 1. If this is the case for all the running jobs, then the algorithm works exactly like the original EASY algorithm: all the termination events come from the running jobs' terminations by user estimates, and therefore the algorithm works in a very deterministic way.

5   Results

The probabilistic backfilling scheme described above was evaluated by comparing it with EASY backfilling, using simulations of several workloads available from the Parallel Workloads archive [10] (Table 1). In these workload logs, jobs that are canceled before they start have 0 runtime and also 0 processors. These jobs were removed from the simulation. If a job requires more processors than the machine has, the requirement is aligned to the machine size.

Table 1. Workloads used in the analysis and simulations. Average wait and run times are in minutes.

log	duration	jobs	avg wait	avg run
CTC SP2	6/96–5/97	77,222	425.7	188.0
KTH SP2	9/96–8/97	28,489	334.6	161.8
SDSC SP2	4/98–4/00	59,725	429.6	123.6
SDSC Blue	4/00–1/03	243,314	720.2	95.5

The runtime distributions were modeled using a Hidden-Markov Model with 16 states, where each state corresponds to a runtime distribution. The model grouped jobs arriving within a 15-minute slice of time together. The runtime distribution was modeled using logarithmic bins, with ranges that grow by a factor of 1.8. The details of the modeling are presented in detail in [12]. The threshold used for the probabilistic backfilling was $\tau = 0.05$.

In order to avoid the influence of the runtime differences between the traces we used waiting time for the performance metric. The system is a multi-user system, therefore fairness is also an issue. Therefore, the L_1-type metrics that take the average or sum of all the jobs' metric values are not enough — a job that suffers from bad service is not compensated by the fact that in average the jobs wait little in the queue. In order to present the complete picture of what is going on for all the jobs the full CDFs of the waiting times are presented.

Figure 2 compares the conventional EASY scheduler with the probability-based scheduler. The X-axis is the waiting times of the jobs in a logarithmic scale, and the Y-axis its CDF. The CDF doesn't start from 0, since there a large fraction of the jobs don't wait in the queue at all: around 50% of the jobs for SDSC Blue and KTH, slightly less for SDSC SP2, and more than 75% of the jobs for CTC.

As the results are shown in the form of a CDF, a curve that is lower and more to the right implies higher wait times and thus worse performance. Conversely, a curve that is higher and to the left indicates lower wait times and better performance. The arrows represent the fraction of jobs for which waiting time improved due to the probabilistic approach — this is the interval of the CDFs where the results for the probabilistic scheme (dashed line) are to the left of and above the EASY results (solid line).

The conclusions of this chart is that usually most of the jobs that had to wait at all are better off using the probabilistic approach. Note that the X-axis is logarithmic, and actually covers a very large range — it changes by a factor of 2.5×10^6. Therefore, when the line moves left even for a little, this may represent an improvement factor of 2. Also, it looks that if the job started waiting, it usually waits for at least a minute. Another finding is that there is a place in the chart where the line is almost straight. This means that the waiting time distribution at some intervals is close to a log-uniform distribution.

Tables 2 and 3 summarize the improvements in the wait time metric in the form of the arithmetic and geometric means. The formula for calculating the

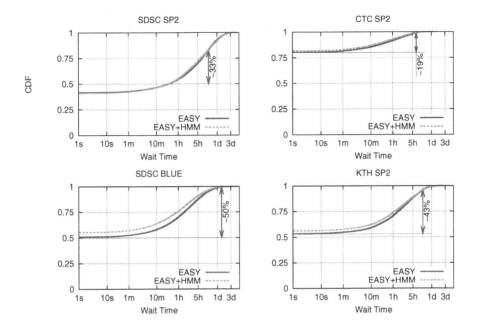

Fig. 2. CDF of waiting time for Probabilistic EASY vs. base EASY. The arrows show the jobs that benefit from the probabilistic approach.

Table 2. Arithmetic mean of waiting times

Trace name	EASY	Probabilistic	
CTC SP2	21.3 min	18.1 min	-15.2%
SDSC SP2	364 min	373 min	+2.6%
SDSC Blue	131 min	105 min	-19.5%
KTH SP2	114 min	113 min	-0.6%
Total			-8.7%

Table 3. Geometric mean of waiting times

Trace name	EASY	Probabilistic	
CTC SP2	28.2 sec	25.3 sec	-10.1%
SDSC SP2	639 sec	635 sec	-0.7%
SDSC Blue	203 sec	135 sec	-33.6%
KTH SP2	181 sec	147 sec	-18.9%
Total			-16.7%

geometric mean is $\exp(\int f(w) \ln \max\{w, w_{\min}\} \mathrm{d}w)$, where w is the job's waiting time, $f(w)$ is its PDF and $w_{\min}$ is the commonly used threshold of 10 seconds, see for instance [13]. Therefore, the improvement in the geometric mean metric value is exactly the area between the lines of the chart that are to the right of $w = w_{min}$.

6 Conclusions

Scheduling algorithms such as backfilling and SJF require job runtimes to be known, or at least predicted. Previous work has always assumed that such predictions have to be point estimates. In contradistinction, we investigate the option of predicting the *distribution* from which the actual runtime will be drawn. This is then integrated into the EASY backfilling algorithm, and shown to reduce the expected waiting time and improve the wait-time distribution.

Once a distribution-based probabilistic backfilling algorithm is in place, several courses of additional research suggest themselves. One is a comparison with the performance obtained by other (single value) prediction schemes. Another is a deeper investigation of alternative ways to predict distributions. In this work we used a rather complex HMM-based prediction scheme. A possible alternative is to just use the empirical distribution of jobs by the same user. This holds promise because it provides more focus on the local process, as opposed to the HMM which takes a global view at the possible expense of predictions for a single job. But a thorough experimental study is needed to verify and quantify the relative performance of the two approaches.

References

1. Lifka, D.: The ANL/IBM SP scheduling system. In: Feitelson, D.G., Rudolph, L. (eds.) JSSPP 1995. LNCS, vol. 949, pp. 295–303. Springer, Heidelberg (1995)
2. Mu'alem, A.W., Feitelson, D.G.: Utilization, predictability, workloads, and user runtime estimates in scheduling the IBM SP2 with backfilling. IEEE Trans. Parallel and Distributed systems 12(6), 529–543 (2001)
3. Feitelson, D.G., Mu'alem Weil, A.: Utilization and predictability in scheduling the IBM SP2 with backfilling. In: International Parallel Processing Symposium, Number 12, pp. 542–546 (1998)
4. Zotkin, D., Keleher, P.J.: Job-length estimation and performance in backfilling schedulers. In: International Symposium on High Performance Distributed Computing, Number 8 (1999)
5. Chiang, S.H., Arpaci-Dusseau, A., Vernon, M.K.: The impact of more accurate requested runtimes on production job scheduling performance. In: Feitelson, D.G., Rudolph, L., Schwiegelshohn, U. (eds.) JSSPP 2002. LNCS, vol. 2537, pp. 103–127. Springer, Heidelberg (2002)
6. Tsafrir, D., Feitelson, D.G.: The dynamics of backfilling: solving the mystery of why increased inaccuracy may help. In: IEEE International Symposium on Workload Characterization, pp. 131–141 (2006)
7. Tsafrir, D., Etsion, Y., Feitelson, D.G.: Backfilling using system-generated predictions rather than user runtime estimates. IEEE Trans. Parallel and Distributed systems 18(6), 789–803 (2007)

8. Gibbons, R.: A historical application profiler for use by parallel schedulers. In: Feitelson, D.G., Rudolph, L. (eds.) JSSPP 1997. LNCS, vol. 1291, pp. 58–77. Springer, Heidelberg (1997)
9. Smith, W., Foster, I., Taylor, V.: Predicting application run times using historical information. In: Feitelson, D.G., Rudolph, L. (eds.) JSSPP 1998. LNCS, vol. 1459, pp. 122–142. Springer, Heidelberg (1998)
10. Parallel workloads archive,
    http://www.cs.huji.ac.il/labs/parallel/workload/
11. Feitelson, D.G.: Locality of sampling and diversity in parallel system workloads. In: 21st International Conference on Supercomputing, pp. 53–63 (2007)
12. Nissimov, A.: Locality and its usage in parallel job runtime distribution modeling using HMM. Master's thesis, The Hebrew University (2006)
13. Feitelson, D.G., Rudolph, L., Schwiegelshohn, U., Sevcik, K.C., Wong, P.: Theory and practice in parallel job scheduling. In: Feitelson, D.G., Rudolph, L. (eds.) JSSPP 1997. LNCS, vol. 1291, pp. 1–34. Springer, Heidelberg (1997)

Impact of Reservations on Production Job Scheduling

Martin W. Margo, Kenneth Yoshimoto, Patricia Kovatch, and Phil Andrews

San Diego Supercomputer Center,
University of California, San Diego
{mmargo, kenneth, pkovatch, andrews}@sdsc.edu

Abstract. The TeraGrid is a closely linked community of diverse resources: computational, data, and experimental, e.g., the imminent very
large computational system at the University of Texas, the extensive data
facilities at SDSC, and the physics experiments at ORNL. As research
efforts become more extensive in scope, the co-scheduling of multiple
resources becomes an essential part of scientific progress. This can be
at odds with the traditional management of the computational systems,
where utilization, queue wait times, and expansion factors are considered
paramount and anything that affects their performance is considered
with suspicion. The only way to assuage concerns is with intensive investigation of the likely effects of allowing advance reservations on these
performance metrics.

To understand the impact, we developed a simulator that reads our
actual production job log and reservation request data to investigate
different scheduling scenarios. We explored the effect of reservations and
policies using job log data from two different months within consecutive
years and present our initial results. Results from the simulations suggest
that utilization, expansion factor and queue wait time indeed can be
affected negatively by significant numbers and size of reservations, but
this effect can be mitigated with appropriate policies.

1 Introduction

Scientists need to reserve computational resources for different reasons. For instance, a scientist may need resources at a specific time to meet a deadline or
perform a demonstration. A scientist may also want to co-schedule multiple resources. Creating reservations is one way of allowing jobs to run simultaneously
at more than one site or resource and guarantees that a resource is available at
a specific time. Many local schedulers can implement policies and operate independently from a centralized scheduler without requiring coordination between
sites with different scheduling goals. This is in contrast with other co-scheduling
mechanisms [1,2,3].

Reservations may reduce batch job throughput of a system, as measured by
utilization, average expansion factor and average queue wait time. A study of
the effect of reservations on utilization and expansion factor [4] concluded that

E. Frachtenberg and U. Schwiegelshohn (Eds.): JSSPP 2007, LNCS 4942, pp. 116–131, 2008.

meta-scheduled reservations equivalent to up to 15 percent of the workload result in less impact than fixed time slots set aside for cross-site jobs. In that study, a real workload was used to compare baseline utilization and expansion factor in the presence and absence of synthetic reservations. In this study, we sample real user reservations to find the point at which user reservations interfere unacceptably with the batch workload. We seek to determine whether policies restricting reservation creation can moderate the negative effect of reservations on utilization, expansion factor and queue wait time. In some cases, the effect of reservations can even be advantageous: allowing a "clean start" with an opening for large, efficient jobs to begin.

The San Diego Supercomputer Center [5] offers several compute resources including DataStar. DataStar consists of 2,528 Power4+ processors connected via IBM's Federation High Performance Switch (HPS). 272 of the nodes have eight processors per node and 11 of the nodes have 32 processors. In aggregate, the machine has over 7 TB of memory. This machine has been in production since April of 2004 and delivers over 14 million service units (SU, representing one hour of processor wall-clock time) per year. DataStar runs LoadLeveler [6] as the resource manager and Catalina [7] as the scheduler. DataStar is also part of the TeraGrid.

The TeraGrid [8] is a multi-year effort sponsored by the National Science Foundation (NSF) to construct the nation's largest grid. The TeraGrid hosts a variety of diverse resources including over 100 TF of High Performance Computing (HPC) power and a spallation neutron resource: an accelerator-based neutron source [9]. These resources are connected via a dedicated high-speed network of 10-30 Gb/s. User allocations are fungible at different sites throughout the TeraGrid. A General Parallel File System (GPFS) [10] is exported from SDSC enabling users to access the same files at different sites without copying files around. This capability facilitates metascheduling.

The TeraGrid currently consists of nine sites: the National Center Supercomputing Applications, San Diego Supercomputer Center (SDSC), Argonne National Laboratory, the National Center for Atmospheric Research, Pittsburgh Supercomputer Center, Texas Advanced Computing Center, Indiana University, Purdue and Oak Ridge National Laboratory.

The TeraGrid is interested in metascheduling capabilities including user-settable reservations [11]. User-settable reservations are favored since they are more efficient with staff time. A Metascheduling Requirements Analysis Team (RAT) [12] was formed to explore the capabilities, Resource Provider (RP) requirements, and software technologies required to assist in the formal adoption of metascheduling capabilities. RPs have expressed concerns about how their local scheduling goals will be affected by metascheduling capabilities, including reservations. Most sites are planning to implement reservations but are unsure how reservations will impact their queues and overall machine utilization. They are considering how to set policies that would help ameliorate the effect.

Using a simulator with real job log data from the actual production queue on DataStar, we can see how local jobs are affected by the reservations from the co-scheduled jobs and compare the results without the reservations. The simulator gives us a controlled and repeatable environment to see the outcomes of the scheduling decisions made by the policies of the scheduler. With this we can assess the impact of reservations and make appropriate policies. For instance, a site may want to limit the impact of reservations created by a specific user. This site could create a policy within the scheduling software to only allow a limited number of reservations created by that user. Some sites want to offer the co-scheduling feature with reservations and are willing to balance any potential decrease in their overall utilization by introducing increased charges for reservations.

The evaluation of parallel job scheduling algorithms is fraught with problems, a long but probably not exhaustive list forms the "Frachtenberg pitfalls" [13]. It is beyond the scope of this paper to demonstrate the avoidance of all 32 of these, but the great majority are circumvented by the technique of using a real workload, rather than a simulated one. The jobs are actual submissions to the SDSC machine DataStar, with the addition of putative reservations to determine the impact on the gross queuing parameters such as usage and queue waits, with and without throttling restrictions.

2   Hypothesis

While user-settable reservations would enable co-allocated grid jobs and make efficient use of staff time, system administrators are often reluctant to allow users to make reservations at will. This stems from a fear that injecting reservations will disrupt the job queue, resulting in degraded utilization, average expansion factor and average queue wait time. We hypothesize that the impact of user-settable reservations on the job queue can be controlled through policies throttling reservation creation. The scheduler used at SDSC and in this simulation study allows users to create reservations only after all eligible jobs have been given reservations. This means that the existing job queue is not affected by user-settable reservations. Subsequent jobs would need to be scheduled around those reservations.

The policy we use to throttle user-settable reservations is that the total node-seconds of user-settable reservations within any sliding 7 day period must not exceed 256 nodes * 12 hours worth of node-seconds. This represents all unshared batch nodes in the system for half a day each week.

3   The Simulator

We developed a simulator to explore the impact of reservations on a real production workload. The simulator allows us to replay the exact workload, vary the number of reservations and observe the effects. We selected three parameters to evaluate the effects of reservations: machine utilization, expansion factor and queue wait time.

Diagram 1 depicts the five major components of our simulator: Simulation Core, Catalina, LoadLeveler simulators, and accounting and reservation databases. The core is written in Python and uses SimPy simulation framework [14]. The simulation core depends heavily on the simulation clock. Our simulator is designated DES (Discrete Event Simulator). In DES, time can be advanced into a discrete time where an event is happening; other times of non-activity are simply skipped. The core is responsible for keeping track of active jobs, queued jobs, and exiting jobs, adjusting the discrete simulation clock, and keeping track of current and future reservations.

The next component is Catalina [7]. Catalina is our production scheduler on SDSC's Datastar. It is written in Python. Catalina is stateless. A scheduling iteration is independent than that of the past and that of the future.

LoadLeveler [6] is Datastar's resource manager software from IBM. It is responsible for accepting job submissions and to signal the nodes to run jobs. It has many different components and a set of APIs to access its functions. To become an external scheduler, Catalina uses many of the LoadLeveler API calls to perform its duty. For example, it uses API calls to query the status of jobs, machines, resources, adapters, etc. Catalina also uses the API to instruct LoadLeveler to run a job on a node. Since we are going to run a discrete event simulator, LoadLeveler behavior must be simulated. LoadLeveler is not stateless; therefore it is impossible for the simulator to advance the simulation clock discretely. To overcome this problem, we wrote LoadLeveler wrapper scripts.

The LoadLeveler API calls that we need are qj_ll, llq, and rj_ll. qj_ll or query job LoadLeveler queries LoadLeveler for all jobs known to LoadLeveler. qj_ll outputs the name of the job, owner, group, node amount requested, wall clock time requested, switch adapter window requirement, along with other job properties. When a job is queued, its information will be included in qj_ll output.

llq or LoadLeveler query works similarly to qj_ll. llq records current job information and display them in human readable format.

rj_ll or run job LoadLeveler is a wrapper script written in C to start a job currently in the queue.

SDSC has accounting and reservation databases. These databases are updated regularly. The accounting database consists of finished jobs information; such as job id, owner, group, account, charges, amount of wall clock time used, return code, location to binaries, location to input and output files, etc. For historical purposes, we can query the database and obtain information about jobs that were submitted by a particular user on a particular day in the past.

The reservation database stores information about user settable reservations on Datastar. It has information about the reservation creation date, reservation start date, reservation end date, owner, etc.

The simulation consists of cycles. A cycle is broken down into five steps: the input step (Step 1), the recording step (Step 2), the scheduling step (Step 3), the execution step (Step 4), and the reporting step (Step 5). The simulation terminates if all jobs and reservations in accounting and reservation databases have been completed or the time limit has been reached. The time limit should be set to be the time when all the jobs and reservations finishes plus few days of buffer period.

In the beginning of the simulation, we initialized the simulation clock to zero, read the job accounting and reservation database, and load them to memory in a queue sorted by their relative submit time. Each job and reservation has a relative submit time. For example, a job submitted on midnight, January 2, 2007 has relative start time of 86400 seconds, if the simulation begins on January 1, 2007. This technique allows us to distribute jobs according to real life distribution. Reservations are distributed uniformly across simulation time.

In Step 1, the simulation core reads the value of simulation clock and reads the memory for any job that submits at that time. If such job or reservation exists, it will update the next simulation time to the next job submission time or reservation creation time in memory and dequeue the current job or reservation.

In Step 2, any jobs extracted from Step 1 are inserted to the qj_ll and llq simulator. Effectively, the jobs information are registered to LoadLeveler. This is the recording step. Also, in this step, reservations extracted from Step 1 are submitted to Catalina. If there are no jobs or reservations extracted from Step 1, the simulation continues to Step 3.

In Step 3, the simulator calls Catalina to run a scheduling iteration. In this iteration, Catalina reads qj_ll and llq that are already populated with jobs in Step 2. Therefore, the newly submitted jobs are now being considered for execution. Also in this step, reservation requests are either granted or rejected depending on the active reservation policy. In Step 3, Catalina passes log information about active jobs and reservations to the core. Look at the text below for more detail. To reduce the amount of processing time, the scheduler iteration occurs every fifteen minutes of simulation time between job submission or completion.

```
43258     :: job (ds002.236406.0) requesting (6) node is here
43639     :: job (ds002.236408.0) requesting (6) node is here
44100     :: ********** begin executing catalina_schedule_jobs.py *********
44100     :: ********** executed catalina_schedule_jobs.py ********
44110     :: job(ds002.236408.0) has been waiting for (471) and now it is run-
          ning.
44110     :: total node usage is now (53) or (20.00) percent
44110     :: job(ds002.236406.0) has been waiting for (852) and now it is run-
          ning.
44110     :: total node usage is now (59) or (22.00) percent
44321     :: job(ds002.236408.0) is done running. it ran for (211.0) seconds
44321     :: total node usage is now (53) or (20.00) percent
44334     :: job(ds002.236355.0) is done running. it ran for (31724.0) seconds
44334     :: total node usage is now (51) or (19.00) percent
44795     :: job(ds002.236406.0) is done running. it ran for (685.0) seconds
44795     :: total node usage is now (45) or (17.00) percent
45000     :: ********** begin executing catalina_schedule_jobs.py *********
45000     :: ********** executed catalina_schedule_jobs.py ********
```

In Step 4, Catalina checks its internal tables to see if it can run one or more jobs at present. If so, it calls rj_ll simulator with the eligible job ids as input parameters. It logs this action to simulation core. At the end of this executing step, the simulation cleans finished jobs by flushing their entries from llq and qj_ll simulator internal table. If there is no job to be run at present, Catalina skips this step. Reservations are handled analogously.

In Step 5 or the reporting step, the simulator print logs into standard output. We can see a message with a timestamp for each action performed on the job or reservation. The text above is an example of our simulator output.

At the end of Step 5, simulation clock is advanced to the next event time and Step 1 restarts. Output from Step 5 allows us to calculate wait time for each job, expansion factor for each job, and instantaneous overall utilization at various point in time. With this information, we can calculate higher-level metrics presented in later sections.

The simulation strives to provide the actual production environment with jobs arriving to the queue at the same distribution as the historical job distribution. The jobs we simulate are a copy of actual jobs from Datastar. We also simulate jobs that finished earlier than its requested wall clock time. The simulator uses historical reservation information from TeraGrid. In the base case, we can see how our simulator resembles the historical production schedule. One factor that deviates us from actual production schedule is the fact that we don't simulate node failures, either hardware or software.

We wrote ~1000 lines of code to implement the simulation core and the LoadLeveler simulator components. The code for the Simulator will be freely available after approval by UCSD's Technology Transfer Office. It will work with generic queue-based external schedulers and resource managers.

4   Evaluation Criteria

To judge the impact on our scheduling goals, we examined the average queue wait time for each job, the expansion factor for each job, and total utilization of the machine. Queue wait time measures the length of time between when a job comes into the queue and when it starts running. It is measured in hours. The expansion factor is the ratio of the sum of requested wall-clock time and queue wait time divided by the requested wall-clock time. Expansion factor is unit-less; the lower the expansion factor is, the better. Finally, utilization is the percentage of the entire cluster being used during the simulation.

To measure impact on the job queue, we use utilization, average expansion factor and average system queue wait time:

$$Utilization = \frac{\sum job\_node\_seconds}{Available\_node\_seconds}$$

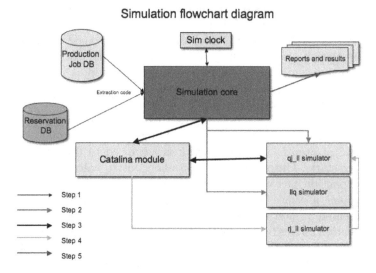

Fig. 1. Simulation Flowchart

$$Average\_expansion\_factor = \frac{\sum\limits_{all jobs} (expansion\_factor \cdot job\_node\_seconds}{\sum\limits_{all jobs} job\_node\_seconds}$$

$$Average\_system\_wait\_time = \frac{\sum\limits_{all\_jobs} job\_wait\_time \cdot job\_node\_seconds}{\sum\limits_{all\_jobs} job\_node\_seconds}$$

5   The Simulation

We wanted to see the effect of real, requested reservations on our normal work-load. We also wanted to see how many reservations it would take to significantly interfere with our scheduling goals. Lastly, we wanted to know if our scheduling goals could be maintained by using policies.

To accomplish these objectives, we planned three runs: (1) a baseline run using only the real production workload, (2) a run including real reservation requests and (3) a run with policies enabled to control the number of reservations. To really show the effect of reservation in our production job mix, we used one year worth of reservations on our system over a month period of time.

Additionally we use two different job mix, one from March 2006 and one from March 2007. The reservation data however, are the same between the two sets of runs. For the simulation, we used DataStar's real production workload from the two months, based on job submission time.

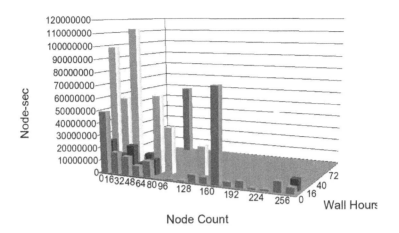

Fig. 2. Job Histogram for March 2006

In the first week of simulation time, there were 767 jobs in the queue. The job mix included jobs from one to 256 nodes (full machine) with a duration of one to 18 hours (the maximum time that can be requested). Six jobs requested the full machine and 29 requested 128 nodes or more. We injected 15 reservations during each week of simulation time,, all actually requested through TeraGrid, with job sizes from eight to 128 with a duration of four to 18 hours.

In 2006, TeraGrid users requested reservations for 60 co-scheduled jobs. We used these real-life requests as the basis for our reservations for both simulations. Compressing a year's worth of actual reservations into a month of simulated job scheduling should overstate the impact of real reservations on the system.

Fig 1 and 2 show the number of jobs requested at each node count for 2006 and 2007. The colors are not significant, only to help identify the jobs. Fig 3 shows the reservations requested for 2006, which was used for both the 2006 and 2007 simulations.

6   Results

From the job data from March 2006, 722 jobs completed during the simulation time. The three scenarios simulated were: baseline, baseline+reservations, baseline+reservations+policy restrictions. For this particular workload, the baseline queue wait time was 6.03 hours, and expansion factor was 2.05. When reservations were added to the schedule, there was a drastic increase in queue wait time to 74.0 hours. Expansion factor also increased to 7.35.

This would be expected, since jobs were scheduled around the obstructing reservations. Some jobs would probably be delayed, resulting in longer queue

Mar 07

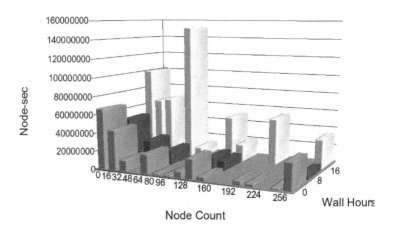

Fig. 3. Job Histogram for March 2007

wait times. When restricting policies were added, to throttle requested reservations, queue wait time dropped to 4.44 hours and expansion factor went to 1.70. This was unexpected, since these metrics are even better than in the baseline, no-reservations scenario. A plausible explanation for this effect is that wide reservations (those spanning much of the machine) create backfill or afterfill windows that allow large jobs to run more quickly than without reservations in place. The reservations would have the effect of preventing small, long jobs from blocking large jobs. In fact, when looking at the simulation data in detail, it became clear that two injected reservations, one for 130 nodes and one for 128 nodes, created a space in the schedule for a 256-node job to run earlier than it would have in the absence of reservations. This case shows that some combinations of workload and reservations may result in increased efficiency.

For the March 2007, 706-job workload, a different pattern occurred. The baseline queue time was 13.7 hours, with expansion factor at 2.53. When reservations were added, queue time went to 107 hours, and expansion factor went to 9.35. With throttling policies, queue wait time recovered to 44.0 hours, and expansion factor went to 5.21. With this workload, reservations had a large negative impact on scheduling metrics. The throttling policies were able to reduce this effect, but scheduling was still less efficient than the baseline case.

One factor to consider is that the simulation does not enforce max jobs per user queued policies, so there can be a hundred one-node, 30 minute jobs waiting to run, giving a very poor expansion factor. On DataStar, we limit the users to six jobs queued at a time, so you wouldn't see the poor expansion factor due to queue stuffing. We would need to examine the individual job expansion factors to know if that's what's going on in the simulation.

2006 Reservations

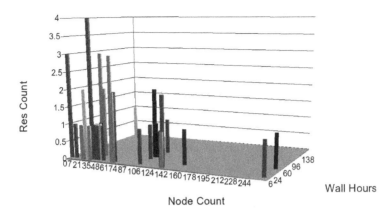

Res Count

Node Count

Wall Hours

Fig. 4. Reservation Histogram for 2006

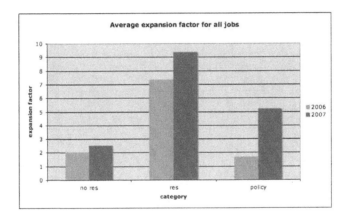

Fig. 5. Average Expansion Factor for All Jobs

Utilization percentage snapshots were taken throughout the simulations. When reservations are counted as utilized parts of the machine, overall utilization remains high. There are some periods in which reservations or reservations+policy results in lower utilization than baseline, but these are not the rule.

To address the effect of a long job queue on user job submission behavior, we examined the length of the job queue as the simulation progressed. Graphs of the queue depth throughout the simulation suggest that in the baseline and baseline+reservations+policy scenarios the queue depth stayed within a realistic regime: 90 waiting jobs for 2006, 150 waiting jobs for 2007. The baseline + reservations queue depth rises much higher than the other two scenarios. Users might be expected to stop submitting jobs before the queue depth reaches that

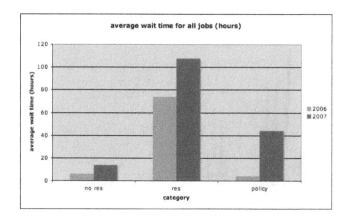

Fig. 6. Average Wait Time for All Jobs

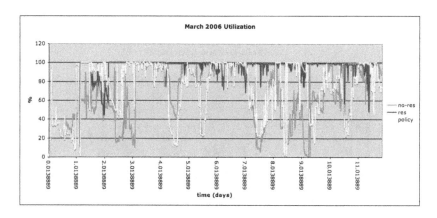

Fig. 7. March 2006 Utilization

point. The baseline+reservation queue depth may represent a worst-case scenario for expansion factor and queue wait time, in which users continue to blindly submit jobs regardless of queue depth.

We wanted to breakdown the components of our expansion factor and wait time changes by job size. The small jobs are one-node jobs, the medium jobs are 2-64 nodes and the large are 65-256. This would allow us to determine whether different size classes of jobs were disproportionately affected by injection of reservations. In 2006, medium-sized jobs suffered more as measured by an expansion factor increase, especially in the baseline+reservations case. In 2007, the expansion factors of large jobs increased over the 2006 simulation. In this simulation, the overall expansion factor with policy did not recover to the baseline case.

In 2006, medium-sized jobs suffered more as measured by an increase in average wait time, especially in the baseline+reservations case. In 2007, the average

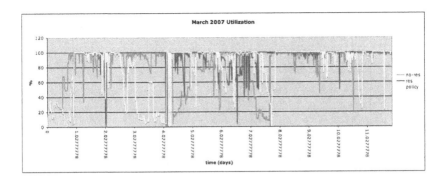

Fig. 8. March 2007 Utilization

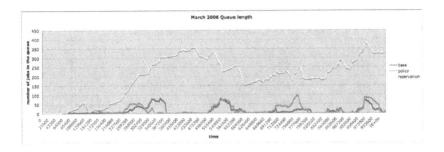

Fig. 9. March 2006 Queue Length

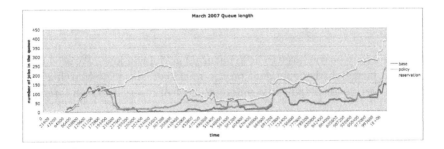

Fig. 10. March 2007 Queue Length

expansion factor and the average wait time for both medium and large jobs suffered in the baseline+reservations scenario. Even after applying our throttling
policy, medium and large jobs did not recover expansion factor and queue wait
time to the baseline case. In general, medium jobs can be expected to suffer
more than small-short or large jobs. In a single-queue, priority-based, reservations
scheduling system, medium jobs may be too small to be granted top priority in

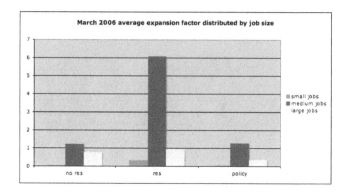

Fig. 11. 2006 Expansion factor (by job size)

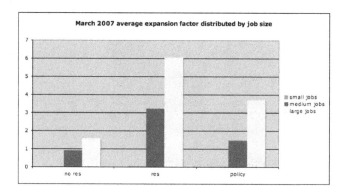

Fig. 12. 2007 Expansion factor (by job size))

the queue and may be too large to fit in natural backfill windows. We see here that the effect on large jobs is dependent on the workload, since the March 2006 and March 2007 workloads displayed a different effect of reservations on large jobs.

7   Future Work

In the next few months we will develop hypotheses on the effects of reservations as a function of reservation size, duration, and advance notice. From these hypotheses we will fashion several postulated policies that attempt to provide the advantages of advanced reservations while reducing the deleterious effects on utilization, queue waits, and expansion factors to a minimum. Indeed, it is possible, that, dependent on the details of the job mix, it may be possible to improve some of these in many situations with an appropriate policy.

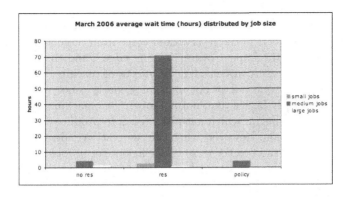

Fig. 13. Average Wait Time for 2006 Based on Job Size

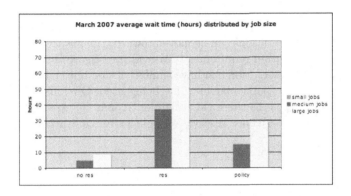

Fig. 14. Average Wait Time for 2007 based on Job Size

8   Conclusions

By running two different production job workloads (from DataStar, March 2006
and March 2007) through three different reservation scheduling scenarios (baseline, baseline+reservations, baseline+reservations+policy), we show that injecting reservations can have a large negative impact on average expansion factor and
average queue wait time. This effect can be moderated by policies that throttle
reservation injection. System utilization was not necessarily worse when reservations were added to the system. The utilization appears to be very dependent on
job mix. One concern with simulating the workload was the effect of extremely
deep job queues on user psychology. In the case of baseline+reservations, queue
depths could run to almost 400 jobs in the queue. Would users continue to submit jobs under that circumstance? On the other hand, with throttling policies
in place, queue depth was comparable to the baseline scenario.

One of the most interesting aspects of this work is that the introduction of advance reservations can, under some circumstances, be advantageous to the existing job mix. The effects of the reservations come from three areas: its "width", or number of nodes, the impact of its "leading edge", and that of its "trailing edge". For simplicity, we can consider the effects of machine-wide reservation, where all nodes are requested (a not unusual scenario, since most reservations tend to be significantly larger than normal jobs). The machine must be drained for the reservation to begin, which naturally tends to produce "holes" in the job mix, reducing utilization. However, when the reservation ends, the job scheduler has had an increased time to try to put an efficient set of jobs together to fully utilize the empty machine at the end of the reservation. Indeed, users will have been continually submitting jobs for the duration of the reservation, increasing the job pool available to the scheduler. This can lead to increased utilization immediately following the reservation.

It is clear that while the deleterious effects of the reservations "leading edge" are independent of the duration of the reservations, the advantageous effects of the "trailing edge" increase with the duration of the reservation. Thus, the effects of allowing reservations can be moved towards the positive by policies that have a minimum duration requirement. We will investigate this in future work. The "width" of the reservation can have similar effects, but these are dependent on the job mix on the particular machine being used. Obviously the history of the job mix is available to the local scheduler: it may be possible to feed back that information into advance reservation policies to again reduce the negative impact.

References

1. Feitelson, D., Rudolph, L., Schwiegelshohn, U.: Parallel Job Scheduling - A Status Report. In: Feitelson, D.G., Rudolph, L., Schwiegelshohn, U. (eds.) JSSPP 2004. LNCS, vol. 3277, Springer, Heidelberg (2005)
2. Singaga, J., Mohamed, H., Epema, D.: Dynamic Co-Allocation Service in Multi-cluster Systems. In: Feitelson, D.G., Rudolph, L., Schwiegelshohn, U. (eds.) JSSPP 2004. LNCS, vol. 3277, Springer, Heidelberg (2005)
3. Sodan, A., Lan, L.: LOMARC - Lookahead Matchmaking for Multi-Resource Coscheduling. In: Feitelson, D.G., Rudolph, L., Schwiegelshohn, U. (eds.) JSSPP 2004. LNCS, vol. 3277, Springer, Heidelberg (2005)
4. Snell, Q., Clement, M., Jackson, D., Gregory, C.: The Performance Impact of Advance Reservation Meta-scheduling. In: Feitelson, D.G., Rudolph, L. (eds.) IPDPS-WS 2000 and JSSPP 2000. LNCS, vol. 1911, pp. 137–153. Springer, Heidelberg (2000)
5. San Diego Supercomputer Center at UCSD, http://www.sdsc.edu
6. IBM LoadLeveler,
   http://publib.boulder.ibm.com/infocenter/clresctr/index.jsp
7. Catalina scheduler, http://www.sdsc.edu/catalina
8. TeraGrid, http://www.teragrid.org
9. Neutron source, http://en.wikipedia.org/wiki/Spallation_Neutron_Source

10. Andrews, P., Jordan, C., Kovatch, P.: Massive High-Performance Global File Systems for Grid Computing. Research Paper, SuperComputing 2005, Seattle, WA (November 2005)
11. Yoshimoto, K., Kovatch, P., Andrews, P.: Co-scheduling with User-Settable Reservations. In: Feitelson, D.G., Frachtenberg, E., Rudolph, L., Schwiegelshohn, U. (eds.) JSSPP 2005. LNCS, vol. 3834, Springer, Heidelberg (2005)
12. Metascheduling Requirement Analysis Team final report, http://www.teragridforum.org/mediawiki/images/b/b4/MetaschedRatReport.pdf
13. Frachtenberg, E., Feitelson, D.G.: Pitfalls in Parallel Job Scheduling Evaluation. In: Feitelson, D.G., Frachtenberg, E., Rudolph, L., Schwiegelshohn, U. (eds.) JSSPP 2005. LNCS, vol. 3834, Springer, Heidelberg (2005)
14. SimPy, http://simpy.sourceforge.net/

Prospects of Collaboration between Compute Providers by Means of Job Interchange

Christian Grimme, Joachim Lepping, and Alexander Papaspyrou

Robotics Research Institute, University Dortmund, 44221 Dortmund, Germany
{christian.grimme, joachim.lepping, alexander.papaspyrou}@udo.edu

Abstract. This paper empirically explores the advantages of the collaboration between different parallel compute sites in a decentralized grid scenario. To this end, we assume independent users that submit their jobs to their local site installation. The sites are allowed to decline the local execution of jobs by offering them to a central job pool. In our analysis we evaluate the performance of three job sharing algorithms that are based on the commonly used algorithms First-Come-First-Serve, EASY Backfilling, and List-Scheduling. The simulation results are obtained using real workload traces and compared to single site results. We show that simple job pooling is beneficial for all sites even if the local scheduling systems remain unchanged. Further, we show that it is possible to achieve shorter response times for jobs compared to the best single-site scheduling results.

1 Introduction

In recent years the demand for computing power has increased significantly as a growing number of science areas rely on extensive simulations, like biotechnology, high energy physics [15], or climate research [13]. In order to provide an on-the-spot support for high performance computing power many Massively Parallel Processing (MPP) systems have been put into service. Those machines are extensively shared by a local user community that submits jobs which are adapted to the local site capabilities, for instance in the jobs' degree of parallelism. As these user communities are still growing, the utilization of such systems is typically very high and computing power is becoming a limited resource.

This, however, is twofold: on the one hand, a high utilization is desirable for the system provider as it allows a profitable operation of the MPP system. On the other hand, this entails longer wait times for the execution of the users' jobs, decreasing customer satisfaction. To ameliorate this, system providers introduce additional queues, restrictive quotas and partitions, or even employ more sophisticated scheduling concepts that allow a flexible prioritization of users, see Franke et al. [11,10]. However, all those approaches favor a certain group of users at best, but do not prevent congestions induced by the overall high demand for compute power.

This has initiated the concept of Computational Grids: the loose coupling [8] of independent and typically diverging MPP installations to a federated source

E. Frachtenberg and U. Schwiegelshohn (Eds.): JSSPP 2007, LNCS 4942, pp. 132–151, 2008.

of ubiquitous computing power. All the more, the world wide growing network infrastructure allows an interchange of jobs among sites with an almost evanescent time delay. In this way locally submitted jobs may—in case of a high local load— also be executed on another MPP system in the federation, utilizing idle resources. However, new scheduling problems arise in the Grid context as interchanging jobs between different sites while keeping or enhancing the performance for all local user communities is a non-trivial problem.

In this paper we study the advantages for local user communities and system providers induced by joining a decentralized Computational Grid where jobs can be interchanged between different MPP installations. We evaluate the concept of a global job pool which can be used by all participating sites to offer or accept available jobs and restrict our evaluation to a small set of sites with simple job-sharing enabled adaptations of common scheduling algorithms.

The rest of the paper is organized as follows. Current developments in the area of research are reviewed in Section 2. Scheduling concepts for local and distributed computing are presented in Section 3. Our model of MPP systems in a decentralized Grid along with job policies and employed algorithms is introduced in Section 4. The experimental setup is described in Section 5, and a detailed evaluation of different heterogeneous site configurations is presented in Section 6. Our paper ends with a conclusion and an outlook on future work in Section 7.

2   Background

Since the first ideas of metacomputing have been formulated by Smarr and Catlett [21], many research activities deal with the development of concepts to connect world wide distributed resources. Nowadays, metacomputing is replaced by the new ideas of Grid Computing [9] which facilitates the aggregation and sharing of heterogeneous resources distributed over large geographical areas. Although the original Grid idea extends the term "'resource"' beyond[1] MPP systems, the area of Computational Grids as the federations of several high performance compute sites is supposed to be the most developed one. To satisfy the growing need for compute power Grids are considered an integral part of the usual business in the near future [22].

Admittedly, every system provider in such a federation aims to retain the control over his system. Futhermore, his main interest lies in reaching short response times for the local user community while keeping the utilization of his machine as high as possible. Against this background it is unrealistic to assume a model where a global resource management system is allowed to decide over the local resources. As such, it is widely agreed that Grid Computing can only be applied beneficially if the resource management and scheduling is appropriately adapted to the environment. Therefore, almost all current Grid projects spend special effort in the development of smart scheduling strategies.

---

[1] For example, storage systems and network links, as well as special purpose devices such as telescopes or satellites.

However, there is a lack of studies that empirically identify potential advantages of the collaboration of compute sites using a decentralized structure and an indirect communication model. A first study by Hamscher et al. [14] shows potential advantages that result from different job sharing strategies. However, their empirical results are not meant to be complete as they mainly focus on the conception of job interchange procedures. Their paper only considers two real workloads and they do not give exclusive single-site scheduling results for comparison. Further, Ernemann et al. identify improvements for the average weighted response time objective assuming hierarchical centralized scheduling structures [4] in multi-site computing [3].

Among the large variety of studies on load balancing Lu et al. [17] developed algorithms for distributed load balancing in a grid environment assuming an additional communication delay. However, their approach requires that the whole local installation is controlled by a central scheduler and their evaluation is founded on statistical workload models that can hardly be compared with real workload traces originating from real-world job submissions. The latter also applies to England and Weissman [2], who analyzed costs and benefits of load sharing, limiting themselves to site configurations and reviewing average slowdown only.

On the theoretical side, Schwiegelshohn [19] proves that the quality of two schedules can be improved concerning the total completion time objective if an interchange of jobs is allowed during the creation of the schedules.

3   Scheduling Concepts for Local and Distributed Computing

In this section, we present the scheduling concepts underlying our evaluations. First, three standard scheduling strategies are briefly recapitulated for single-site MPP systems. Then, we introduce three very simple job-sharing algorithms that are based on the previously introduced standard approaches.

3.1   Local Job Scheduling

The single site scenario has been discussed in research for quite a long time. Various algorithms are available that try to minimize the response time for jobs and to utilize the system properly. The algorithms that we chose for evaluation purposes are most commonly applied in practice. These algorithms are in detail:

First Come First Serve (FCFS) starts the first job of the waiting queue whenever enough idle resources are available. Despite the very low utilization that is produced in the worst case this heuristic works well in practice [20].

List-Scheduling (LIST) as introduced by Graham [12] serves as a template for our LIST algorithm. List-Scheduling is based on a list that is ordered according to static job weights. The scheduler selects from the list the job with the highest weight. In our case, the job arrival time (or release date) is used as the list's weight. The scheduler scans the list in ascending order until finding a job that can be processed immediately on the currently idle resources. Therefore, this algorithm is similar to the *First-Fit* strategy [1].

EASY Backfilling (EASY) requires that a runtime estimation is provided for each job by its user [16]. If the first job of the waiting queue cannot be started immediately, the algorithm allows an allocation of another job if it does not delay the earliest possible start time of the *first job*.

3.2 Distributed Job Scheduling

For local scheduling systems, the aforementioned algorithms have been established as quasi-standard, since they work well for a single parallel computer but they are not optimized for any Grid interaction.

Scheduling in Grid systems can mainly be divided into two distinct layers. The local layer is responsible for the scheduling of jobs in the current waiting queue onto the available local resources. This allows for example the realization of priorities for different user groups which can be formulated by the system provider. Albeit in a very simplistic way, the aforementioned local job scheduling algorithms cover this area, and work well for the single parallel computer view to such an extent that they have been established as quasi-standard for many MPP installations.

The second, higher layer is responsible for the interaction with other Grid participants and might perform (among others) discovery, negotiation, and the migration of jobs to remote sites. This functionality, however, is not provided by the local scheduling algorithms and is subject to research [22].

For the structure of these two layers, a large variety of concepts exists. These can be classified into the following two categories:

Hierarchical Scheduling. The hierarchical scheduling structure utilizes a central scheduler—the so- called meta-scheduler—which accepts the submission of workload independent of its origin and decides on the distribution among available sites. After the decision is made, the given workload is assigned to the local schedulers which in turn are responsible for the assignment on local resources. The advantage of this approach is that different strategies and policies may be applied for the meta-scheduler and the local scheduling systems. The main disadvantage arises from the centralization concept of this approach: it inherently lacks scalability and, since having a single-point-of-failure, has a very bad fault-tolerance—if the meta-scheduler breaks down, workload handling ceases completely.

Decentralized Scheduling. In decentralized scheduling systems the distributed local schedulers interact with each other in a direct or indirect fashion. As there is no single-point-of- failure, the system is more reliable: possible breakdowns of one participant does not necessarily impair the performance of the whole system. The possibility of realizing different policies on the local and global scheduling layers is given as in the hierarchical case, admittedly requiring more sophisticated scheduling concepts due to the lack of a global system view.

As mentioned above, there exist two possibilities to establish the communication of distributed schedulers. In *direct communication* schedulers can transfer/accept jobs to/from remote sites directly. This may imply searching for remote sites and/or keeping a list of potential communication partners. In case that local job execution is not possible, the scheduler may then delegate the execution one of the known remote sites.

The second model is *indirect communication* by sharing a central repository. Whenever local execution is not possible, jobs are offered this repository —for example realized as a job pool— which then can be used by the other participants as a second queue for occupying currently idle local resources. Since this concept is used for the evaluations in this paper, the details are given in Section 4.3.

4   Model

In this Section, we detail the setup and actual environment model that we use for our evaluation. First, we give an description of the site scenario. Then, we describe the scheduling problem for a single site and specify the assumptions that are made for the computational jobs and the formal description.

4.1   Site and Machine Environment

We assume a Computational Grid consisting of $|K|$ independent MPP systems, following referred to as *sites*. Each site $k \in K$ is modeled by m_k parallel processors which are identical such that a parallel job can be allocated on any subset of these machines. Splitting jobs over multiple sites (multi-site computation) is not allowed.

Moreover, we assume that all sites only differ in the number of available processors, but not in their speed. As we focus on the job-sharing algorithms, the differences in execution speeds are neglected.

Still, every site has its own local user demand for computational resources which is reflected by the sites' originating workload. This includes the submission characteristics, but also the adaptation of the submitted jobs' resource demand to the local configuration. That is, jobs that are submitted to the local site scheduler may not be accepted for execution elsewhere because of their resource demand being oversized for some or all of the other sites.

4.2   Job Model

We assume rigid[2] parallel batch jobs for our analysis, which are dominant on most MPP systems. The user provides the number of required machines m_j at the release date r_j of the job. The completion time of job $j \in \pi_k$ in schedule S_k on site k is denoted by $C_j(S_k)$. As preemptions are not allowed in many MPP systems [6], each job starts its execution at time $C_j(S_k) - p_j$.

---

[2] Neither moldable nor malleable, requiring concurrent and exclusive access to the requested resources.

Job scheduling on MPP systems is an online problem as jobs are submitted over time and the processing time p_j of job j is not available at the release date r_j. As the release and processing times are unknown, the problem is often classified as non-clairvoyant online scheduling, see Motwani et al. [18]. In the following, we denote the set of jobs that are submitted to a *local* site k by τ_k. Further, system administrators often require users to provide worst case estimates $\bar{p}_j$ of the processing time p_j to determine faulty jobs whose processing times exceed the estimate.

Furthermore, data management of any files is neglected in this paper. In our multi-site scenario, a job can be transmitted to a common pool without any communication penalty while in a real implementation the transport of data requires additional time. The communication cost can often be hidden by pre- and postfetching before and after the execution. In such a case the overhead is not necessarily part of the scheduling process.

4.3 Job-Sharing Algorithms

In order to establish indirect communication between sites we introduce a central job pool from/to which local schedulers can receive/transfer jobs. All sites joining this collaboration scenario are connected to the central pool as shown in Figure 1. In our model, the pool is realized as a global job queue where all jobs are ordered according to their local submission time. The interaction with the pool requires a policy that decides, whether a job is offered to the job pool or is kept in the local queue. For all our job-sharing algorithms we apply the following universal policy:

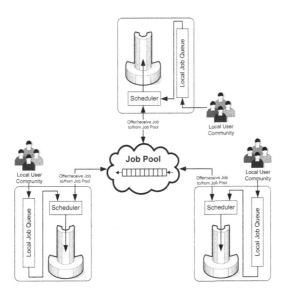

Fig. 1. Decentralized scheduling scenario sharing a central job pool

Whenever a job from the local queue cannot be executed immediately on the local processors, it is offered to the global job pool and removed from the local queue.

Algorithm 1. General template for job-sharing algorithm.

Preconditions: a local job queue l, a global job pool g
1: *algorithm* $\in$ {FCFS, EASY, LIST}
2: apply *algorithm* to l
3: **for all** considered, but locally non-schedulable jobs **do**
4:     offer job to g
5: **end for**
6: **if** no job could be scheduled locally **then**
7:     apply *algorithm* to g
8: **end if**

In the following, we detail how the interaction between local queue and global job pool is implemented by the different job-sharing (JS) algorithms. Our three job-sharing algorithms are based on the template which is described in Algorithm 1. In the beginning, FCFS, EASY, or LIST is applied locally (see Line 2). Following (see Line 4), all jobs that have been considered for the current schedule during the previous step —including all potential backfilling candidates—but could not be scheduled immediately are moved to the pool. If no job from the local queue could be scheduled, the algorithm is executed again, using the global job pool (see Line 7).

For the modified FCFS policy, only the first job of each queue is considered respectively. In the case of adapted EASY policy, the application of the algorithm is completely separate for each queue. As such, backfilling is repeated on the global job pool if and only if local scheduling failed. Note that only the currently treated queue is used for finding backfilling candidates, and not the union of locally and globally available jobs. The changed LIST policy also iterates over the queue stopping as soon as a schedulable job has been found, and also resorts to the global job pool if no local job could be fit into the schedule.

In the remainder of this paper we will denote the FCFS based job-sharing algorithm as **FCFS-JS**, the EASY based as **EASY-JS**, and the LIST based algorithm as **LIST-JS** respectively.

5   Experimental Setup

Before presenting our detailed evaluation results we give an overview on how our experiments have been setup and introduce performance objectives and used input data.

5.1   Performance Objectives

In order to measure the schedule quality and to quantify the effect on jobs interchange we define several objectives. Remember that we denote the set of jobs that have been submitted locally to site k by τ_k and all jobs that have been actually processed on site k by π_k.

Squashed Area and Utilization. The first two objectives are *Squashed Area* SA_k and *Utilization* U_k, both specific to a certain site k. They are measured from the start of the schedule S_k, that is $\min_{j \in \pi_k} \{C_j(S_k) - p_j\}$ as the earliest job start time, up to its makespan $C_{max,k} = \max_{j \in \pi_k} \{C_j(S_k)\}$, that is the latest job completion time and thus the schedule's length.

SA_k denotes the overall resource usage of all jobs that have been executed on site k, see Equation 1.

$$SA_k = \sum_{j \in \pi_k} p_j \cdot m_j \tag{1}$$

U_k describes the ratio between overall resource usage and available resources after the completion of all jobs $j \in \pi_k$, see Equation 2.

$$U_k = \frac{SA_k}{m_k \cdot \left(C_{max,k} - \min_{j \in \pi_k} \{C_j(S_k) - p_j\} \right)} \tag{2}$$

U_k describes the usage efficiency of the site's available machines. Therefore, it is often serving as a schedule quality metric from the site provider's point of view.

However, comparing single-site and multi-site utilization values is illicit: since the calculation of U_k depends on $C_{max,k}$, valid comparisons are only admissible if $C_{max,k}$ is approximately equal between the single-site and multi-site scenario. Otherwise, high utilizations may indicate good usage efficiency, although the corresponding $C_{max,k}$ value is very small and shows that only few jobs have been computed locally while many have been delegated to other sites for remote execution.

As such, we additionally introduce the *Change of Squashed Area* ΔSA_k, which provides a makespan- independent view on the utilization's alteration, see Equation 3.

$$\Delta SA_k = \frac{SA_k}{\sum_{j \in \tau_k} p_j \cdot m_j} \tag{3}$$

From the system provider's point of view this objective reflects the real change of the utilization when jobs are shared between site compared to the local execution.

Response Time. For our third objective we switch focus towards a more users-centric view and consider the *Average Weighted Response Time* $AWRT_k$ relative to all jobs $j \in \tau_k$ that have been initially submitted to site k, see Equation 4. Note that this also respects the execution on remote sites and, as such, the completion time $C_j(S)$ refers to the site that executed job j.

$$AWRT_k = \frac{\sum_{j \in \tau_k} p_j \cdot m_j \cdot (C_j(S) - r_j)}{\sum_{j \in \tau_k} p_j \cdot m_j} \tag{4}$$

A short AWRT describes that on average users do not wait long for their jobs to complete. According to Schwiegelshohn et al. [20], we use the resource consumption $(p_j \cdot m_j)$ of each job j as the weight. This ensures that neither splitting nor combination of jobs can influence the objective function in a beneficial way.

Migration Rate. Finally, we measure the amount of migration in the multi-site scenarios. To this end, we introduce a migration matrix M that shows the ratio of job dissemination with respect to the original submission site, see Equation 5.

$$M = \begin{bmatrix} \dfrac{|\pi_{kk}|}{|\tau_k|} & \dfrac{|\pi_{kl}|}{|\tau_k|} & \cdots \\[2ex] \dfrac{|\pi_{lk}|}{|\tau_l|} & \dfrac{|\pi_{ll}|}{|\tau_l|} & \cdots \\[2ex] \vdots & \vdots & \ddots \end{bmatrix} \tag{5}$$

In this matrix we apply the following notation:

τ_k. Total amount of jobs that have been originally submitted to site k.
π_{lk}. Amount of jobs that have been originally submitted to site l but have been executed on site k.

Remember that the rows denote the site where the jobs have been submitted to while columns specify the actual execution sites. Next, we detail the data source utilized for our investigation.

5.2   Input Data

The Parallel Workloads Archive[3] provides job submission and execution traces recorded on real-world MPP system sites, each of which containing information on relevant job characteristics. For our evaluations, we restricted the set of used workloads to those which contain valid runtime estimations, since the EASY and EASY-JS algorithms depend on this data. Furthermore, we applied various pre-filtering steps to the original—partially erroneous—data: we discard jobs with invalid release dates ($r_j < 0$), processing times ($p_j \leq 0$), node requests ($m_j \leq 0$), and estimates ($\bar{p}_j \leq 0$), as well as unsatisfiable resource demands ($m_j > m$). Furthermore, we assume overuse interdiction, effectively disallowing jobs to run longer than the user provided runtime estimation ($p_j = \min\{p_j, \bar{p}_j\}$). Some details of the examined cleaned traces are given in Table 1.

Naturally, the total number of available processors differs in workloads which makes it possible to model unequally sized site configurations. Further, the original workloads record time periods of different length. In order to be able to combine different workloads in a multi-site simulations we shortened the workloads to the minimum required length of all participating workloads. To reflect different site configurations (e.g. small machine and large machine) we combine only workloads that represent a long record period to obtain meaningful results.

---

[3] http://www.cs.huji.ac.il/labs/parallel/workload/

Table 1. Details of the shortened workloads obtained from the Parallel Workload Archive and the corresponding examined site setups 1-7

Identifier	n	m	Months	Site Setup							SA
				1	2	3	4	5	6	7	
KTH-11	28479	100	11	X			X	X			2017737644
CTC-11	77199	430	11						X		8279369703
LANL96-11	57715	1024	11					X			16701881984
LANL96-13	67043	1024	13				X				19467626464
LANL96-24	110769	1024	24		X	X				X	35426509344
SDSC00-11	29810	128	11	X			X	X			2780016139
SDSC00-24	54006	128	24			X				X	6656350775
SDSC03-11	65584	1152	11								23337438904
SDSC03-13	78951	1152	13				X				27410557560
SDSC03-24	176268	1152	24		X					X	54233113112
SDSC05-13	84876	1664	13				X				34347849760

Therefore, we created shortened versions of the LANL96, SDSC00, SDSC03, and SDSC05 workloads[4]. The resulting seven different site configurations are listed in Table 1.

Note that we do not shift the traces regarding their originating timezones. We restrict our study to workloads which are all submitted within the same timezone. Therefore, the known diurnal rhythm of job submission is similar for all sites in our scenario and time shifts cannot be availed to improve scheduling. In a global grid the different timezones even benefit the job scheduling as idle machines at night can be used by jobs from peak loaded sites at noon, see Ernemann at al. [5]. As we cannot benefit from timezone shifts the presented results might be even better in a global grid.

6   Evaluation

We now provide results obtained for the single site case and for the different site setups which allow the interchange of jobs.

6.1   Reference Results on the Local Sites

As it is our aim to compare the introduced simple job sharing mechanism to the performance of standard algorithms in a single site environment, we show these results first. In Table 2 the AWRT, U, and C_{max} are given when the three standard algorithms FCFS, EASY, and LIST are applied to the 11 different workloads and the corresponding sites given in Table 1. It becomes obvious that EASY outperforms the FCFS algorithm in terms of AWRT and U, what is well known from the literature, see Feitelson and Weil [7]. However, for some workloads the LIST algorithm performs even better than EASY which might be due to the characteristics of some workloads. In general, both queue-iterating procedures are superior to FCFS while there is no significant advantage of LIST scheduling compared to EASY.

---

[4] http://www-ds.e-technik.uni-dortmund.de/~lepping/workloads/

Table 2. AWRT (in seconds), U (in %), and C_{max} (in seconds) for the different workloads. The objective values are shown for the three algorithms and only single site execution ($K = 1$).

Identifier	FCFS			EASY			LIST		
	AWRT	U	C_{max}	AWRT	U	C_{max}	AWRT	U	C_{max}
KTH-11	418171.98	68.67	29381344	75157.63	68.72	29363626	80459.27	68.72	29363626
CTC-11	58592.52	65.70	29306682	52937.96	65.70	29306682	53282.02	65.70	29306682
LANL96-11	13886.61	55.65	29306900	12442.02	55.65	29306355	13082.10	55.65	29307464
LANL96-13	14064.40	56.24	33801984	12467.61	56.24	33802986	13178.91	56.24	33802986
LANL96-24	12265.92	55.54	62292428	11105.15	55.54	62292428	11652.44	55.54	62292428
SDSC00-11	266618.82	71.53	30361813	73605.86	73.94	29374554	74527.98	73.96	29364791
SDSC00-24	2224462.43	75.39	68978708	112040.42	81.78	63591452	116260.72	82.26	63618662
SDSC03-11	72417.87	68.58	29537543	50772.48	68.74	29471588	48015.99	68.87	29413625
SDSC03-13	82149.66	69.92	34030926	54546.9	70.12	33932665	52012.84	70.14	33921090
SDSC03-24	166189.54	73.22	64299555	70774.86	73.91	63696120	72220.28	73.91	63695942
SDSC05-13	72690.44	61.08	33793591	56990.23	61.08	33793591	55250.72	61.08	33793591

6.2 Interchange of Jobs between Two Sites

To investigate the effect of site collaboration applying the job-sharing approach described in Section 4.3 we define three simple setups of two sites respectively connected to the central job-pool. Every site in this setup corresponds to the machine represented by the workload trace it processes.

In Table 3 the results of our examined setup with two collaborating sites are listed. The objectives are given for each job-sharing algorithm compared to the results of the corresponding single-site algorithm (denoted by Δ) and the best single-site algorithm (denoted by Δ_b) respectively. This distinction has been made to illustrate the effect of applying job-sharing algorithms as well as to review whether a general improvement compared with the single-site approach is possible. To analyze the behavior systematically, we first discuss the results compared to the related single-site scheduling algorithms.

For the constellation of two small sites, represented by KTH and SDSC00 workloads, a significant improvement in AWRT with respect to the corresponding local setup can be observed. This is achieved even without affecting the utilization or squashed area significantly. However, this does not hold for two large sites, processing workloads like LANL96 and SDSC03. Especially for the FCFS-JS strategy, the AWRT of site 1 increases drastically. It is obvious that in the non-cooperating case and the LANL96 workload short AWRT values are achieved for all standard algorithms. This may be due to a comparably low utilization and a special manner of use where only jobs are allowed that (a) require a number of processors equal to a power of two and (b) use at least 32 processors. For the job-sharing algorithms one may argue that even slight changes in utilization as well as violations of the policies may result in a significant growth of AWRT. Thus, for a low utilized system the job-sharing may be disadvantageous.

A completely different behavior can be observed when a small site (SDSC00) cooperated with a large site (LANL96). Here, the small site migrates a higher percentage of its jobs to the large site than vice versa. Obviously, the AWRT of the small site improves strongly while the utilization decreases. Concerning

Table 3. Objective values for site setups 1-3 each with two participants ($K = 2$). $AWRT_k$ and $C_{max,k}$ values are given in seconds while the U_k, SA_k, and all comparative objectives (Δ, Δ_b, and matrix M) are given in %.

Site Setup	1		2		3	
Workload	KTH-11	SDSC00-11	LANL96-24	SDSC03-24	LANL96-24	SDSC00-24
m	100	128	1024	1152	1024	128
k	1	2	1	2	1	2
FCFS-JS						
$AWRT_k$	128043.42	139380.14	33487.04	67584.37	14277.15	40764.89
U_k	70.12	72.94	64.59	65.44	58.91	55.57
$C_{max,k}$	29571802	2957587	62440050	64151102	62303391	63638145
SA_k	2073589120	2724164663	41300491136	48359131320	37584312832	4498547287
$\Delta\ AWRT_k$	69.38	47.72	100.00	59.33	-16.40	98.17
$\Delta\ U_k$	2.11	0.63	16.31	-10.62	6.07	-26.71
$\Delta\ SA_k$	2.77	-2.01	16.58	-10.83	6.07	-32.42
$\Delta\ C_{max,k}$	-0.65	2.59	-0.24	0.23	-0.02	7.74
$\Delta_b\ AWRT_k$	-70.37	-89.36	-201.55	4.51	-28.56	63.62
$\Delta_b\ U_k$	2.04	-2.68	16.31	-11.46	6.07	-32.47
$\Delta_b\ SA_k$	2.77	-2.01	16.58	-10.83	6.09	-32.42
$\Delta_b\ C_{max,k}$	-0.71	-0.68	-0.24	-0.71	-0.02	-0.07
$M =$	82.86	17.14	88.69	11.31	97.35	2.65
	13.95	86.05	9.51	90.49	15.41	84.59
EASY-JS						
$AWRT_k$	66115.56	59015.97	13579.91	54019.88	12583.95	41441.88
U_k	68.95	74.80	63.20	67.24	58.33	60.28
$C_{max,k}$	29363626	29364791	62303135	63694187	62292428	63618367
SA_k	2024644907	2773108876	40318878368	49340744088	37204951541	4877908578
$\Delta\ AWRT_k$	12.03	19.82	-22.28	23.67	-13.32	63.01
$\Delta\ U_k$	0.34	-0.21	13.79	-9.02	5.02	-26.75
$\Delta\ SA_k$	0.34	-0.25	13.81	-9.02	5.02	-26.72
$\Delta\ C_{max,k}$	0.00	0.03	-0.02	0.00	0.00	-0.04
$\Delta_b\ AWRT_k$	12.03	19.82	-22.28	23.67	-13.32	63.01
$\Delta_b\ U_k$	0.34	-0.21	13.79	-9.02	5.02	-26.75
$\Delta_b\ SA_k$	0.34	-0.25	13.81	-9.02	5.02	-26.72
$\Delta_b\ C_{max,k}$	0.00	0.03	-0.02	0.00	0.00	-0.04
$M =$	79.63	20.37	88.69	13.37	97.21	2.79
	15.04	84.96	9.99	90.01	17.01	82.99
LIST-JS						
$AWRT_k$	61016.52	58354.18	13509.25	51150.19	13001.56	38655.67
U_k	68.98	74.84	63.45	67.01	59.11	54.04
$C_{max,k}$	29363626	29339969	62317990	63694095	62303391	63588898
SA_k	2025505127	2772248656	49172388088	49172388088	37711932960	4370927159
$\Delta\ AWRT_k$	24.16	21.70	-15.93	29.17	-11.52	66.75
$\Delta\ U_k$	0.38	-0.19	14.24	-9.33	6.43	-34.30
$\Delta\ SA_k$	0.38	-0.28	14.29	-9.33	6.45	-34.33
$\Delta\ C_{max,k}$	0.00	0.08	-0.04	0.00	-0.02	0.05
$\Delta_b\ AWRT_k$	18.82	20.72	-21.65	27.73	-17.08	65.50
$\Delta_b\ U_k$	0.38	-0.16	14.24	-9.33	6.43	-34.33
$\Delta_b\ SA_k$	0.38	-0.28	14.29	-9.33	6.45	-34.33
$\Delta_b\ C_{max,k}$	0.00	0.12	-0.04	0.00	-0.02	0.00
$M =$	77.77	22.23	83.20	16.80	96.62	3.38
	19.61	80.39	11.35	88.65	14.88	85.12

the large site similar effects as in the case of two large sites, discussed above, are observed. Due to the large amount of jobs migrated from the small to the large site the AWRT becomes longer while the utilization increases. However, the impact of these jobs is smaller than in the previous case which may again result from the use policy of LANL96 so that small jobs from SDSC00 can be used to fill a gap.

The comparison of the job-sharing algorithms with the results for EASY as the best single-site algorithm yields structurally similar results. However, for two small sites, the EASY-JS and LIST-JS approaches even outperform EASY with respect to AWRT. Summarizing we can formulate the following statement from our experiments:

1. Adapting the local algorithms to job-sharing can lead to an overall AWRT improvement for sites with high utilization and rather equal size.
2. Combining a site with low utilization and short AWRT with a more loaded one resembles a load balancing behavior which may involve a significant deterioration concerning AWRT for the less loaded site.
3. For disparate sized sites a significant higher percentage of job migrates from the small to the large site than vice versa. While many jobs from the large site cannot be executed on the small site due to oversized resource demands, jobs from the small site may fill gaps in the schedule of the large site.

6.3   Interchange of Jobs between Three Sites

For the setup with three collaborating sites we omit a complete presentation of the obtained simulation results and refer to the accompanying Table 4 and 5 in the appendix. Instead we present figures of AWRT improvements and the change in SA compared to EASY as the best single-site algorithm.

Again, we find that job-sharing yields shorter AWRT values for all participating sites. However, the utilization at the largest site (CTC) increases in a load balancing behavior, see Figure 2, but this does not affect the AWRT for EASY-JS and LIST-JS.

Since the sharing of jobs results in less utilization on two sites and more on one site while preserving or even improving the AWRT, this can be interpreted as benefit of job-sharing: on the less utilized site the system providers have more capabilities to serve additional customers.

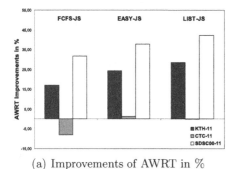
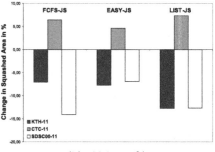

(a) Improvements of AWRT in %   (b) ΔSA_b in %

Fig. 2. AWRT and $\Delta_b SA$ for setup 6 with KTH-11 ($m_1=100$), CTC-11 ($m_2=430$), and SDSC00-11 ($m_3=128$) workloads and all three algorithms FCFS-JS, EASY-JS, and LIST-JS

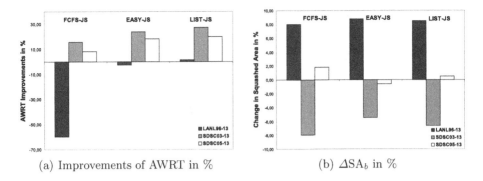

(a) Improvements of AWRT in %   (b) ΔSA_b in %

Fig. 3. AWRT and Δ_bSA for setup 4 with LANL96-13 ($m_1=1024$), SDSC03-13 ($m_2=1152$), and SDSC05-13 ($m_3=1664$) workloads and all three algorithms FCFS-JS, EASY-JS, and LIST-JS

A similar effect can be observed in Figure 3 for three large collaborating sites. Here, however, the aforementioned characteristics of LANL96 seem to influence the results. Nevertheless, for EASY- JS and LIST-JS we can identify a constant or improved AWRT, while U_1 increases for LANL96 and remains rather constant or decreases for the other sites.

Analogous to the two site setups, the results shown in Figure 4 for two small and one large sites yield a significant improvement of the small sites' AWRT to the expense of the large. It is possible to argue that many jobs are migrated from the small sites with high utilization to the large site with relatively low utilization.

In the last evaluation setting of two large and one small site, see Figure 5, the constellation behaves similar to the two large sites setup, discussed in Section 6.2. Again, LANL96 takes most of the shared jobs which leads to a strong deterioration in AWRT for FCFS-JS. This effect is even intensified by jobs

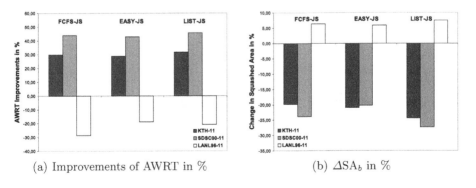

(a) Improvements of AWRT in %   (b) ΔSA_b in %

Fig. 4. AWRT and Δ_bSA for setup 5 with KTH-11 ($m_1=100$), SDSC00-11 ($m_2=128$), and LANL96-11 ($m_3=1024$) workloads and all three algorithms FCFS-JS, EASY-JS, and LIST-JS

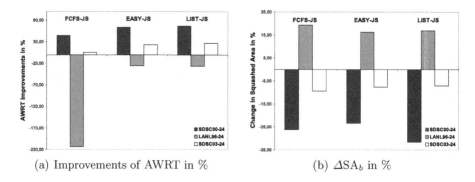

(a) Improvements of AWRT in %   (b) ΔSA_b in %

Fig. 5. AWRT and $\Delta_b SA$ for setup 7 with SDSC00-24 (m_1=128), LANL96-24 (m_2=1024), and SDSC03-24 (m_3=1152) workloads and all three algorithms FCFS-JS, EASY-JS, and LIST-JS

offered by the small site SDSC00. Note that this behavior was also observed in the two-site case with one large and one small site. For the other algorithms the situation is alike while the AWRT deterioration is less strong.

6.4   Job Pool Size Variation during Interchange

To conclude our evaluation we finally measure the job pool size to determine the amount of jobs residing in the pool during execution. To this end, we determine

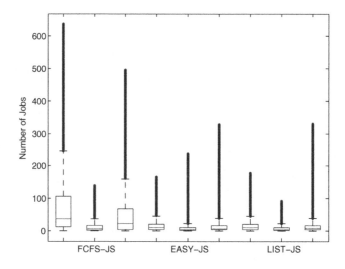

Fig. 6. Box plots of the job pool size for the two-site case considering the three job-sharing algorithms. For each algorithm three box plots are depicted, from left to right, KTH-11/SDSC00-11, LANL96-24/SDSC03-24, and LANL96-24/SDSC00-24.

the pool size every time a job is added to or removed from the job pool for a two site setup. The box plots in Figure 6 show the median, 25% quantile, 75% quantile as well as 5% and 95% quantile (at end of the whiskers) of the measured data. From these results we can conclude that in comparison with the total number of jobs processed the pool is not overcrowded. As the median values are comparably small jobs do not reside in the pool for a long time.

7   Conclusion and Future Work

In this work we explored the behavior of collaborating MPP systems in a decentralized scenario. In this context, we assumed independent users who submit jobs to their local compute sites, while the site schedulers were allowed to place released jobs into a global job pool instead of starting them locally. Respectively, the site schedulers may incorporate not only local, but also globally offered jobs into their scheduling decision.

To this end, we analyzed common performance metrics such as average weighted response time and utilization for the single-site, non-cooperating case, using standard algorithms. Then, we compared them to the results for collaborating setups in varying configurations. To this end, we defined three simple job-sharing algorithms that are based on modified variants of the standard algorithms, adding the ability to manage the interaction with the job pool.

Our results show that in case of an unchanged local scheduling algorithm many configurations benefit from the ability to additionally use a global job pool, especially in the cases of machines with a high local load. Furthermore, it could be shown that in some cases the job-sharing algorithms yield even better results than the best standard algorithm. Against this background it is noteworthy that our proposed job-sharing algorithms are very simple and leave ample room for improvements.

Regarding the extension of our analysis, the possibilities are twofold: first, an extension within the given model could be considered, including more sophisticated algorithms that make better use of the global job pool as well as dedicated distribution policies for local schedulers regarding non-schedulable jobs. An extension to the model itself could for example impose incentives and penalties for the runtime of jobs that are migrated between sites with highly diverging performance characteristics.

In our next steps, we will continue to examine our current setup, introducing more sophisticated distribution strategies and extend our evaluation to other standard algorithms such as Greedy-Scheduling with different queue ordering policies. On the medium term we plan to replace the indirect communication model we currently use by a direct communication model where each site scheduler may not only decide whether to migrate a job at all, but also to which target machine, allowing a fully decentralized scheduling model for computational jobs.

Acknowledgement

The authors would like to thank Christian Fisseler and Cesare Foltin for their extensive support in creating and verifying the simulation results.

Joachim Lepping is member of the Collaborative Research Center 531, "Computational Intelligence", at the University Dortmund with financial support of the Deutsche Forschungsgemeinschaft (DFG).

References

1. Aida, K.: Effect of Job Size Characteristics on Job Scheduling Performance. In: Feitelson, D.G., Rudolph, L. (eds.) IPDPS-WS 2000 and JSSPP 2000. LNCS, vol. 1911, pp. 1–17. Springer, Heidelberg (2000)
2. England, D., Weissman, J.B.: Cost and Benefits of Load Sharing in the Computational Grid. In: Feitelson, D.G., Rudolph, L., Schwiegelshohn, U. (eds.) JSSPP 2004. LNCS, vol. 3277, pp. 160–175. Springer, Heidelberg (2005)
3. Ernemann, C., Hamscher, V., Schwiegelshohn, U., Streit, A., Yahyapour, R.: Enhanced algorithms for multi-site scheduling. In: Parashar, M. (ed.) GRID 2002. LNCS, vol. 2536, pp. 219–231. Springer, Heidelberg (2002)
4. Ernemann, C., Hamscher, V., Schwiegelshohn, U., Streit, A., Yahyapour, R.: On advantages of grid computing for parallel job scheduling. In: Proceedings of the 2nd IEEE/ACM International Symposium on Cluster Computing and the Grid (CCGRID 2002), pp. 39–46. IEEE Computer Society Press, Los Alamitos (2002)
5. Ernemann, C., Hamscher, V., Yahyapour, R.: Benefits of global grid computing for job scheduling. In: Proceedings of the Fifth IEEE/ACM International Workshop on Grid Computing (GRID 2004), pp. 374–379. IEEE Computer Society Press, Los Alamitos (2004)
6. Feitelson, D.G., Rudolph, L., Schwiegelshohn, U., Sevcik, K.C., Wong, P.: Theory and practice in parallel job scheduling. In: Feitelson, D.G., Rudolph, L. (eds.) IPPS-WS 1997 and JSSPP 1997. LNCS, vol. 1291, pp. 1–34. Springer, Heidelberg (1997)
7. Feitelson, D.G., Weil, A.M.: Utilization and Predictability in Scheduling the IBM SP2 with Backfilling. In: Proceedings of the 12th International Parallel Processing Symposium and the 9th Symposium on Parallel and Distributed Processing, pp. 542–547. IEEE Computer Society Press, Los Alamitos (1998)
8. Foster, I.: What is the Grid? - A Three Point Checklist. GRIDtoday, 1(6) (July 2002)
9. Foster, I., Kesselman, C.: The Grid: Blueprint for a New Computing Infrastructure. Morgan Kaufmann, San Francisco (1999)
10. Franke, C., Lepping, J., Schwiegelshohn, U.: Greedy Scheduling with Complex Objectives. In: Proceedings of the 2007 IEEE Symposium Series in Computational Intelligence, IEEE Computer Society Press, Los Alamitos (to appear, 2007)
11. Franke, C., Lepping, J., Schwiegelshohn, U.: On Advantages of Scheduling Using Genetic Fuzzy Systems. In: Frachtenberg, E., Schwiegelshohn, U. (eds.) JSSPP 2006. LNCS, vol. 4376, pp. 68–93. Springer, Heidelberg (2007)
12. Graham, R.L.: Bounds on multiprocessing timing anomalies. SIAM Journal of Applied Mathematics 17(2), 416–429 (1969)

13. Grimme, C., Langhammer, T., Papaspyrou, A., Schintke, F.: Negotiation-based choreography of data-intensive applications in the c3grid project. In: Proceedings of the German e-Science Conference (GES) (to appear, 2007)
14. Hamscher, V., Schwiegelshohn, U., Streit, A., Yahyapour, R.: Evaluation of job-scheduling strategies for grid computing. In: Buyya, R., Baker, M. (eds.) GRID 2000. LNCS, vol. 1971, pp. 191–202. Springer, Heidelberg (2000)
15. Keahey, K., Fredian, T.W., Peng, Q., Schissel, D.P., Thompson, M.R., Foster, I., Greenwald, M.J., McCune, D.: Computational Grids in Action: The National Fusion Collaboratory. Future Generation Computer Systems 18(8), 1005–1015 (2002)
16. Lifka, D.A.: The ANL/IBM SP scheduling system. In: Feitelson, D.G., Rudolph, L. (eds.) IPPS-WS 1995 and JSSPP 1995. LNCS, vol. 949, pp. 295–303. Springer, Heidelberg (1995)
17. Lu, K., Subrata, R., Zomaya, A.Y.: Towards decentralized load balancing in a computational grid environment. In: Chung, Y.-C., Moreira, J.E. (eds.) GPC 2006. LNCS, vol. 3947, pp. 466–477. Springer, Heidelberg (2006)
18. Motwani, R., Phillips, S., Torng, E.: Nonclairvoyant scheduling. Theoretical Computer Science 130(1), 17–47 (1994)
19. Schwiegelshohn, U.: Preemptive weighted completion time scheduling of parallel jobs. SIAM Journal of Computing 33, 1280–1308 (2004)
20. Schwiegelshohn, U., Yahyapour, R.: Fairness in parallel job scheduling. Journal of Scheduling 3(5), 297–320 (2000)
21. Smarr, L., Catlett, C.E.: Metacomputing. Commun. ACM 35(6), 44–52 (1992)
22. Tonellotto, N., Wieder, P., Yahyapour, R.: A proposal for a generic grid scheduling architecture. In: Gorlach, S., Danelutto, M. (eds.) Proceedings of the Integrated Research in Grid Computing Workshop, November 2005, pp. 337–346 (2005)

A   Complete Results for Three Sites

Table 4. Objectives for site setup 4 and 5 each with three participants ($K = 3$). AWRT_k and $C_{max,k}$ values are given in seconds while the U_k, SA_k, and all comparative objectives (Δ, Δ_b, and matrix M) are given in %.

Site Setup	4			5		
Workload	LANL96-13	SDSC03-13	SDSC05-13	KTH-11	SDSC00-11	LANL96-11
m	1024	1152	1664	100	128	1024
k	1	2	3	1	2	3
FCFS-JS						
AWRT_k	19916.00	45870.87	52242.80	52851.95	41162.32	16021.66
U_k	60.74	64.68	62.03	55.11	57.15	59.15
$C_{max,k}$	33799198	33861823	33884574	29363626	29333220	29332006
SA_k	2122884048	25230465816	34972683920	1618211181	2116457552	17764967064
$\Delta\ \mathrm{AWRT}_k$	-41.61	44.16	28.13	87.36	84.56	-15.38
$\Delta\ \mathrm{U}_k$	8.00	-7.49	1.55	-19.75	-21.16	6.27
$\Delta\ \mathrm{SA}_k$	7.99	-7.95	1.82	-19.80	-23.87	6.37
$\Delta\ C_{max,k}$	0.01	0.50	-0.27	0.06	3.39	-0.09
$\Delta_b\ \mathrm{AWRT}_k$	-59.74	15.91	8.33	29.68	44.08	-28.77
$\Delta_b\ \mathrm{U}_k$	8.00	-7.79	1.55	-19.80	-23.76	6.27
$\Delta_b\ \mathrm{SA}_k$	7.99	-7.95	1.82	-19.80	-23.87	6.37
$\Delta_b\ C_{max,k}$	0.01	0.18	-0.27	0.00	0.14	-0.09
	83.82	7.19	8.98	85.22	4.51	10.27
$M =$	5.89	88.07	6.04	4.71	84.22	11.07
	6.28	5.64	88.08	4.52	1.64	93.85
EASY-JS						
AWRT_k	12790.98	41567.04	46570.09	53582.19	42083.57	14797.40
U_k	61.17	66.43	60.55	54.36	59.87	58.88
$C_{max,k}$	33802986	33861823	33884573	29363626	29333220	29332215
SA_k	21171896400	25914567656	34139569728	1596217383	2217375861	17686039823
$\Delta\ \mathrm{AWRT}_k$	-2.59	23.80	18.28	28.71	42.83	-18.93
$\Delta\ \mathrm{U}_k$	8.75	-5.29	-0.87	-20.71	-20.12	5.80
$\Delta\ \mathrm{SA}_k$	8.75	-5.46	-0.61	-20.89	-20.24	5.89
$\Delta\ C_{max,k}$	0.00	0.18	-0.27	-20.89	0.14	-0.09
$\Delta_b\ \mathrm{AWRT}_k$	-2.59	23.80	18.28	28.71	42.83	-18.93
$\Delta_b\ \mathrm{U}_k$	8.75	-5.29	-0.87	-20.89	-20.12	5.80
$\Delta_b\ \mathrm{SA}_k$	8.75	-5.46	-0.61	-20.89	-20.24	5.89
$\Delta_b\ C_{max,k}$	0.00	0.18	-0.27	0.00	0.14	-0.09
	80.85	8.50	10.65	85.09	4.39	10.52
$M =$	5.45	86.75	7.79	4.33	84.10	11.57
	7.03	7.24	85.73	2.04	3.12	94.83
LIST-JS						
AWRT_k	12308.17	39608.98	45554.56	51470.82	39959.20	15031.02
U_k	61.03	65.61	61.21	51.97	54.61	59.79
$C_{max,k}$	33796660	33861823	33884573	29363626	29333220	29320703
SA_k	21120338112	25591989520	34513706152	1526159515	2022449972	17951026280
$\Delta\ \mathrm{AWRT}_k$	6.61	23.85	17.55	36.03	46.38	-14.94
$\Delta\ \mathrm{U}_k$	8.51	-6.47	0.21	-24.36	-27.17	7.43
$\Delta\ \mathrm{SA}_k$	8.49	-6.63	0.48	-24.36	-27.25	7.48
$\Delta\ C_{max,k}$	0.02	0.17	-0.27	0.00	0.11	-0.05
$\Delta_b\ \mathrm{AWRT}_k$	1.28	27.39	20.07	31.52	45.71	-20.86
$\Delta_b\ \mathrm{U}_k$	8.51	-6.46	0.21	-24.36	-27.15	7.43
$\Delta_b\ \mathrm{SA}_k$	8.49	-6.63	0.48	-24.36	-27.25	7.48
$\Delta_b\ C_{max,k}$	0.02	0.18	-0.27	0.00	0.14	-0.05
	78.13	10.37	11.51	85.20	4.59	10.21
$M =$	6.44	85.51	8.06	4.05	84.76	11.19
	7.99	8.31	83.71	2.63	3.39	93.98

Table 5. Objectives for site setup 6 and 7 each with three participants ($K = 3$). $AWRT_k$ and $C_{max,k}$ values are given in seconds while the U_k, SA_k, and all comparative objectives (Δ, Δ_b, and matrix M) are given in %.

Site Setup	6			7		
Workload	KTH-11	CTC-11	SDSC00-11	SDSC00-24	LANL96-24	SDSC03-24
m	100	430	128	128	1024	1152
k	1	2	3	1	2	3
FCFS-JS						
$AWRT_k$	62338.86	57201.08	50232.14	62101.21	34797.44	66909.13
U_k	63.89	69.93	64.48	60.36	66.13	66.56
$C_{max,k}$	29363626	29308287	29331912	63983290	62404360	64089508
SA_k	1875983688	8813151320	2387988478	4912160835	42260968454	49142843942
Δ $AWRT_k$	85.09	2.37	81.16	97.21	-183.69	59.74
Δ U_k	-6.97	6.44	-11.04	-20.41	19.08	-9.09
Δ SA_k	-7.03	6.45	-14.10	-26.20	19.29	-9.39
Δ $C_{max,k}$	0.06	-0.01	3.39	7.24	-0.18	0.33
Δ_b $AWRT_k$	17.06	-8.05	31.76	44.57	-213.35	5.46
Δ_b U_kL	-7.03	6.44	-13.98	-26.66	19.08	-9.94
Δ_b SA_k	-7.03	6.45	-14.10	-26.20	19.29	-9.39
Δ_b $C_{max,k}$	0.00	-0.01	0.15	-0.62	-0.18	-0.62
	80.01	14.59	5.39	80.69	9.70	9.61
$M =$	3.94	92.15	3.91	2.60	86.54	10.86
	5.17	14.50	80.34	2.32	8.43	89.25
EASY-JS						
$AWRT_k$	56824.14	52231.77	45829.72	40991.60	13975.35	54443.17
U_k	63.41	68.67	68.90	63.07	64.40	68.23
$C_{max,k}$	29363626	29333225	29349199	63588898	62404876	63694151
SA_k	1861958410	8662107095	2553057981	5100935288	41152934711	50062103232
Δ $AWRT_k$	24.39	1.33	37.74	63.41	-25.85	23.08
Δ U_k	-7.72	4.53	-8.08	-23.36	15.95	-7.69
Δ SA_k	-7.72	4.62	-8.16	-23.37	16.16	-7.69
Δ $C_{max,k}$	0.00	-0.09	0.09	0.00	-0.18	0.00
Δ_b $AWRT_k$	24.39	1.33	37.74	63.41	-25.85	23.08
Δ_b U_k	-7.72	4.53	-8.08	-23.36	15.95	-7.69
Δ_b SA_k	-7.72	4.62	-8.16	-23.37	16.16	-7.69
Δ_b $C_{max,k}$	0.00	-0.09	0.09	0.00	-0.18	0.00
	75.66	18.02	6.32	78.48	7.83	13.69
$M =$	4.99	88.69	6.32	1.41	84.62	13.97
	5.33	17.09	77.58	2.08	9.56	88.36
LIST-JS						
$AWRT_k$	53667.36	53030.53	42517.13	37582.73	14032.26	52078.06
U_k	59.96	70.54	65.54	56.22	64.86	68.66
$C_{max,k}$	29363626	29308287	29331912	63588898	62321145	63694095
SA_k	1760513685	8889577981	2427031820	4547218912	41391071039	50377683280
Δ $AWRT_k$	33.30	0.47	42.95	67.67	-20.42	27.89
Δ U_k	-12.75	7.36	-12.60	-31.65	16.78	-7.11
Δ SA_k	-12.75	7.37	-12.70	-31.69	16.84	-7.11
Δ $C_{max,k}$	0.00	-0.01	0.05	0.05	-0.05	0.00
Δ_b $AWRT_k$	28.59	-0.17	42.24	66.46	-26.36	26.42
Δ_b U_k	-12.75	7.36	-12.60	-31.68	16.78	-7.11
Δ_b SA_k	-12.75	7.37	-12.70	-31.69	16.84	-7.11
Δ_b $C_{max,k}$	0.00	-0.01	0.05	0.00	-0.05	0.00
	73.93	18.75	7.32	80.82	7.07	12.10
$M =$	5.73	87.74	6.53	1.82	81.99	16.19
	4.42	16.97	78.61	2.62	10.63	86.75

GridARS: An Advance Reservation-Based Grid Co-allocation Framework for Distributed Computing and Network Resources

Atsuko Takefusa, Hidemoto Nakada, Tomohiro Kudoh, Yoshio Tanaka, and Satoshi Sekiguchi

National Institute of Advanced Industrial Science and Technology (AIST)
{atsuko.takefusa,hide-nakada,t.kudoh,yoshio.tanaka,
s.sekiguchi}@aist.go.jp

Abstract. For high performance parallel computing on actual Grids, one of the important issues is to co-allocate the distributed resources that are managed by various local schedulers with advance reservation. To address the issue, we proposed and developed the GridARS resource co-allocation framework, and a general advance reservation protocol that uses WSRF/GSI and a two-phased commit (2PC) protocol to enable a generic and secure advance reservation process based on distributed transactions, and provides the interface module for various existing resource schedulers. To confirm the effectiveness of GridARS, we describe the performance of a simultaneous reservation process and a case study of GridARS grid co-allocation over transpacific computing and network resources. Our experiments showed that: 1) the GridARS simultaneous 2PC reservation process is scalable and practical and 2) GridARS can co-allocate distributed resources managed by various local schedulers stably.

1 Introduction

Grid technologies allow large-scale parallel computing, namely metacomputing, over distributed computing resources managed by different organizations. A crucial issue for achieving high effective performance of fine-grain message passing applications over Grid environments is Grid co-allocation of various distributed resources.

At this point, we perform Grid co-allocation as follows:

(1) Manual reservation and job execution by SSH
The user reserves distributed resources by human negotiations such as e-mail and phone for each resource manager and performs metacomputing over the reserved resources at the reserved time. Some academic Grid test beds apply this strategy, but the problems are: it is difficult to use resources effectively, someone might use the reserved resources, and it is unrealistic to expect to have a local account on all of the available resources in large-scale Grid environments.

(2) Manual reservation of resources managed by resource schedulers
The user reserves resources manually as in (1), and administrators of the corresponding cluster managed by a batch queuing system configure a reservation

E. Frachtenberg and U. Schwiegelshohn (Eds.): JSSPP 2007, LNCS 4942, pp. 152–168, 2008.

queue according to the requirements. Then, the user submits jobs to the queues and performs metacomputing. The Tera Grid project in the US[1] adopts this strategy, which allows management of resources based on each organization's policy. On the other hand, many manual configuration errors have been reported.

(3) Automatic reservation of resources managed by resource schedulers

Resources are managed by a local batch queuing system with an advance reservation capability and a global scheduler co-allocates distributed resources for user requirements. Then the user submits jobs to the reserved queue. This strategy allows resource management based on each organization's own policy, as well as (2) avoiding human configuration errors. However, there have been several technical issues standing in the way of automatic reservation by global schedulers, as described in Section 2.

We propose GridARS (Grid Advance Reservation-based System framework), a Grid co-allocation framework for distributed resources, such as computers and network, and we developed a general advance reservation protocol over WSRF (Web Services Resource Framework)[2].

GridARS co-allocation architecture consists of a Global Resource Scheduler (GRS) and Resource Managers (RM, local schedulers), and automatically co-allocates required resources via WSRF. It enables a simultaneous reservation process for multiple resources by using a hierarchical two-phase commit (2PC) protocol between the User-GRS and GRS-RMs.

The main components of GridARS are the GridARS-Coscheduler and GridARS-WSRF. The GridARS-Coscheduler finds suitable resources for each user and co-allocates the resources by distributed transactions. GridARS-WSRF is an interface module for the proposed 2PC advance reservation protocol over WSRF. Our GridARS-WSRF implementation, called GridARS-WSRF/GT4, has been developed using Globus Toolkit 4 (GT4)[3].

To confirm the effectiveness of GridARS, we present the basic performance of our 2PC reservation process between GRS and 8 RMs over WSRF/GSI using GridARS, and describe a case study of GridARS Grid co-allocation of transpacific computing and network resources. Our experiments showed that: 1) the GridARS simultaneous 2PC reservation process is scalable and practical and 2) GridARS can co-allocate distributed resources managed by various local schedulers stably.

2   Issues for Grid Co-allocation

Various resources, such as computers, network, and storage, on Grids are generally used by local domain users. In Grid co-allocation, resource schedulers have to provide their resources for both local users and global users, and thus must aim for co-allocation over Grids, efficiently. To resolve this situation, there are the following issues:

Co-allocation of various resources. Existing Grid global scheduling system, such as Moab[4] and CSF[5] actually address only computing resources.

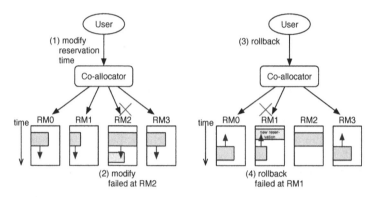

Fig. 1. An example of rollback failure by one-phase commit

However, high performance parallel computing over distributed environments requires not only computing resources, but also network resources, such as bandwidth. A global scheduling system co-allocates various resources with assured performance.

Coordination with existing resource schedulers. In order to use resources efficiently under differing domain policies, most Grid resources have been managed by resource schedulers such as GridEngine[6], TORQUE[7] or other commercial batch queuing systems. Global schedulers have to provide resources for global users in coordination with existing resource schedulers.

Advance reservation. Local resource schedulers basically allocate each user job based on strategies such as FCFS. In this situation, it is difficult to estimate when a user job will start. To co-allocate resources without losing each local resource, an advance reservation capability is required for local and global schedulers.

WSRF/GSI. WSRF is a standard interface for stateless services. Most resource schedulers provide a command line interface or a graphical interface. To provide resources for various global users, who usually do not access resource scheduler hosts by SSH or other schemes, resource schedulers and global schedulers should provide a standard WSRF interface with secure communication, such as GSI (Grid Security Infrastructure).

Two-phase commit. Resource schedulers should support a two-phase commit (2PC) reservation interface so that global schedulers can allocate distributed resources simultaneously based on distributed transactions. As shown in Fig. 1, we assume modification of reservation time on reserved resources managed by distributed resource schedulers using a one-phase commit (1PC) protocol, which most resource schedulers support. (1) After User sends a modification request to the global scheduler, called Co-allocator, Co-allocator sends the request to related resource managers. (2) In this case, RM2 has failed to modify the reservation time but the other RMs have succeeded. Then, (3) User and Co-allocator send a rollback request of the reservation time to RM0, RM1, and RM3. But at (4), the rollback has failed fatally because the rollback on RM1 has failed due to another reservation being inserted in advance.

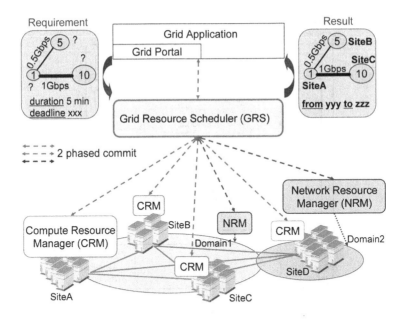

Fig. 2. Overview of the GridARS co-allocation framework

3   GridARS Grid Co-allocation Framework

In order to resolve the above issues, we propose, and have developed, a GridARS (Grid Advance Reservation-based System framework) co-allocation framework, which allows co-allocation of widely-distributed resources managed by various organizations and resource schedulers.

An overview of the GridARS co-allocation framework is shown in Fig. 2. GridARS consists of a Global Resource Scheduler (GRS) and Resource Managers (RM) for computers (CRM), network (NRM), and other resources. In each RM, existing resource schedulers manage a reservation table of their resources for advance reservation. A User sends requirements on resources and reservation time to GRS, and then GRS co-allocates suitable resources in coordination with related RMs.

The dotted lines between User-GRS and CRS-RMs in Fig. 2 indicate a two-phase commit (2PC) advance reservation process so that GRS can book distributed resources simultaneously based on distributed transactions. As shown in Fig. 2, GridARS provides a hierarchical 2PC process so that GRS can be one of the resource managers, because it is easy to coordinate with other global schedulers.

GRS consists of GridARS-Coscheduler and GridARS-WSRF. Grid-Coscheduler selects suitable resources for user requirements for resources and co-allocates the resources based on distributed transactions. GridARS-WSRF is an interface module of this 2PC WSRF reservation process. Each RM consists of GridARS-WSRF and an existing local resource scheduler.

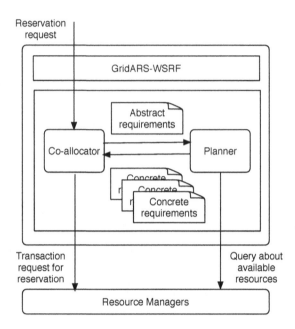

Fig. 3. GridARS-Coscheduler System Architecture

3.1   GridARS-Coscheduler

GridARS-Coscheduler consists of a Co-allocator and a Planner, as shown in
Fig. 3. Co-allocator receives user resource requirements via GridARS-WSRF
and sends the requirement to Planner. From the user request and current resource status, Planner determines candidates from among concrete resources
and then returns the planning results to Co-allocator. One solution to get distributed resource information is a centralized global information service to collect and provide local resource information. However, a commercial resource
manager cannot expose resource information, and the amount of reservation
timetable information is larger than current resource information as managed
by current information services, such as Ganglia[8]. Therefore, GridARS GRS
requests resource information from each RM directly. Planner is replaceable for
each manager strategy or user requirement.

Then, Co-allocator negotiates with the related RMs and books the resources
selected by Planner simultaneously based on distributed transactions. Details
of the reservation process will be described in Section 4. After the reservation
process has finished, Co-allocator monitors the status of the reserved resources
periodically.

3.2   GridARS-WSRF

GridARS-WSRF is a polling-based 2PC interface module for advance reservation. In a polling-based situation, the number of communications between client

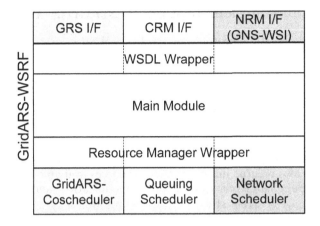

Fig. 4. GridARS-WSRF System Architecture

and server will increase, and the client detects a change of resource status behind the actual change. On the other hand, this enables asymmetric communication, e.g., a client does not have global address or firewall problems. WS-Notification[9] has been proposed for notification over web services and it also requires polling from the client side in order to detect network or server failures. Therefore, GridARS is based on polling and applies WS-Notification, optionally.

GridARS-WSRF consists of a WSDL Wrapper, a Main Module, and a Resource Manager Wrapper. Fig. 4 is an example of GRS, with CRM for the computing resource, and NRM for the network resource. WSDL Wrapper is in between the various resource interfaces and the Main Module. GridARS applies a common advance reservation protocol for reservation, modification, and release, and different resource parameter representations for each resource, because some resource representations such as JSDL[10] have already been standardized.

Main Module enables a polling-based 2PC reservation process for reservation, modification, and release. When a client invokes the reserve operation, Main Module returns a response to the client in a non-blocking manner, and sends the reserve request to resource schedulers or to the GridARS-Coscheduler. After pre-reservation has finished, it completes the reservation using the client commit request. A non-blocking manner is important for distributed systems. It avoids hang ups because of server or client side troubles, and enables recovery of each process from the failure, easily. Main Module also checks the status of reserved resources managed by the resource scheduler periodically in a polling-based manner, so that the client can get the status via the WSRF interface.

Resource Manager Wrapper provides an API for the GridARS-Coscheduler or resource schedulers. Implementing this API, existing schedulers can provide a GridARS WSRF interface without complicated WSRF coding.

4   Design and Implementation of GridARS-WSRF

The advance reservation protocol of GridARS-WSRF is based on GNS-WSI (Grid Network Service - Web Services Interface)[11] version 2 (GNS-WSI2)[12]. GNS-WSI has been defined by the G-lambda project[13], which is a collaboration of AIST, KDDI R&D Laboratories, NTT, and NICT. It is a web services-based interface for network resources for Grid middleware and applications. While the version 1 is based on pure web services, GNS-WSI2 is based on WSRF.

GridARS-WSRF provides the following services:

ReservationFactoryService. Receives registration requests to book Grid resources. It also returns information on resources available on the Grid.
ReservationService. Receives reservation, modification, and release requests. It also manages current status of reserved resources.
ReservationCommandService. Supports 2PC. It manages the status of prereserve, -modify, and -release processes, and abort or commit for each process by order of users.

ReservationResource and ReservationCommandResource are service instances for ReservationService and ReservationCommandService for each user request, respectively.

4.1   Service Operations

Table 1 shows service operations related to reservation, modification, and release for each GridARS-WSRF service. ReservationFactoryService creates ReservationResource which manages each set of reservation information and provides a query operation which provides information on available resources. The create operation returns EPR(End Point Reference) to the created ReservationResource. We call this EPR rsvEPR.

ReservationService provides operations for resource reservation / modification / release and acquisition of reserved resource status and reserved resource information. For reserve and modify, ReservationService receives requirements on resources, such as the number of clusters and CPUs, and bandwidth and reservation times, such as duration, deadline, or exact start and end time. At this point, ReservationService just returns an EPR called cmdEPR for ReservationCommandResource which manages the reserve / modify / release process. reserve, modify, and release are triggers of each command, and the actual process is managed by ReservationCommandResource.

ReservationCommandService provides notification of each command status and completes or destroys the command by order of the user. ReservationCommandService enables the 2PC WSRF reservation process.

4.2   Resource Status Transition and Advance Reservation Protocol

ReservationStatus is a property of ReservationResource and represents the current reservation status for each reservation request. The ReservationStatus transition process is shown in Fig. 5. The ReservationStatus transition process consists of the following:

Table 1. Service operations related to reservation, modification, and release

Operation name	Action	Input / Output
ReservationFactoryService		
create	Creates *ReservationResource*	- / *rsvEPR*
getAvailableResources	Provides available resource information	conditions / available resource information
ReservationService (Accessed using *rsvEPR*)		
reserve	Makes resource reservation	Requirements on resources and reservation time / *cmdEPR*
modify	Modifies reserved resources	Requirements on resources and reservation time / *cmdEPR*
release	Releases reserved resources	- / *cmdEPR*
getReservationStatus	Returns reserved resource status	- / reserved resource status
getResourceProperty (*GridResources*)	Returns reservation result	Resource property name / Reserved resource information
ReservationCommandService (Accessed using *cmdEPR*)		
commit	Completes reserve/modify/ release process	- / -
abort	Destroys reserve/modify/ release process	- / -
getReservation-CommandStatus	Returns current status of (pre-)reserve/modify/release	- / status of the pre-process

Created. *ReservationResource* is created.
Reserved. Requested resources are booked.
Activated. The resources are activated.
Released. The resources are released.
Error. Errors have occurred.

create, *reserve*, *modify*, and *release* in Fig. 5 indicate operations of Table 1 invoked by a client. *S* and *F* represent success and failure or destruction by the client of each command. The gray squares represent status changes at the server side.

ReservationCommandStatus is a property of *ReservationCommandResource* and represents the current command status of each *ReservationCommandResource* created by a reservation-related operation such as *reserve*, *modify*, or *release*. The *ReservationCommandStatus* transition process is shown in Fig. 6. The *ReservationCommandStatus* transition process consists of the following:

Initial. *reserve/modify/release* command has been sent to an actual resource manager, but the request has not been completed yet.
Prepared. The requested command has been prepared.
Committed. The command has been completed.
Aborted. The requested resources are not available or the pre-command has expired.

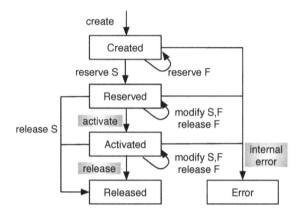

Fig. 5. The ReservationStatus transition process

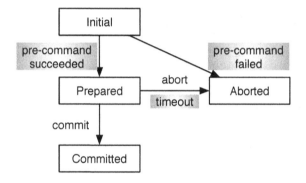

Fig. 6. The ReservationCommandStatus transition process

commit and *abort* in Fig. 6 are invoked by the client, and the gray squares also represent status changes at the server side. After *ReservationCommandStatus* has changed to *Prepared*, the client invokes *commit* and *abort*.

We use a modified two-phase commit protocol. Fundamentally, a two-phase commit is a blocking protocol. If a coordinator fails after a *reserve* request, *ReservationCommandStatus* may be left in the *Prepared* state until the coordinator is repaired and the requested resources are blocked for that duration. Moreover, a coordinator and its cohorts are loosely coupled on the Grid, and the coordinator may not issue a *commit* or *abort* request.

We applied an automatic "time out" to the transit from *Prepared* to *Aborted*. In our system, *Prepared* waiting for a commit or abort request times out at $T_{timeout}$ as follows:

$$T_{timeout} = T_{transit} + \epsilon \tag{1}$$

$T_{transit}$ indicates the state transit time from *Initial* to *Prepared*.

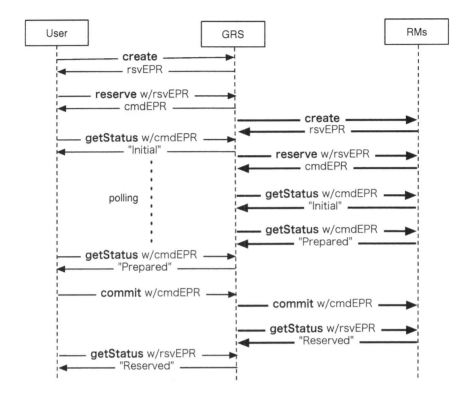

Fig. 7. Protocol sequence of advance reservation process

4.3   Protocol Sequence of the Advance Reservation Process

We describe the protocol sequence of our advance resource reservation process in Fig. 7. As described in Section 3.2, each operation is non-blocking and based on a polling method.

User calls the *create* operation provided by GRS *ReservationFactoryService*, *ReservationResource* is created and the EPR (*rsvEPR*) is returned to User. After User calls *reserve* using *rsvEPR*, GRS starts to co-allocate the requested resources.

GRS collects available resource information, such as CPUs and bandwidth, by the *getAvailableResources* operation provided by RMs. Using the information obtained, GRS selects suitable resources and co-allocates the resource in coordination with related RMs based on distributed transactions. The bold lines in Fig. 7 represent a simultaneous process by transactions between GRS and RMs.

The reservation process between GRS and each RM is performed in the same manner between User and GRS.

After all of related RMs' *ReservationCommandStatus* have been changed to *Prepared*, GRS's *ReservationCommandStatus* is changed to *Prepared* and GRS waits for a user *commit* or *abort* request. If User detects a *Prepared* status, User sends GRS the *commit* request and then GRS sends *commit* to the related RMs.

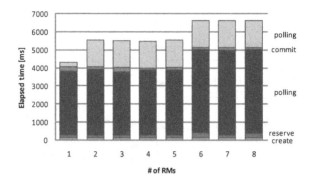

Fig. 8. Elapsed time of simultaneous resource reservation processes (no additional latency)

After the reservation process has completed at the related RMs, *ReservationStatus* of GRS and the appropriate RMs is changed to *Reserved*. User can search for success for the resource reservation to check the *ReservationStatus* via the *getReservationStatus* operation. Then, User acquires the reserved resource information.

4.4   Reference Implementation of GridARS-WSRF

We have developed a reference implementation of GridARS-WSRF named GridARS-WSRF/GT4 using Globus Toolkit4 (GT4). GridARS-WSRF/GT4 allows user authentication and authorization by GSI (Grid Security Infrastructure) as provided by GT4. GSI supports capabilities of authentication by certificates based on PKI (Public Key Infrastructure) and authorization by the grid-mapfile which maps global user name in the certificate on local user name. GRS also adopts a GSI delegation capability and books resources by each user authority.

We apply JSDL for compute resources and GNS-WSI2 for network resources, and extend them to represent advance reservation requirements.

5   Performance Measurement

The elapsed time of simultaneous resource reservation processes based on distributed transactions, compared to the number of RMs is shown in Fig. 8, Fig. 9, and Fig. 10. In these experiments, we emulate an actual Grid environment in our cluster, where all the hosts of GRS and eight RMs are deployed. User is located on the GRS host. Latencies between the hosts of GRS and RMs are 200 [us] in this cluster. In the experiments in Fig. 9 and Fig. 10, we configured additional 186 [ms] latencies on the paths to one RM or all RMs. 186 [ms] equals the latency between Tokyo and North Carolina, where the GRS and one of the RMs in US were located in the experiment described in Section 6. It takes 2 [sec]

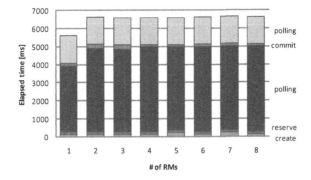

Fig. 9. Elapsed time of simultaneous resource reservation processes (additional latency on the path to RM1)

for each pre-reservation and 1 [sec] for completion of each requested reservation at each RM.

For all graphs, the horizontal axis indicates the number of RMs invoked simultaneously in a reservation request, and the vertical axis indicates the elapsed time of the entire resource reservation process. Details of elapsed times are shown on the right hand side. create / reserve / polling / commit / polling in all graphs correspond to User's invocation in Fig. 7. All of the results show the shortest elapsed time for ten trials over WSRF/GSI, respectively.

Comparing the three graphs, the elapsed times of Fig. 9 and Fig. 10 are comparable, and longer than those of Fig. 8; this is because the latest reservation process at an RM determines the total elapsed time in transactions. On the other hand, when the number of RMs increases, the elapsed times increase because of the load at GRS, but they are around 6.7 [sec]. Therefore, the GridARS co-allocation framework works efficiently on Grids on which GRS and RMs are widely-distributed.

6   Case Study: A Trans-Pacific Experiment Using GridARS

We conducted a demonstration[14] at GLIF2006[15] and SC06[16]. In this demonstration, a user booked trans-pacific computing and network resources managed by different organizations, and we performed operations an actual parallel applications over the reserved resources. The demonstration was in cooperation with G-lambda and the EnLIGHTened Computing project[17].

In this experiment, a user submits requirements on resources from the portal system, GridARS makes corresponding reservations, and then the user invokes a parallel application via WS GRAM of GT4. The parallel application starts at the reserved time, automatically. We use QM/MD simulation developed using GridMPI[18] for the application program.

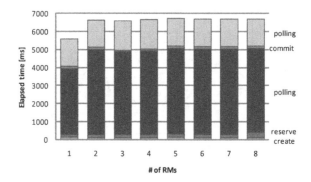

Fig. 10. Elapsed time of simultaneous resource reservation processes (additional latencies on the paths to all RMs)

QM/MD simulation simulates a chemical reaction process based on the Nudged Elastic Band (NEB) method[19]. In this simulation, the energy of each image is calculated by combining classical molecular dynamic (MD) simulation with quantum mechanics (QM) simulation, in parallel. MD and QM simulations were performed on distributed clusters in Japan and the US using GridMPI, which is a Grid-enabled reference implementation of MPI.

The experimental environment is as follows:

- # of sites (clusters) = 10 (7 sites in Japan and 3 sites in the US)
- # of network domains = 4 (3 domains in Japan and 1 domain in the US)
- CRM composition: GridARS-WSRF/GT4, PluS[20] and GridEngine[6] (Japan), Maui[21] and TORQUE[7] (US)
- NRM composition: NRMs developed by KDDI R&D Labs, NTT*EnLIGHTened Computing* C and AIST, respectively. *EnLIGHTened Computing* and AIST NRMs were developed using GridARS-WSRF/GT4.

We booked compute and network resources in the US via HARC (Highly-Available Resource Co-allocator)[22] developed by EnLIGHTened. The EnLIGHTened and G-lambda teams developed wrappers to enable interoperability across our middleware stacks, so that GRS could book resources in the US with our distributed transactions. PluS and Maui are plugin schedulers which allow advance reservation on existing batch queuing systems.

Fig. 11 shows the reservation resource monitor service display and the simulation results output at the experiment.

In this demonstration, we sent 10 [min] reservation requests, submitted a QM/MD simulation into local scheduler queues in the reserved sites, and performed the simulation, continuously. Although the reservation cycle is shorter than that of general use cases, GridARS worked stably during the demonstrations.

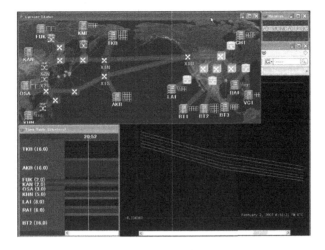

Fig. 11. The reservation resource monitor service display and the simulation results output at the experiment

7   Related Work

There have been several global schedulers which allow metacomputing over distributed computing environment. In Moab Grid Suites[4], the Moab Grid Workload Manager can co-allocate distributed computing resources managed by the Maui Cluster Scheduler and TORQUE Resource Manager. Moab is a commercial Grid scheduling suite, and it also provides monitoring and reporting tools and a portal system for end users In general use, only administrators can make reservations, but users can submit a reservation request and their jobs from the portal.

CSF4 (Community Scheduler Framework)[5] developed using GT4 is a WSRF-based scheduling framework for computing resources. The CSF MetaScheduler can submit user jobs to queuing systems, Platform LSF[23], GridEngine, and Open PBS[24]. CSF supports an advance reservation capability for LSF clusters. CSF is open source and provides a Portlet GUI, but LSF is a commercial queuing system.

GUR[25] is a global scheduler which supports advance reservation. It is offered in cooperation with the Catalina external scheduler, and can work with TORQUE and LoadLeveler. GUR finds and books available resources to communicate with Catalina schedulers, one by one. Communication between GUR and Catalina is SSH or GSI-enabled SSH.

While Moab, CSF, and GUR support only computing resources, the VIOLA MetaScheduling Service (MSS)[26] can co-allocate both computing and network resources as well as work with GridARS. MSS works on UNICORE[27]-based Grid environments. The communication between MSS and the other components will be based on WS-Agreement[28] for establishing agreement between a service provider and consumer.

HARC developed by the EnLIGHTened Computing project is a co-allocation system, which consists of Acceptors and Resource Managers. HARC applies the Paxos commit protocol[29] to enhance fault-tolerancy of the Acceptor (coordinator) side. Each requirement on resources is represented by an XML documents and sent to the HARC Acceptors and Resource Managers by REST-styled HTTP messaging.

However, there are no other co-allocation systems which support a safe transaction process by 2PC over the standard WSRF interface and that satisfies all the requirements as described in Section 2.

8   Conclusions

We propose the GridARS Grid co-allocation framework for management of various distributed resources such as computers and network, and we developed a general 2PC advance reservation protocol over WSRF.

The GridARS co-allocation architecture consists of Global Resource Scheduler (GRS) and Resource Managers (RM) and automatically co-allocates required resources, simultaneously. The main components of GridARS are GridARS-Coscheduler and GridARS-WSRF. GridARS-Coscheduler finds suitable resources for each user and co-allocates the resources based on distributed transactions. GridARS-WSRF is an interface module for the proposed advance reservation protocol.

Using a reference implementation, called GridARS-WSRF/GT4, we investigated the basic performance of the 2PC reservation process over WSRF/GSI on emulated Grid environments. The results showed that the GridARS co-allocation framework and the simultaneous reservation process worked efficiently on Grids on which GRS and RMs are widely-distributed.

Also, we described a case study of Grid co-allocation for transpacific computing and network resources using GridARS-WSRF/GT4. The experiment shows GridARS can co-allocate distributed computing and network resources managed by various multiple-domain local schedulers, stably.

For future work, we plan to make the reservation protocol more practical and investigate suitable co-allocation algorithms for multiple resources. We also plan to collaborate with other Grid co-allocation systems, such as VIOLA MSS.

Acknowledgements

We thank all of the members of G-lambda and the EnLIGHTened Computing project. This work is partly funded by the Science and Technology Promotion Program's "Optical Paths Network Provisioning based on Grid Technologies" of MEXT, Japan.

References

1. TeraGrid, `http://www.teragrid.org/`
2. OASIS Web Services Resource Framework (WSRF) TC: Web Services Resource 1.2 (WS-Resource) Committee Specification (2006)
3. Foster, I.: Globus Toolkit Version 4: Software for Service-Oriented Systems. In: Jin, H., Reed, D., Jiang, W. (eds.) NPC 2005. LNCS, vol. 3779, pp. 2–13. Springer, Heidelberg (2005)
4. Moab Grid Scheduler (Silver) Administrator's Guide, version 4.0, `http://www.clusterresources.com/products/mgs/docs/`
5. Community Scheduler Framework, `http://sf.net/projects/gcsf`
6. Grid Engine, `http://gridengine.sunsource.net/`
7. TORQUE Resource Manager, `http://www.clusterresources.com/resource-manager.php`
8. Ganglia Monitoring System, `http://ganglia.info/`
9. OASIS Web Services Notification (WSN) TC: Web Services Base Notification 1.3 (WS-BaseNotification) Public Review Draft 02 (2005)
10. Anjomshoaa, A., Brisard, F., Drescher, M., Fellows, D., Ly, A., McGough, S., Pulsipher, D., Savva, A.: Job Submission Description Language (JSDL) Specification v1.0 (2005)
11. Takefusa, A., Hayashi, M., Nagatsu, N., Nakada, H., Kudoh, T., Miyamoto, T., Otani, T., Tanaka, H., Suzuki, M., Sameshima, Y., Imajuku, W., Jinno, M., Takigawa, Y., Okamoto, S., Tanaka, Y., Sekiguchi, S.: G-lambda: Coordination of a Grid Scheduler and Lambda Path Service over GMPLS. Future Generation Computing Systems 22(2006), 868–875 (2006)
12. Takefusa, A., Hayashi, M., Hirano, A., Okamoto, S., Kudoh, T., Miyamoto, T., Tsukishima, Y., Otani, T., Nakada, H., Tanaka, H., Taniguchi, A., Sameshima, Y.: GNS-WSI2 Grid Network Service - Web Services Interface, version 2, OGF19, GHPN-RG (2007)
13. The G-lambda project, `http://www.g-lambda.net/`
14. Thorpe, S.R., Battestilli, L., Karmous-Edwards, G., Hutanu, A., MacLaren, J., Mambretti, J., Moore, J.H., Sundar, K.S., Xin, Y., Takefusa, A., Hayashi, M., Hirano, A., Okamoto, S., Kudoh, T., Miyamoto, T., Tsukishima, Y., Otani, T., Nakada, H., Tanaka, H., Taniguchi, A., Sameshima, Y., Jinno, M.: G-lambda and EnLIGHTened: Wrapped In Middleware Co-allocating Compute and Network Resources Accross Japan and the US. In: Proc. GridNets (to appear, 2007)
15. GLIF: Global Lambda Integrated Facility, `http://www.glif.is/`
16. SC06, `http://sc06.supercomputing.org/`
17. The EnLIGHTened Computing project, `http://enlightenedcomputing.org/`
18. GridMPI, `http://www.gridmpi.org/`
19. Ogata, S., Shimo, F., Kalia, R., Nakano, A., Vashisha, P.: Hybrid Quantum Mechanical/Molecular Dynamics Simulations on Parallel Computers: Density Functional Theory on Real-space Multigrids. Computer Physics Communications, p. 30
20. Nakada, H., Takefusa, A., Ookubo, K., Kishimoto, M., Kudoh, T., Tanaka, Y., Sekiguchi, S.: Design and Implementation of a Local Scheduling System with Advance Reservation for Co-allocation on the Grid. In: Proc. CIT 2006 (2006)
21. Maui Cluster Scheduler, `http://www.clusterresources.com/pages/products/maui-cluster-scheduler.php`

22. HARC: The Highly-Available Robust Co-allocator,
    http://www.cct.lsu.edu/~maclaren/HARC/
23. Zhou, S.: LSF: Load sharing in large-scale heterogeneous distributed systems. In:
    Proc. Workshop on Cluster Computing (1992)
24. OpenPBS, http://www.openpbs.org/
25. Yoshimoto, K., Kovatch, P., Andrews, P.: Co-scheduling with User-Settable Reser-
    vations. In: Feitelson, D.G., Frachtenberg, E., Rudolph, L., Schwiegelshohn, U.
    (eds.) JSSPP 2005. LNCS, vol. 3834, pp. 146–156. Springer, Heidelberg (2005)
26. Barz, C., Pilz, M., Eickermann, T., Kirtchakova, L., Waldrich, O., Ziegler, W.: Co-
    Allocation of Compute and Network Resources in the VIOLA Testbed, TR-0051,
    CoreGrid (2006)
27. UNICORE, http://www.kfa-juelich.de/unicore/
28. Andrieux, A., Czajkowski, K., Dan, A., Keathey, K., Ludwig, H., Nakata, T.,
    Pruyne, J., Rofrano, J., Tuecke, S., Xu, M.: Web Services Agreement Speci-
    fication (WS-Agreement) (2005), https://forge.gridforum.org/sf/docman/do/
    downloadDocument/projects.graap-wg/docman.root.current_drafts/doc6090
29. Gray, J., Lamport, L.: Consensus on Transaction Commit, MSR-TR-2003-96, Mi-
    crosoft Research (2004)

A Self-optimized Job Scheduler for Heterogeneous Server Clusters

Elad Yom-Tov and Yariv Aridor

IBM Haifa Research Lab, Haifa 31905, Israel
yomtov@il.ibm.com, yariv.aridor@gmail.com

Abstract. Heterogeneous clusters and grid infrastructures are becoming increasingly popular. In these computing infrastructures, machines have different resources, including memory sizes, disk space, and installed software packages. These differences give rise to a problem of over-provisioning, that is, sub-optimal utilization of a cluster due to users requesting resource capacities greater than what their jobs actually need. Our analysis of a real workload file (LANL CM5) revealed differences of up to two orders of magnitude between requested memory capacity and actual memory usage. This paper presents an algorithm to estimate actual resource capacities used by batch jobs. Such an algorithm reduces the need for users to correctly predict the resources required by their jobs, while at the same time managing the scheduling system to obtain superior utilization of available hardware. The algorithm is based on the Reinforcement Learning paradigm; it learns its estimation policy on-line and dynamically modifies it according to the overall cluster load. The paper includes simulation results which indicate that our algorithm can yield an improvement of over 30% in utilization (overall throughput) of heterogeneous clusters.

1 Introduction

1.1 Background

Heterogeneous clusters and grid infrastructures are becoming increasingly popular. In these computing infrastructures, the machines have different computing power and resources (memory, networking, etc.). Additionally, machines can dynamically join and leave the systems at any time. Job schedulers provide a means of sending jobs for execution on these computing clusters. A job is defined as a set of processes that run, in parallel, on a single computer or on multiple computers. Dynamic approaches to resource management play a significant role in the management and utilization of these infrastructures. With these approaches, the job submitted together with a specification of the type and capacity of resources required for successful execution e.g., amount of memory and disk space, and prerequisite software packages. When a job is scheduled, its job request is matched with the available resources. If all the required resources are found, they are allocated and the job is launched for execution.

E. Frachtenberg and U. Schwiegelshohn (Eds.): JSSPP 2007, LNCS 4942, pp. 169–187, 2008.

Dynamic resource matching between jobs and resources has been extensively researched over the years, initially for homogeneous clusters and more recently for heterogeneous and grid computing environments [3]. However, one problem that has rarely been examined is over-provisioning. That is, jobs are allocated more resources than what they actually need due to users overestimating the job requirements. With over-provisioning, we specifically refer to resources in a given computing machine that can affect the completion of the job execution. That is, if the capacity of these resources falls below a certain level, the job cannot complete successfully. Examples of such resources are memory size, disk space, and even prerequisite software packages. This paper focuses on the over-provisioning problem. We do not deal with the problem of over-provisioning the number of machines requested for parallel jobs. This is a complicated problem, which is heavily dependent on the programming model used (i.e., whether the number of machines is hard-coded in the job source program).

Over-provisioning affects machine utilization as best explained by the following scenario. Assume two machines, M1 and M2, and two jobs, J1 and J2. Assume M1 has a larger memory size than M2. Initially, J1 can run on either M1 or M2. However, the resource allocation matches it with machine M1 because the user requests a memory size larger than that of M2, but possible for M1. Later, J2 arrives. Due to its memory size request, the only machine it can use is M1. Now J2 is blocked until J1 completes or a new node with at least the same memory size as M1 is added to the cluster.

The over-provisioning problem is demonstrated in Figure 1. This figure shows a histogram of the ratio of requested to used memory in the LANL CM5 log [19]. As this figure demonstrates, less than 70% of jobs correctly estimate their required memory. In over 30% of jobs there is a mismatch by a factor of two or more between requested memory and used memory. The regression line in the figure shows the fit of the over-provisioning ratio to the percentage of jobs. The R^2 coefficient[1] for this regression line is 0.69. This fitting shows that it is possible to estimate, with high accuracy, the fraction of jobs with a given over-provisioning ratio in future log files from similar systems. This is an important design consideration in some learning algorithms.

Unfortunately, it is frequently difficult for most users to correctly specify the needs of their jobs. Therefore, this is a persistent problem which causes waste of computing resources. Ideally, the scheduler in a parallel system should independently overcome this problem by estimating actual user needs. This article attempts to show how such an autonomic scheduler could be used.

Research of the over-provisioning problem is difficult, in part because there are few workload files that contain information on requested resources versus actual used resources per job. One workload file we found useful is the LANL CM5 [19] workload file. It contains a record of 122,055 jobs submitted to a Thinking Machines CM-5 cluster at the Los Alamos National Lab (LANL) over

---

[1] R^2 is a measure of fitness between the points on the graph and the regression line [17]. It represents the percentage of the data variance explained by the regression line. A high R^2 (i.e., closer to 1) represents a better fit.

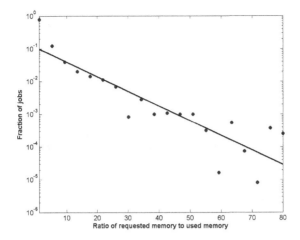

Fig. 1. A histogram of the ratio between requested memory size and actual memory used, per job, in the LANL CM5 workload file. The vertical axis is logarithmically scaled.

approximately two years. We used this workload file in our simulations for estimation of memory capacity per job (see Section 3).

1.2   Related Work

Resource management, including monitoring, matching, and allocation, is a well documented area of research. Basic dynamic resource matching is already implemented by all common scheduler systems (e.g., LoadLeveler [7], Condor [9], PBS [5], and LSF [20]) for mostly homogeneous clusters. Condor [1] suggests a declarative language (called ClassAd) and system infrastructure to match job requests for resources with resource owners. Jobs and resources declare their capabilities, constraints, and preferences using ClassAds. Each job is matched with a single machine to run the job; that is, two ClassAds are matched against each other. The basic match-making process deals only with a single resource, hence, one-to-one matching. Also, successful matching occurs when the available resource capacity is equal to or greater than the job request [13].

Several works already extend and optimize dynamic resource allocation specifically for heterogeneous computing environments. An extension for optimal one-to-many matching between a single job and multiple heterogeneous resources is described in [10]. The optimal co-matching of resources is based on application-specific global and aggregation constraints (e.g., total memory size, running all application tasks in the same grid domain). Still, in its essence, it follows the basic matching where on every machine, the amount of resources is equal to or greater than the job request. A similar problem is also solved by [14].

A linear programming approach for the resource-matching problem in a grid is described in [12]. This approach deals with sharing (not necessarily dedicated) resources and many-to-many matching between all jobs in the queue and available resources. Using linear programming instead of a user-specified mechanism as in [10], matching is optimized for different global objectives such as load balancing, throughput (matching as many jobs as possible), and minimizing the number of grid resources used.

A fuzzy resource management framework is proposed in [8]. In this framework, resource allocation is based on a quantitative model as opposed to a binary model. Every resource (e.g., machine) is given a fuzzy value between 0 and 1, which indicates its capabilities (e.g., high/low memory, high/low MFLOPS). Every job is also assigned a fuzzy value, which indicates its nature (e.g., IO intensive, CPU-bound). The matching process tries to maximize the matching of different resource capabilities with the job's nature. Depending on the categorization of job and resource capabilities, this approach can solve the under-utilization scenario, described in Section 1.1, using a completely different approach from the one proposed in this paper.

Another approach from a different perspective replaces the user's runtime estimate with automatic learning of the job runtimes needed to optimize the backfilling scheduling algorithms [16]. While this is not a resource-matching problem *per se*, it is an example of using a learning method to optimize over-estimation of the user's input in scheduling systems, which is very similar in spirit to the approach suggested in this paper.

Previously, we addressed the problem of resource estimation in cases where similar jobs can be identified [21]. If there exists a metric which identifies two jobs that use similar resource capacities based on the job parameters, a simple learning algorithm can be used to estimate required resources. This is explained briefly below.

2   Learning to Estimate Job Requirements

2.1   The General Approach

All known approaches for dynamic matching between jobs and resources select resources whose available capacity is greater than or equal to the users' specifications. We propose an approach that can select resources whose capacity might also be lower than the job request.

Our approach is based on using automatic learning techniques to estimate the actual job requirements. These requirements assist the job scheduler in matching the jobs to computers with lower resource capacity than that specified by the job requests. These jobs have a high probability of successful termination even though they are assigned fewer resources (e.g., memory capacity) or even no resources at all (e.g., ignore some software packages that are defined as prerequisites), based on experience learned from earlier submitted jobs (e.g., how many actual resources they used). As such, our approach deals efficiently with the basic scenario described in Section 1.1.

In principle, we envision a resource estimation phase prior to resource allocation (see Figure 2). When a job is submitted to the scheduler, its actual job requirements are estimated, based on past experience with previously submitted jobs. Then, the resource allocator matches these estimated job requirements with available resources instead of matching them based on the original job require- ments. Once a job completes (either successfully or unsuccessfully), the estimator gathers feedback information to improve its resource approximation for future job submissions (e.g., actual resources used). If jobs terminate unsuccessfully due to insufficient resource capacities they will be resubmitted for execution either by the users or automatically by the scheduling system (see below).

In this work we assume that job requirements are always equal to or greater than the actual used resources. We do not attempt to approximate actual job re- quirements in cases where the original job resources requested are insufficient for successful execution of the job. Also, the proposed estimator is independent and can be integrated with different scheduling policies (e.g., FCFS, shortest-first- job), backfilling and different resource allocation schemes. Finally, the primary goal of the estimator is to free unused resources, which otherwise would have been allocated to jobs. As such, it is oriented towards heterogeneous cluster environ- ments in which high throughput (and derived measurements such as slowdown) are the primary goals.

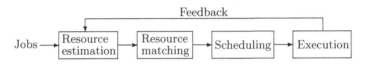

Fig. 2. Schematic diagram of the scheduling process with estimation of job requirements

2.2 Usability Issues

Our approach for automatic resource estimation in job schedulers has several implicit assumptions regarding jobs and user experience:

1. Potential side-effects of job failures due to insufficient resources, for exam- ple, temporary opened files and allocated storage, are no different than side- effects due to other type of failures, e.g., user aborts or segmentation viola- tion. Moreover, they are handled by similar methods and techniques such as postmortem reset and cleanup processes.
2. Users will be made aware of automatic resource allocation and the possibil- ity of job failures due to insufficient resources. They can disable or enable automatic resource estimation for various reasons, on a per job basis, for example by adding a corresponding Boolean flag in the job request files.
3. Users have means (e.g., error logs and traces) to identify job failures due to insufficient resources. Otherwise, they may decide to disable automatic resource allocation for specific jobs. Also, if the system needs to identify these failures and resubmit jobs in an automatic fashion, some policies need to be identified. For example, many jobs allocate their memory at the initialization

Table 1. Algorithms for resource estimation

		Feedback type	
		Implicit	Explicit
Identification of similar jobs	Yes	Successive approximation	Last instance identification
	No	RL with classification	RL with regression

phase. Thus, if job execution lasts for more than one minute, it indicates that the job will not fail due to low memory resources [11].

4. Jobs with insufficient resources will eventually fail. For example, jobs which may have different behavior because of insufficient memory, i.e., intensive swapping operations, are outside the scope of our paper.

2.3 Methods for Estimation of Job Requirements

Estimating job requirements depends on two main factors: the ability to infer similarity of jobs and the type of feedback offered by the scheduling system. Table 1 suggests four possible algorithms for estimating resource capacity, based on these two factors.

Similar jobs are defined as jobs that require similar amounts of resource capacity, where similar refers to capacity values that are all within a specific range (hence similarity range), for example, 10%. This range value is a qualitative measurement for the similarity of jobs within a group (i.e., there isn't a criterion for non-similar jobs). The lower the value, the more similar the jobs. It is beneficial to identify similarity groups with very low ranges. This improves the effectiveness of the resource estimator.

In this context, the resources are all system resources handled by the estimator and available for running jobs. If a job does not use a specific resource, we consider it to consume zero capacity of this resource. The similar jobs are **disjoint** groups of job submissions that use similar amounts of resource capacities.

The most simple case of similar jobs is repeated job submissions. Assume every job is assigned a unique identifier (ID), which can be used to recognize repeated submissions of the exact same job (i.e., same program, input data, and input parameters). In this case, a similarity group would include all the repeated submissions of a specific job and the resource estimator would use the experience gathered from previous submissions of that job to estimate the actual job requirements. Unfortunately, in many cases, such job IDs are not available. For example, most of the workload files in [19] do not include job IDs. Also, job IDs (assigned by users) may be a restrictive approach, narrowing the job space in which similar jobs are detected.

A more general method is to determine a set of job request parameters that can be used to identify similarity groups. This can be done by observation, where we find parameters that indicate jobs using similar resources. Alternatively, one can partition a set of jobs into groups that use similar resources and train a classifier to classify new jobs into their similarity group. By default, this process will be done offline (i.e., not as part of the resource matching process itself), using traces of feedback from previous job submissions, as part of the training (customization) phase of the estimator.

As noted above the second factor which affects estimation of job requirements is the type of feedback gathered after each job is executed. Feedback can range from implicit to explicit. **Implicit feedback** refers to a Boolean value indicating whether the job completed successfully or not. This is a basic indication supported by every cluster and scheduling system. **Explicit feedback** also includes the actual amount of resources used by a job upon its termination. Explicit feedback depends on the availability of a cluster infrastructure to gather and report this information. The feedback information is used to refine the approximation and get closer to the actual job requirements.

In practice, some balance between explicit and implicit feedback can probably be expected. That is, explicit feedback will be available for some resources, but not all of them. Explicit feedback is more informative and it is therefore expected that resource estimation will achieve better performance compared to cases where only implicit feedback is given. An additional drawback of resource estimation using implicit feedback is that it is more prone to false positive cases. These cases are, for example, job failures due to faulty programming (e.g., a job generating an exception) or faulty machines. These failures might mislead the estimator into assuming that the job failed due to insufficient estimated resources. In the case of explicit feedback, however, such confusion can be avoided by comparing the resource capacities allocated to the job and the actual resource capacities used.

The following paragraphs provide a description of methods for resource estimation that do not assume similar jobs can be identified. Methods that require the detection of similar jobs were described in detail in [21] and are not further elaborated on for lack of space. In this paper we focus here on the practical on-line algorithms (that do not require an off-line training phase for their operation).

The estimation of actual job requirements without job similarity is best approached using Reinforcement Learning (RL) [6]. RL is a class of learning algorithms where an agent learns a behavior policy by exploring a state-space. The agent can take actions, where it receives rewards for good actions or penalties for poor actions. The goal of the agent is to maximize its cumulative reward by modifying its behavior policy. RL has been applied to autonomous systems before, for example for improving load balancing by applications in server farms [15].

In the context of resource estimation, at each step the RL agent (the resource estimator) attempts to determine a policy of whether a job can be submitted for execution. The policy is learned on-line, based on the system state, (i.e., the status of each node whether idle or busy, and if busy, for how long), the resources of each machine, and the requested resource capacities of the jobs in the queue. A reward would be an improvement in utilization or slowdown, whereas a penalty would be a decrease in these parameters. The RL policy is initially random, but converges to a stable policy over time, via a process of trial and error. RL algorithms can also adjust the policy over time if system behavior changes. The main differences with methods that use similarity groups is that in RL, the policy is global and applied to all jobs, and that learning is performed on-line (i.e., with no training phase).

RL is general enough to be applied with either explicit or implicit feedback. Explicit feedback will help reach a more fine-grained policy, with a better estimation of the average actual resource capacities through learning of a regression model. This is done by estimating the actual resource requirements. If implicit feedback is available, a classification model will be employed which, at each time step, would decide whether or not the job can be submitted using currently available resources.

In this work, we unified the two methods (classification and regression) by using a non-linear Perceptron for estimating the job requirements. In the case of explicit feedback, the Perceptron attempts to estimate the actual resources required, after which it can be decided whether the job can be submitted using currently available resources. If only implicit feedback is available, the Perceptron only decides whether or not the job can be submitted for execution.

Pseudo-code of the reinforcement learning algorithm is shown in Algorithm 1. This algorithm is based on the SoftMax strategy [18]. The algorithm is initiated (line 1) with a separate weight vector $\mathbf{w}$ for each resource capacity. For simplicity, in the following we assume only a single resource capacity should be estimated. In our simulations we attempted to estimate the required memory capacity for each job.

When a job is submitted, its required resources are estimated by the Perceptron (line 3). The Perceptron uses as input a feature vector derived from parameters of the job request file (for example, the requested resource capacities) and from system measurements such as the number of free nodes, the load on the input queue, etc.

If the estimated resources can be satisfied using currently available resources, the job is executed. However, even if current resource capacities cannot satisfy the estimated resources, the job might still executed. A random number is generated (line 7) and if it is larger than a threshold, the job will be sent for execution with zero estimated resources. The threshold is the probability determined by a Gibbs distribution of the parameter p, which is the fraction of successful executions so far. This is the exploration stage of the RL paradigm.

If explicit feedback is available (lines 12-13) a successfully executed job (i.e., one that was allocated sufficient resource capacities) reports the utilized capacity. If it failed, it reports the maximal allocated capacity. This means that learning in the case of failure is hindered by the fact that the estimator only knows that the allocated resource capacity was insufficient, but not what the job would have required for a successful execution. If implicit feedback is available (lines 15-16), only a Boolean indicator of success or failure is given.

Algorithm 1. Reinforcement learning algorithm for estimating job requirements. J denotes a job, E' denotes the estimated resource capacity, E the available resource capacity, and U the used resource capacity. $\mathbf{w}$ is the weight vector of the Perceptron operating on a job feature vector $\mathbf{x}$, $f\left(\cdot\right)$ the activation function of the Perceptron and $f'\left(\cdot\right)$ the derivative of this function with respect to w. p is the fraction of successful executions so far. $rand$ denotes a random number chosen uniformly from $[0, 1]$. η is a learning constant and τ the decay constant for the RL algorithm.

```
 1: Initialize w = 0, p = 0.5
 2: for each submitted job J do
 3:     The estimated resource capacity E' = f (w · xᵀ).
 4:     if E' ≤ E then
 5:         Submit job to scheduler using E' as required resource capacity
 6:     else
 7:         if rand > eᵖ/ᵗ / (eᵖ/ᵗ + e⁽¹⁻ᵖ⁾/ᵗ) then
 8:             Submit job to scheduler using zero as the required resource capacity
 9:         end if
10:     end if
11:     if explicit feedback is available then
12:         t = { U  if J terminated successfully
               { E  if J terminated unsuccessfully
13:         z = E'
14:     else
15:         t = { +1  if J terminated successfully
               { −1  if J terminated unsuccessfully
16:         z = { +1  if E' ≤ E
               { −1  if E' > E
17:     end if
18:     dE = f' (w · xᵀ)
19:     dw = η · (t − z) · dE · xᵀ
20:     w = w + dw
21:     Update p such that p is the fraction of successful job executions.
22: end for
```

Finally, the Perceptron weights and the exploration threshold p are updated according to the execution results (lines 18-21). The Perceptron is updated with the object of minimizing the error between the estimator and the actual results, where both estimation and actual results are dependent on feedback type, as defined in lines 12-16.

3 Simulations

3.1 Metrics for Evaluation

The rate at which jobs are submitted for execution on a computing cluster is measured by the **offered load**. The higher the rate, the higher the offered load.

Given a set of jobs arriving at time a_i, each requiring M_i nodes for a run-time of T_i seconds $(i = 1, 2, \ldots, N)$, the offered load is computed as:

$$Offered\ Load\ =\ \sum_{i=1}^{N} M_i \cdot T_i / (M_T \cdot (a_N + T_N)) \tag{1}$$

where M_T is the total number of nodes in the cluster.

We used two main metrics, **slowdown** and **utilization**, to evaluate the proposed algorithm. Slowdown [4] is a measure of the time users' jobs wait for execution, calculated using the following formula:

$$Slowdown\ =\ \frac{1}{N} \sum_{i=1}^{N} (W_i + M_i) / M_i \tag{2}$$

where W_i is the time that the i-th job waited in the input queue. One possible analogy of slowdown is latency in a network.

Utilization [4] is a measure of the clusters' activity. It is computed as:

$$Utilization\ =\ \sum_{i=1}^{N} M_i \cdot T_i / (M_T \cdot T_T)) \tag{3}$$

where T_T the total simulation time.

In our experiments we changed the rate of job submissions within the workload files and measured the slowdown and utilization as a function of the offer load. Utilization always grows linearly as the offered load increases until the scheduling system becomes saturated. This is when, for the first time, jobs are queued in the input queue of the scheduler awaiting available resources. The higher the offered load at the saturation point, the better the computing cluster is utilized [4].

Utilization is usually computed under the assumption that all jobs performed a useful function. However, in the current setup, some jobs will ultimately fail because insufficient resource capacities are allocated to them, without performing a useful function. We therefore report **effective utilization**, which is the utilization of successfully executed jobs and **total utilization**, which is the utilization associated with both successful and unsuccessful jobs.

3.2   Simulation Setup

We used the LANL CM5 [19] as a real workload file to simulate a scheduling process where we estimated the memory capacity per job. The reason for using this workload file was because to our knowledge it is the only publicly-available workload file which reports both requested and used memory capacities. Figure 3 shows histograms of the distribution of run-time, requested and used memory, and requested processors in the CM5 workload.

In our simulations we dealt with two possibilities: Explicit feedback where if a job successfully completed it reported actual memory usage (if it did not,

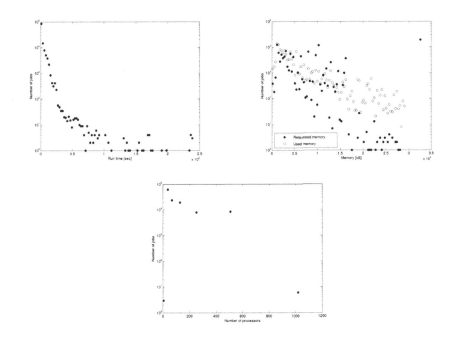

Fig. 3. Distribution of run-time, requested and used memory, and requested processors for the CM5 workload

only allocated memory capacity is known), and implicit feedback where the only feedback was whether a job completed successfully (because it had ample resource capacity) or not.

The CM-5 cluster had 1024 nodes, each with 32 MB physical memory. For our experiments, we needed to run this workload file on a heterogeneous cluster. Thus, we had to change the workload file. We found that the minimum change would be to remove six entries for jobs that required the full 1024 nodes of the original CM5 cluster. This removal enabled us to rerun the workload file for a heterogeneous cluster with 512 original machines (32 MB memory) and another 512 machines with lower memory sizes.

We also used the algorithm in Section 2.3 to estimate the actual memory capacity for jobs. The learning constant η was set to 0.1 and the decay constant τ to 10. We used a hyperbolic tangent activation function for the Perceptron, such that $f(x) = a \cdot M \cdot tanh(b \cdot x)$, where $a = 1.716$ and $b = 2/3$ (set according to the recommendations in [2], pg. 308) and M the largest memory size in the cluster (i.e., 32 MB).

In the simulation we used a scheduling policy of first-come-first-served (FCFS). We expect that the results of cluster utilization with more aggressive scheduling policies such as backfilling will be correlated with those for FCFS. However, these experiments are left for future work. We assumed no job pre-emption. Moreover, when a job is scheduled for execution, but not enough resources are allocated for it, it fails after a random time, drawn uniformly between zero and the execution run-time of that job. We assume that jobs do not fail except for insufficient resources. Moreover, once failed, a job is automatically resubmitted for execution.

The offered load (see Equation 1) in each run was modified by multiplying the submission time of all jobs by a constant factor so as to achieve a required load.

In our simulations the estimator used as features the following measurements to estimate the required memory resources:

1. The fraction of available processors in the cluster with a given memory size
2. The fraction of available processors in the cluster required to complete the job
3. Logarithm of the requested memory capacity for the current job
4. Logarithm of the number of jobs in the queue (i.e., the queue length)

These features represent a heuristic of indicators that could be useful and relatively easy to obtain. However, system designers can choose to use other measurements for the estimation process.

3.3   Results

In our first experiment, we measured the effect of resource estimation on effective utilization. We experimented with a cluster of 512 machines, each with 32 MB memory, and an additional 512 machines, each with 24 MB memory. Figures 4 and 5 show a comparison of the effective utilization [4], with and without resource estimation, for both the implicit and explicit feedback scenarios. The difference between utilization with implicit and explicit feedback is small (approximately 1%). This is surprising since explicit feedback provides much additional information for the learning algorithm. We hypothesize that this is related to the naive learning method we used (Perceptron), which failed to utilize the additional information, as well as the fact that when a job fails the feedback only contains the (insufficient) allocated capacity, not the required capacity. We address these issues further in Section 4. Figures 4 and 5 further show that effective utilization with resource estimation improved by approximately 33% for the case of implicit feedback and 31% for the case of implicit feedback.

The reason for the improvement in utilization with resource estimation is as follows. At low effective loads, most of the jobs are likely to have sufficient resources as defined by the corresponding user requests. However, as the load increases, fewer jobs are likely to have available resources that match the job requests. Resource estimation increases the number of these jobs; once scheduled, it enables them to run on the cluster instead of waiting in the queue for more resources that they don't actually need.

Figure 6 compares the effective utilization to the total utilization in the case of implicit feedback. The difference between the effective utilization and the total utilization is the utilization caused by jobs which terminated unsuccessfully due to insufficient resources. This difference represents the overhead (in terms of

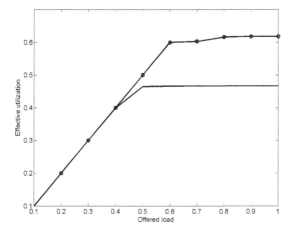

Fig. 4. Effective utilization with resource estimation (dotted line) and without resource estimation (solid line) with implicit feedback

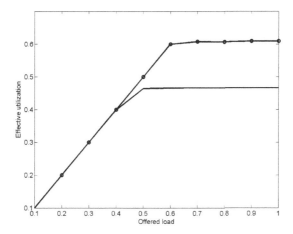

Fig. 5. Effective utilization with resource estimation (dotted line) and without resource estimation (solid line) with explicit feedback

computing resources, electricity, etc.) which the system administrator has to pay for the learning process to find a useful policy.

Figures 7 and 8 show the effect of resource estimation on slowdown for both types of feedback. As shown, over most of the range of offered load, resource estimation halves the slowdown compared to the case where no resource estimation is performed, and never causes slowdown to increase beyond the case where no resource estimation is performed. Moreover, slowdown decreases dramatically (by a factor of approximately 10) around loads of 50%. The reason for this peak in performance can be explained by the fact that a FCFS scheduling policy is

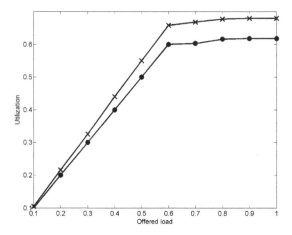

Fig. 6. Effective utilization (dotted line) compared to the total utilization (line marked by crosses) in the case of resource estimation with implicit feedback

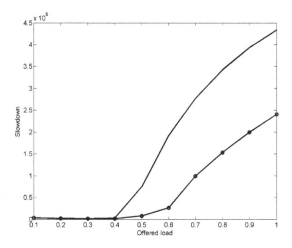

Fig. 7. Slowdown with resource estimation (dotted line) and without resource estimation (solid line) with implicit feedback

used. The higher the loads, the longer the job queue, and the relative decrease in slowdown is less prominent. The 50% load is a point at which the job queue is still not extremely long and resource estimation is already useful in reducing the wait-time of jobs in the queue.

Reinforcement Learning finds a policy for submitting jobs. In our case, the policy was indirect in that the RL algorithm was required to estimate the memory requirements rather than the actual scheduling policy. This was done to make the proposed system independent of the scheduling policy. Clearly, the policy

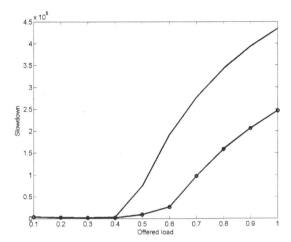

Fig. 8. Slowdown with resource estimation (dotted line) and without resource estimation (solid line) with explicit feedback

should also affect the submission policy. For example, if a good policy would be to try and submit all the jobs regardless of their memory requirements and the available processors, we would expect RL to estimate the required memory as lower than the minimal available memory so the jobs would be submitted with minimal requested resources.

Figure 9 shows the feature weights versus load. Feature 1 is the fraction of available 32 MB nodes. Feature 2 is the fraction of available 24 MB nodes. Feature 3 is the requested memory and Feature 4 the length of the queue. The weights associated with the fraction of available processors required to complete the job is not shown because it is highly correlated with Features 3 and 4. As Figure 9 shows, all weights tend to lower values as the load increases. This implies that as the load becomes higher, more and more jobs will be estimated as requiring low memory, and will thus be submitted whenever enough processors of *any* capacity are available. This is to be expected because at high loads it makes sense to try and use whatever resources are available.

This effect is visible in Figure 10, which shows the number of unsuccessful job submissions as a function of the load[2]. Clearly, as the load increases, more jobs are submitted with a low memory usage estimate and later fail. However, even at this high failure rate, effective utilization still increases by 30%.

Another interesting trend can be seen in Figure 9. The top row shows almost linear decline in the weights ($R^2 > 0.85$), while the lower row shows a much less linear decline ($R^2 = 0.85$ for Feature 3 and $R^2 = 0.66$ for Feature 4). We interpret this behavior by noting that at low loads the queue length is usually very short

---

[2] We note that although the values on the vertical axis are large, one should bear in mind that the total number of jobs in the workload file is approximately 122,000 and that each job can fail multiple times.

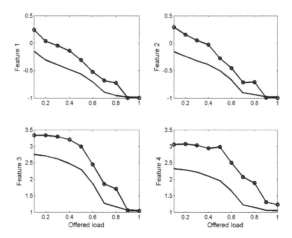

Fig. 9. Feature weights versus load. Feature 1 is the fraction of available 32 MB processors. Feature 2 is the fraction of available 24 MB processors. Feature 3 is the requested memory and Feature 4 the length of the queue. Solid lines represent learning with explicit feedback. Lines marked by circles denote learning with implicit feedback.

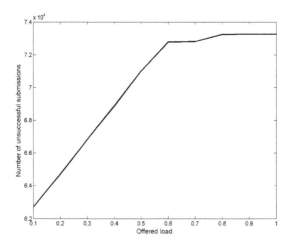

Fig. 10. Number of unsuccessful job submissions as a function of the load (Implicit feedback)

and computing resources are usually available. Therefore, these weights have little effect on the memory estimation. These weights only play an important role when the load is high, as shown on the graph.

All the above experiments were done with one particular heterogeneous cluster. In the following experiment, we measured the cluster utilization with and without resource estimation for different clusters. We used 512 machines with

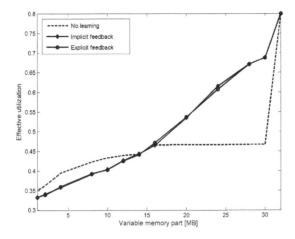

Fig. 11. Utilization with and without resource estimation for the implicit and explicit feedback cases

32 MB of memory and an additional 512 machines with different memory sizes between 1 MB and 32 MB. All other simulation parameters remained as in the previous experiments.

Figure 11 shows the ratio of utilization when using memory estimation, compared to using user requirements, as a function of the variable memory part of the cluster. The greatest improvement in utilization was obtained for clusters with the 512 machines whose memory size was modified to between 16 MB and 28 MB. The utilization at the rightmost part of the graph, when all machines have 32 MB of memory, is the same with and without learning because at this point the cluster is homogeneous and any job can be successfully executed on the available machines. There is a slight decrease in utilization for clusters where the machine had memory below 15 MB. For such configurations only a small proportion of jobs could be run with lower memory. Consequently, utilization decreases because of repeated attempts to create a good estimator that is only applicable for a few jobs.

4   Discussion

This paper presents an autonomic module for assessing the actual resources required by jobs submitted to distributed computation systems. Its huge benefits were demonstrated by extremely significant improvements in utilization and slowdown. It is estimated that these improvements would not be easy to achieve through modification of user behavior.

The proposed system can utilize both implicit feedback, which only informs the learning system whether the job submission was successful, and explicit feedback, which provides more information on resource usage. Interestingly, our simulations show almost identical performance for the two types of feedback. This is surprising because it is to be expected that when additional information exists, better performance will ensue. We hypothesize that the reason for this behavior is due to the type of learning algorithm we used. We expect that better algorithms, such as Support Vector Machines (SVM) or neural networks, will show the superiority of explicit feedback over implicit feedback.

Finally, we note that the problem we addressed in this paper is prevalent in many other cases. These cases are characterized by settings where users give (poor) estimates of their needs or requirements, but where it is possible to automatically improve these estimates by learning from larger populations. One such example is setting parameters to achieve given service level objectives (SLOs) in complicated systems and creating policies for storage systems. We are currently applying the algorithms described in this paper to such problems.

References

1. Basney, J., Livny, M., Tannenbaum, T.: High throughput computing with condor. HPCU news 1(2) (1997)
2. Duda, R.O., Hart, P.E., Stork, D.G.: Pattern classification. John Wiley and Sons, Inc, New-York, USA (2001)
3. Feitelson, D.G., Rudolph, L., Schwiegelshohn, U.: Parallel job scheduling: a status report. In: Feitelson, D.G., Rudolph, L., Schwiegelshohn, U. (eds.) JSSPP 2004. LNCS, vol. 3277, pp. 1–16. Springer, Heidelberg (2005)
4. Feitelson, D.G.: Metrics for parallel job scheduling and their convergence. In: Feitelson, D.G., Rudolph, L. (eds.) JSSPP 2001. LNCS, vol. 2221, pp. 188–206. Springer, Heidelberg (2001)
5. Henderson, R.L.: Job scheduling under the portable batch system. In: Proceedings of the Workshop on Job Scheduling Strategies for Parallel Processing (IPPS 1995), pp. 279–294. Springer, London, UK (1995)
6. Kaelbling, L.P., Littman, M., Moore, A.: Reinforcement learning: A survey. Journal of Artificial Intelligence Research 4, 237–285 (1996)
7. Kannan, S., Roberts, M., Mayes, P., Brelsford, D., Skovira, J.F.: Workload Management with LoadLeveler. IBM Press (2001)
8. Kumar, K.P., Agarwal, A., Krishnan, R.: Fuzzy based resource management framework for high throughput computing. In: IEEE International Symposium on Cluster Computing and the Grid (CCGrid 2004), pp. 555–562. IEEE Computer Society Press, Los Alamitos (2004)
9. Litzkow, M., Livny, M., Mutka, M.: Condor - a hunter of idle workstations. In: Proceedings of the 8th International Conference of Distributed Computing Systems (June 1988)
10. Liu, C., Yang, L., Foster, I., Angulo, D.: Design and evaluation of a resource selection framework for grid applications. In: HPDC 2002: Proceedings of the 11th IEEE International Symposium on High Performance Distributed Computing HPDC-11 20002 (HPDC 2002), p. 63. IEEE Computer Society Press, Washington, DC, USA (2002)
11. Livny, M.: Personal communication (2005)
12. Naik, V., Liu, C., Yang, L., Wagner, J.: On-line resource matching in a heterogeneous grid environment. In: IEEE International Symposium on Cluster Computing and the Grid (CCGrid 2005), IEEE Computer Society Press, Los Alamitos (2005)

13. Raman, R., Livny, M., Solomon, M.: Matchmaking: Distributed resource management for high throughput computing. In: Proceedings of the Seventh IEEE International Symposium on High Performance Distributed Computing (HPDC7), July 1998, Chicago, IL (1998)
14. Raman, R., Livny, M., Solomon, M.: Policy driven heterogeneous resource co-allocation with gangmatching. In: 12th IEEE International Symposium on High Performance Distributed Computing (HPDC-12 2003), pp. 80–89 (2003)
15. Tesauro, G., Jong, N.K., Das, R., Bennani, M.N.: A hybrid reinforcement learning approach to autonomic resource allocation. In: Proceedings of the IEEE International Conference on Autonomic Computing (ICAC) 2006, Dublin, Ireland, pp. 65–73 (2006)
16. Tsafrir, D., Etsion, Y., Feitelson, D.G.: Backfilling using runtime predictions rather than user estimates. Technical Report TR 2005-5, School of Computer Science and Engineering, Hebrew University of Jerusalem (2003)
17. Upton, G., Cook, I.: Oxford Dictionary of Statistics. Oxford University Press, Oxford, UK (2002)
18. Vermorel, J., Mohri, M.: Multi-armed bandit algorithms and empirical evaluation. In: Gama, J., Camacho, R., Brazdil, P.B., Jorge, A.M., Torgo, L. (eds.) ECML 2005. LNCS (LNAI), vol. 3720, pp. 437–448. Springer, Heidelberg (2005)
19. Parallel workloads archive, `http://www.cs.huji.ac.il/labs/parallel/workload`
20. Xu, M.Q.: Effective metacomputing using lsf multicluster. In: CCGRID 2001: Proceedings of the 1st International Symposium on Cluster Computing and the Grid, p. 100. IEEE Computer Society Press, Los Alamitos (2001)
21. Yom-Tov, E., Aridor, Y.: Improving resource matching through estimation of actual job requirements. In: IBM Research Report H-0244 (2006)

Author Index

Lecture Notes in Computer Science

Sublibrary 1: Theoretical Computer Science and General Issues

For information about Vols. 1– 4666
please contact your bookseller or Springer

Vol. 4848: M.H. Garzon, H. Yan (Eds.), DNA Computing. XI, 292 pages. 2008.

Vol. 4847: M. Xu, Y. Zhan, J. Cao, Y. Liu (Eds.), Advanced Parallel Processing Technologies. XIX, 767 pages. 2007.

Vol. 4846: I. Cervesato (Ed.), Advances in Computer Science – ASIAN 2007. XI, 313 pages. 2007.

Vol. 4838: T. Masuzawa, S. Tixeuil (Eds.), Stabilization, Safety, and Security of Distributed Systems. XIII, 409 pages. 2007.

Vol. 4835: T. Tokuyama (Ed.), Algorithms and Computation. XVII, 929 pages. 2007.

Vol. 4818: I. Lirkov, S. Margenov, J. Waśniewski (Eds.), Large-Scale Scientific Computing. XIV, 755 pages. 2008.

Vol. 4800: A. Avron, N. Dershowitz, A. Rabinovich (Eds.), Pillars of Computer Science. XXI, 683 pages. 2008.

Vol. 4783: J. Holub, J. Žďárek (Eds.), Implementation and Application of Automata. XIII, 324 pages. 2007.

Vol. 4782: R. Perrott, B.M. Chapman, J. Subhlok, R.F. de Mello, L.T. Yang (Eds.), High Performance Computing and Communications. XIX, 823 pages. 2007.

Vol. 4771: T. Bartz-Beielstein, M.J. Blesa Aguilera, C. Blum, B. Naujoks, A. Roli, G. Rudolph, M. Sampels (Eds.), Hybrid Metaheuristics. X, 202 pages. 2007.

Vol. 4770: V.G. Ganzha, E.W. Mayr, E.V. Vorozhtsov (Eds.), Computer Algebra in Scientific Computing. XIII, 460 pages. 2007.

Vol. 4769: A. Brandstädt, D. Kratsch, H. Müller (Eds.), Graph-Theoretic Concepts in Computer Science. XIII, 341 pages. 2007.

Vol. 4763: J.-F. Raskin, P.S. Thiagarajan (Eds.), Formal Modeling and Analysis of Timed Systems. X, 369 pages. 2007.

Vol. 4759: J. Labarta, K. Joe, T. Sato (Eds.), High-Performance Computing. XV, 524 pages. 2008.

Vol. 4746: A. Bondavalli, F. Brasileiro, S. Rajsbaum (Eds.), Dependable Computing. XV, 239 pages. 2007.

Vol. 4743: P. Thulasiraman, X. He, T.L. Xu, M.K. Denko, R.K. Thulasiram, L.T. Yang (Eds.), Frontiers of High Performance Computing and Networking ISPA 2007 Workshops. XXIX, 536 pages. 2007.

Vol. 4742: I. Stojmenovic, R.K. Thulasiram, L.T. Yang, W. Jia, M. Guo, R.F. de Mello (Eds.), Parallel and Distributed Processing and Applications. XX, 995 pages. 2007.

Vol. 4739: R. Moreno Díaz, F. Pichler, A. Quesada Arencibia (Eds.), Computer Aided Systems Theory – EUROCAST 2007. XIX, 1233 pages. 2007.

Vol. 4736: S. Winter, M. Duckham, L. Kulik, B. Kuipers (Eds.), Spatial Information Theory. XV, 455 pages. 2007.

Vol. 4732: K. Schneider, J. Brandt (Eds.), Theorem Proving in Higher Order Logics. IX, 401 pages. 2007.

Vol. 4731: A. Pelc (Ed.), Distributed Computing. XVI, 510 pages. 2007.

Vol. 4728: S. Bozapalidis, G. Rahonis (Eds.), Algebraic Informatics. VIII, 291 pages. 2007.

Vol. 4726: N. Ziviani, R. Baeza-Yates (Eds.), String Processing and Information Retrieval. XII, 311 pages. 2007.

Vol. 4719: R. Backhouse, J. Gibbons, R. Hinze, J. Jeuring (Eds.), Datatype-Generic Programming. XI, 369 pages. 2007.

Vol. 4711: C.B. Jones, Z. Liu, J. Woodcock (Eds.), Theoretical Aspects of Computing – ICTAC 2007. XI, 483 pages. 2007.

Vol. 4710: C.W. George, Z. Liu, J. Woodcock (Eds.), Domain Modeling and the Duration Calculus. XI, 237 pages. 2007.

Vol. 4708: L. Kučera, A. Kučera (Eds.), Mathematical Foundations of Computer Science 2007. XVIII, 764 pages. 2007.

Vol. 4707: O. Gervasi, M.L. Gavrilova (Eds.), Computational Science and Its Applications – ICCSA 2007, Part III. XXIV, 1205 pages. 2007.

Vol. 4706: O. Gervasi, M.L. Gavrilova (Eds.), Computational Science and Its Applications – ICCSA 2007, Part II. XXIII, 1129 pages. 2007.

Vol. 4705: O. Gervasi, M.L. Gavrilova (Eds.), Computational Science and Its Applications – ICCSA 2007, Part I. XLIV, 1169 pages. 2007.

Vol. 4703: L. Caires, V.T. Vasconcelos (Eds.), CONCUR 2007 – Concurrency Theory. XIII, 507 pages. 2007.

Vol. 4700: C.B. Jones, Z. Liu, J. Woodcock (Eds.), Formal Methods and Hybrid Real-Time Systems. XVI, 539 pages. 2007.

Vol. 4699: B. Kågström, E. Elmroth, J. Dongarra, J. Waśniewski (Eds.), Applied Parallel Computing. XXIX, 1192 pages. 2007.

Vol. 4698: L. Arge, M. Hoffmann, E. Welzl (Eds.), Algorithms – ESA 2007. XV, 769 pages. 2007.

Vol. 4697: L. Choi, Y. Paek, S. Cho (Eds.), Advances in Computer Systems Architecture. XIII, 400 pages. 2007.

Vol. 4688: K. Li, M. Fei, G.W. Irwin, S. Ma (Eds.), Bio-Inspired Computational Intelligence and Applications. XIX, 805 pages. 2007.

Vol. 4684: L. Kang, Y. Liu, S. Zeng (Eds.), Evolvable Systems: From Biology to Hardware. XIV, 446 pages. 2007.

Vol. 4683: L. Kang, Y. Liu, S. Zeng (Eds.), Advances in Computation and Intelligence. XVII, 663 pages. 2007.

Vol. 4681: D.-S. Huang, L. Heutte, M. Loog (Eds.), Advanced Intelligent Computing Theories and Applications. XXVI, 1379 pages. 2007.

Vol. 4672: K. Li, C. Jesshope, H. Jin, J.-L. Gaudiot (Eds.), Network and Parallel Computing. XVIII, 558 pages. 2007.

Vol. 4671: V.E. Malyshkin (Ed.), Parallel Computing Technologies. XIV, 635 pages. 2007.

Vol. 4669: J.M. de Sá, L.A. Alexandre, W. Duch, D.P. Mandic (Eds.), Artificial Neural Networks – ICANN 2007, Part II. XXXI, 990 pages. 2007.

Vol. 4668: J.M. de Sá, L.A. Alexandre, W. Duch, D.P. Mandic (Eds.), Artificial Neural Networks – ICANN 2007, Part I. XXXI, 978 pages. 2007.